RUSSIAN SATIRIC COMEDY

Library of Congress Cataloging in Publication Data
Russian Satiric Comedy
CONTENTS: *The Milliner's Shop, The Headstrong Turk, The Fourth Wall, The Power of Love, Sundown, Ivan Vasilievich*
Library of Congress Catalog Card No.: 83-61195
ISBN: 0-933826-52-4 (cloth)
ISBN: 0-933826-53-2 (paper)

Graphic Design: Gautam Dasgupta

Printed in the United States of America

Publication of this book has been made possible in part by grants received from the National Endowment for the Arts, Washington, D.C., a federal agency, and the New York State Council on the Arts.

General Editors of the PAJ Playscript Series:
Bonnie Marranca and Gautam Dasgupta

The Publishers would like to dedicate their own work on the publication of this volume to their good friend and colleague Earl Ostroff (1927-1982) who loved the Russian drama.

RUSSIAN SATIRIC COMEDY

Six Plays

Edited and Translated, with an Introduction, by

LAURENCE SENELICK

Performing Arts Journal Publications
New York

For the veterans of HARPO

Contents

Textual Note

The purpose of this anthology is to enlarge the repertoire of Russian drama in English. Although the works of Gogol and Chekhov are regularly retranslated, a wealth of interesting plays remain inaccessible to the non-Russian reader. Of the comedies in this collection, only the Babel has previously appeared in English and is available only in a back issue of an out-of-print journal. My translation of *Ivan Vasilievich* and *The Power of Love* were first published in the magazine, *Modern Drama International*, in 1977, and have been revised for their reappearance here.

The translations are meant for American readers and actors, and I have not hesitated to use American idioms and dialects to convey equivalent tones. If this means that Krylov's peasants sound as if they were bred in Dogpatch and his Frenchmen as if they learned English on the vaudeville stage, the effect is intentional. Babel's Jews sound as exotic and outlandish in Russian as they do in English. The main liberty I have taken is in *The Power of Love*: two alcoholic wedding guests are referred to, in the original, as Lyov Nikolaevich and Anton Pavlovich. To any literate Russian, those are immediately recognized as the names and patronymics of two of Russia's greatest writers. To smuggle the joke into English, I have had to dub them, more crudely, Comrade Tolstoy and Comrade Chekhov.

L.S.

INTRODUCTION

When George S. Kaufman said that "Satire is what closes on Saturday night," he was not talking about Russia. Despite repressive regimes and centuries of censorship, satire has been a persistent element in Russian art and literature. In the theatre, a public forum zealously muzzled by the powers-that-be and -have-been, satire crept in in many guises. The longest-lived, most widely-spread Russian folk dramas are imbued with a caustic distrust of religion and society. Local landowners and judges were favorite butts in folk plays, such as "The Farce of the Boyar," which survived well into the nineteenth century. It exhibited a magistrate who was bribed with wicker-baskets full of rubbish and eventually thrashed by his petitioners for his stupid verdicts.

The ever popular *Tsar Maximilian and his disobedient son Adolph* which evolved in the seventeenth century featured a heathen king who executed his Christian (or in some versions, robber chieftain) son. Some have thought this to be a not-very-subtle allusion to the reigning monarch Peter the Great, suspected of having persecuted and murdered his son Alexis. Since the Westernizing, innovative Peter was seen by the conservative majority of the population as Anti-Christ, and his priest-ridden son as a popular upholder of the old-fashioned way, the Tsar was a ripe target for satire in folk plays, and, more Aesopically, as the greedy cat in *lubki*, cheap colored woodcuts.

Such simple representations of corruption and injustice were audacious, but Soviet scholars overstate the case when they deem such plays manifestations of widespread social protest at the grass roots level. Unrest and discontent were alleviated by the laughter these plays evoked; no true propaganda or programmatic dissent emanated from them. In fact, similar stereotypical caricatures of the gentry as callous and self-indulgent, and the people as long-suffering, are the stuff of most European folklore. Russian dramatic satire at this level is not particularly savage or exceptional.

Still, these plays do, to some extent, meet the criteria for satire set down by Northrup Frye in his *Anatomy of Criticism*. According to Frye, satire requires a (token) fantasy; a recognizably grotesque content; a moral judgment that is at least implicit; and a "militant attitude to experience." These qualities characterize Russian literature in general, and Russian comedy in particular.

The fantasy requirement may show up merely as wish-fulfillment, as in the folk play *The Boat*, in which a local squire is drowned by a gang of bandits, or it may be the extended phantasmagoria of the Hoffmanesque tales of Prince Odoevsky, Bulgakov's novel *The Master and Margarita*, or, in the theatre, the allegorical fairy tales of Evgeny Shvarts. The grotesque has been cited as an outstanding feature of Russian comedy since Gogol, although critics have not agreed on a definition of that elusive term. Emphasis on the disturbing detail, "hyperbole," the juxtaposition of the everyday with the supernatural are some of the distinctions proposed to explain it. "Grotesque" has become a blanket term to characterize Gogol, Sukhovo-Kobylin and comic writers of the NEP period, just as "absurd" was the critical catchall that lumped together Beckett, Genet, Pinter and Ionesco into one undifferentiated mass.

Moral judgments and a "militant attitude to experience" are ubiquitous in Russian literature. In a society whose means of subversive or deviant expression have always been scant, where education and enlightenment were for the chosen few, where obliquity and covert meanings are still common tools of art, literature was obliged to instruct, to criticize, to be encyclopedic. Belinsky and the "civic critics" of the 1840s and 1850s spelled this out in no uncertain terms, and an even more prescriptive injunction to art to serve the people was handed down by innumerable Party Congresses after the Revolution. Almost by nature the Russian writer has been aware of this need to do more than practice "art for art's sake." Among the greatest writers, this instinct has been at odds with the impulse for self-expression and experimentation, and the tension has produced brilliant results.

The earliest literary comedies on the Russian stage were based on French models, particularly the plays of Molière and his followers, in which the emphasis was on character rather than plot, and satire was directed either at French institutions or universal conditions. Only gradually was the satiric searchlight directed at Russian life. Even then, eighteenth-century comedies tended to be *na litso, ad hominem* attacks on specific individuals engaged in literary or political polemic, as in the plays of Sumarokov and Lukin. Even Catherine the Great, herself the author of satiric comedies attacking social foibles and recalcitrant conservatism, did not escape veiled portrayal as a lecherous old woman in other persons' works.

Otherwise, the playwright created types of general abuses. Vasily Kapnist's verse comedy, *Chicanery* (*Yabeda*, 1798), was a pungent indictment of corruption in the law courts, embodied by a rollicking gallery of rogues; in this, he foreshadowed Gogol and others who made dramatic hay out of the bureaucracy. It was typical that in Kapnist's last act, the Government, all-seeing and all-wise like the King in Molière's *Tartuffe*, steps in and sets everything to rights. A similar tactic resolves the first major Russian comedy, Denis Fonvizin's *The Minor* (*Nedorosl*, 1782). By creating caricatures of ignorant and arbitrary landowners, Fonvizin obliquely castigated the evils of unsupervised power; characters like Prostakova (Mrs. Simpleton) and Skotinin (Mr. Beastly) became bywords for benighted provincial backwardness. But, here too, the happy ending was contrived by the intervention of the imperial authorities, whose Argus-eyed wisdom prevents anything dire from occurring.

Fonvizin's first comedy *The Brigadier* (*Brigadir*, 1766) had satirized the safe and common subject of Gallomania. The Russian fad for all things French had been prompted by the court and the educational system and led to what some considered an unpatriotic preference for European modes and manners over homespun virtues. Peter the Great's attempt to make Russia a European country was thus trivialized, and virtually every Russian comedy written between 1765 and 1823 aims a shaft at this crotchet. Its first dramatic appearance was in Sumarokov's *Monstrosities* (*Chudovishcha*, 1750) and it gets definitive treatment in Krylov's *The Milliner's Shop* (Modnaya Lavka, 1805; an alternative rendering might be *The Fashionable Boutique*).

Ivan Krylov is best remembered as a fabulist, whose verses and aphorisms are imbedded in the consciousness of every literate Russian; pithy and perfectly phrased, they mirror Krylov's eminently sensible mind. In literature he disliked extremes; both pseudo-classical moralizing and romantic sentimentality excited his mirth. He sacrificed the former in a bombastic and almost surrealistic parody called *Trumphus* (*Trumf*, 1800), and the latter in the more realistic *School for Daughters* (*Urok dochkam*, 1807). But *The Milliner's Shop* may be his stage masterpiece. At first sight, it looks to be a traditional "New Comedy": two lovers are kept apart by cranks—in this case, the girl's father, a pigheaded booster of Russian customs, and her stepmother, a ridiculous provincial dandizette—but are brought together through the wiles of a clever servant. The freshness of the play derives from the alacrity of the action, the ambiguity of the characters, and the naturalism of the language.

None of the characters in *The Milliner's Shop* is quite the stereotype he seems. Lestov is, of course, a handsome and rich young gentleman who gets the girl; but he is also a rake and a gambler, who would have been either scorned or made to reform in a sentimental comedy of the period. Madame Carié and Monsieur Tricher are French malaprops who mangle the Russian language but they are no longer portrayed as fools. Krylov's patriotism and morality conduce to the characterization of the French as criminals and subversives: Madame smuggles and acts the go-between, Monsieur blackmails and acts the spy. Even old Sumburov's thickness is redeemed by his bluff candor.

The Milliner's Shop, in this respect, exemplifies Northrup Frye's criterion of moral militancy towards experience in its arguments for common sense and sensible behavior. Masha, the "female Figaro," may be the traditional cunning underling who contrives intricate plots to aid her betters; but she is also a hard-working serf, longing like a slave in Plautus for her freedom. Her backchat and interference, unlike those of a French Dorine, can be punished by exile, flogging or even sale. Yet Krylov seems to make her his hero, precisely because of her level-headedness. The rest of the characters err through their extremism. Lestov is given to novelistic emotionalizing; Sumburov is bigoted and suspicious; his wife is foppish and selfish; the French amoral and underhanded. Only the relatively unspoilt peasant lass, who can keep her head when hiding contraband or thwarting an elopement, has no ridiculous traits: she becomes the play's norm. It is curious to note that she is the only character shown at work, and, without going so far as to suggest that Masha is an archetype of the epic tractor-drivers of socialist realism, one may still conjecture that Krylov looked to the common folk for a standard of reasonable conduct.

In accordance with Krylov's published statements about stage diction, the characters speak *in* character. There is no fireworks display of wit to show off the author's cleverness, and, compared to the tendentious moralizing and conventionalized lovemaking of Fonvizin's virtuous characters, the dialogue of Liza and Lestov seems positively breezy. Unhampered by self-conscious messages of verbal exhibitionism, the play moves smoothly and rapidly to its climactic scenes and its efficient dénouement.

Satire is a dominant chord in the two greatest Russian comedies of the nineteenth century, Griboedov's *Woe from Wit* (*Gore ot uma*, 1821-23) and Gogol's *The Inspector* (*Revizor*, 1836), though in differing modes. Griboedov emerges from the *vaudeville* tradition, the school of light topical farces interspersed with verses and songs set to popular tunes; *Woe from Wit* surpasses all of his earlier attempts by its complexity and polish. It is usually compared to Molière's *Misanthrope*: in verse of epigrammatic coruscation, its young protagonist Chatsky lashes out at Moscow society for its heartlessness and toadyism, and flees in desperation at the play's end. But, as the poet Pushkin noted, Chatsky is not the most intelligent voice in the play, because his complaints are wasted on the old grannies at the ball. The intelligent voice belongs to Griboedov himself, who regards Chatsky's salon Byronism with the same jaundiced eye he casts on the sycophants and blockheads of society. The government found the play dangerous and took years before granting permission to stage it. In the meantime, Russians learned its dialogue by heart from manuscript copies passed from hand to hand.

Gogol's *Inspector* was passed for the stage, owing, according to legend, to the personal intervention of Tsar Nicholas II. It seems to be following the well-beaten track of Fonvizin and Kapnist in its portrayal of peccadillos in officialdom, and was censured by the government literary party for casting aspersions on officeholders and dignitaries. As a matter of fact, Gogol's play is less grounded in reality than it seems and than the critic Belinsky claimed. Gogol wanted the stage to be a tribune from which moral lessons could be preached, but in the event his plays are hopelessly and gloriously amoral. Although the small town and its citizens in *The Inspector* appear superficially to be realistic portrayals of an average community, Gogol actually creates *ex nihilo* (as Leo Shestov said less accurately of Chekhov). He is not so much satirizing small-time corruption and provincial airs as confecting an elaborate fantasy. It is more than coincidence that most of the characters are liars, gossips, logorrhoetics and obsessionals; they verbally construct a world that has no more objective reality than they do themselves as fictional characters. Gogol endows his creations with the same genius for embroidering the truth than he himself possesses, and it is the exercise of this genius that passes for "action" or "plot." Not surprisingly, a play like *Chicanery* that attacks specific malpractices is never revived; whereas *The Inspector* survives in every repertory in the world.

The combination of Griboedov and Gogol dominated Russian satire and comedy for decades. Griboedov's example helped to perfect the *vaudeville*, which became more adept at skewering current vogues and more polished in its dialogue and verses; it even nurtured a form of minor realism. Those plays that most elaborated Gogol's grotesque side, on the other hand, received no stage hearing until shortly before the Revolution. Saltykov-Shchedrin's caustic satire *Pazukhin's Death* (*Smert Pazukhina*, 1857) follows Gogol's lead in setting its scene in a backwoods town, in avoiding a love interest, and in presenting no "positive" characters (Gogol had insisted that the positive character in *The Inspector* was Laughter itself). But Shchedrin partakes more of Ben Jonson in his contempt for his characters and his indictment of their sins. Relatives and friends conspire over the deathbed of a millionaire merchant, a situation reminiscent of *Volpone*; but in this case, the man is actually dying. And when his scheming son manages to beat out the scheming son-in-law, justice is not seen to be done. As the curtain speech puts it, "Vice has been punished, and virtue—oops, just where is virtue anyway?"

The dramatic trilogy of Sukhovo-Kobylin also begins from established satiric conventions but soon divagates to wilder territory, to what Simon Karlinsky has called the "alogical and absurd" tradition. *Krechinsky's Wedding* (*Svadba Krechinskogo*, 1852-54) starts as a satire on fortune hunters and social-climbing and ends as a domestic tragedy; *The Case* (*Delo*, 1861) gives every appearance of another lampoon on the bureaucracy and red-tape, but devolves into a Kafkaesque black comedy in which the persecuted hero dies and the monstrous villains survive; and *Tarelkin's Death* (*Smert Tarelkina*, 1869) gets under way as a farcical exchange of identities and finishes as a macabre, nightmarish, virtually surreal clown show. These plays would come into their own only after the Revolution when directors could tap into the avant-garde artistic movements of their own times for modes of presentation that could match Sukhovo-Kobylin's unique creations.

The difficulties in getting satire on the stage in the Russia of Nicholas I are evident in the case of the vaudeville *Fantasy* (*Fantasya*) by Kozma Petrovich Prutkov (1802-1863). Of Prutkov, it may be said, as Betsy Prig said of Mrs. Harris, "there ain't no sich a pusson." Prutkov was, in fact, a fictional civil servant in the Assay Office dreamt up by the brothers Aleksey, Aleksandr and Vladimir Zhemchuzhnikov and their cousin Aleksey Konstantinovich Tolstoy. Prutkov (whose name translates loosely as "Cosmo Twigly") was envisaged as the compleat Philistine, whose literary ventures foundered on bathos and nonsense. Under Prutkov's aegis, the cousins parodied sentimental German verse, fatuous aphorisms, and all the literary excesses of the period. The great man's alleged first dramatic composition, *Fantasy*, was a bizarre send-up of the vaudeville, with a Pirandellian ending in which one character steps forward and asks the audience what it all means. As a lark, the cousins submitted it to the censorship and it was passed, albeit with numerous cuts that were as arbitrary and lunatic as anything in the play. But on opening night at the Alexandra Theatre in St. Petersburg in 1851, after a scene in which several dogs dance across the stage to the storm music from *The Barber of Seville*, the Tsar stamped out of his box, saying, "I've seen a good deal of rubbish in my time, but never anything like this." The play was immediately banned as a stage-piece, but was published, with the censor's comments printed as footnotes to enhance the absurdity of the thing.

The Headstrong Turk Or Is It Nice to Be a Grandson? (*Oprometchiviy turka: ili Prilichno li byt vnukom?*) is, to some slight degree, a sequel, employing some of the same characters. Its prime target was the playwright Aleksandr Ostrovsky, whose works began to infiltrate the Russian stage in the 1850s and 1860s. Ostrovsky had been heralded by the critic Apollon Grigoriev as a "new word" in Russian literature and was associated, not entirely with reason, with the Slavophile party, who professed adherence to old Russian traditions and creeds. As sophisticated young gentlemen, the Zhemchuznikov brothers and Tolstoy had nothing but scorn for the merchant and peasant milieux so carefully reproduced in Ostrovsky's plays, and found his dialogue, composed of authentic dialects and colloquialisms, incoherent and inept failures to create dramatic speech. *The Headstrong Turk*, which first appeared in the anti-Slavophile journal *The Contemporary* in 1863 as part of Prutkov's "obituary," is full of in-jokes aimed at the Slavophiles (including Prince Batog-Batyev's quotation from a poem by one of their number).

For the modern audience, the play has quite a different interest. While parodying Ostrovsky's "realistic-conversational" style, its inconsequential speeches and inconclusive ending point toward Ionesco and the absurdists. The meaningless garrulity, linked only by mental association, the unseen protagonist whose fate was determined by so trivial an item as rosin, and the framing devices of the prefatory poet and the apologetic editorial note are familiar ploys in the twentieth century. If *The Headstrong Turk* were published with the authorship attributed to Alfred Jarry or Georges Courteline, not an eyebrow would be raised.

Prutkov's other dramatic endeavors made a mockery of metaphysical German allegories, eighteenth-century comic opera, and romantic melodrama; but none were produced in his "lifetime." Aleksey Tolstoy went on to become Russia's greatest writer of light verse, and his blank verse dramatic trilogy on Ivan the Terrible and his successors demonstrates what he thought theatre ought to be. In the teens of the next century, however, Prutkov was adopted as the patron saint of the cabaret movement, and his works were staged by Nikolay Evreinov.

The removal of the government monopoly on theatres in 1882 might have proven an impetus to satire, had it not been coupled with increased political repression and censorship. In the artistic doldrums of the 1880s and 1890s, comedy tended to the trivial, the most popular successes being translations of the bedroom farces of the Parisian *boulevards*. Chekhov rehearses some of the themes of his major plays in his one-act *shutki* or jokes; but neither in form nor content are they particularly original. The resurgence of satire on stage accompanied the rise of the theatre of miniatures in the early twentieth century.

The causes for this were numerous: a growing liberal movement and a chipping away at the autocracy under Nicholas II; a new *intelligentsia*, composed in part of millionaire merchants and upwardly-mobile professionals capable of supporting such private and non-commercial ventures as the Moscow Art Theatre; exciting movements in art and literature that challenged the assumptions of traditional realism and social purpose, and spun off such organs of comic criticism as the journal *New Satyricon*; a breed of actors and directors, trained in conservatories and universities and *amateurs* in the best sense of the word. Affluence, a more widely-disseminated literacy, and eased restrictions fostered a number of influential club theatres.

The Moscow Art Theatre's annual cabbage-parties, "rag nights" when the actors performed circus acts and self-parodies, had become so popular that there was a demand for public performances. One offshoot was the Bat (known in the West as the Chauve-Souris), founded by the MAT actor Nikolay Baliev; its repertoire included colorful vignettes based on folksongs, short stories and pantomimes, in a revue format M.C.'d by Baliev himself. More pointed in its satire was the Crooked Mirror Theatre in St. Petersburg, created by the actress Kholmskaya and her husband, the influential critic and editor, A. R. Kugel. Their intention was to poke fun at excesses in the theatrical art of the time. Kugel was a pragmatist and a traditionalist, who disliked the growing supremacy of the director (evinced by Meyerhold's work) and extremism in either naturalism or stylization. His audience was made up of well-informed playgoers, *au courant* of the latest innovations, and alert to satirical jabs at sacred cows.

The Crooked Mirror's first hit was *Vampuka, or the Bride of Africa* (1909), an hilarious spoof of grand opera, with special attention paid to *Aida* and *L'Africaine*. Nowadays, opera seems a cheap and stale target; but in 1910, *Vampuka's* exuberant and poker-faced compilation of operatic clichés was fresh and necessary. "Vampuka" became a byword for fusty staging techniques, and the verb "to vampukicize" entered the Russian language as a synonym for rendering something ridiculous by exaggerating its worst features. The success of *Vampuka* led the Kugels to hire a larger theatre and to invite Nikolay Evreinov to join them as artistic director.

Evreinov, a thirty-one-year-old ex-law and music student, had a motley theatrical background as a playwright, director and actor. His Merry Theatre for Grownup Children had revived Prutkov's *Fantasy* in 1909; and he had become celebrated for his much-publicized theories of monodrama and theatricality. Evreinov brought the Crooked Mirror a new emphasis, theatrical rather than literary; under his sway, a favored format was to present a given situation in a number of styles. Typical were Evreinov's own *Inspector* (*Revizor*, 1912) in which excerpts from Gogol's comedy were staged as they might be presented by a provincial troupe, the Moscow Art Theatre, Max Reinhardt, Gordon Craig, and a silent film starring Larry Semon; and *The Laughter Kitchen* (*Kukhnya smekha*, 1913) in which a short scenario was dramatized according to the *vis comica* of the English, Russians, German, French and Americans. Boris Geyer's *The Evolution of Drama* (*Evolyutsiya dramy*, 1910) presented a love triangle in the manner of Gogol, Ostrovsky, Chekhov and the morbid symbolism of Leonid Andreev. He also moved beyond this straightforward parodic format to more complex explorations of human perception, without ceasing to be comic. Geyer's plays exhibit the transformation in a man's environment as he grows progressively drunker; a wedding scene as reviewed through the eyes of various members of the party; and a proto-O'Neill drama in which the character's real thoughts are spoken in advance of the actual lines.

Evreinov's own favorite play for the Crooked Mirror was *The Fourth Wall* (*Chetvyortaya stena*, 1915), a *reductio ad absurdum* of naturalistic tenets. The shaft was aimed, to some degree, at the Moscow Art Theatre, famous for its veristic sets and costumes and the psychological realism of its acting; but a more immediate butt was the St. Petersburg Theatre for Opera, a group whose aim was to "unvampukicize" opera by rendering it as realistic as possible. It did succeed in demolishing outworn conventions and injecting sense and logic into its productions; Stanislavsky and Nemirovich-Danchenko both learned from it when they turned to staging opera. But the Theatre had its own humorless excesses, apt for ridicule; in the last act of *Carmen*, for example, a first-aid squad milled about the stage, presumably to deal with wounded bull-fighters. Another of Evreinov's laughingstocks may be the director Fyodor Kommissarzhevsky, a former colleague, who had directed Goethe's *Faust* at Nezlobin's Theatre in Moscow, a production in which Mephistopheles was portrayed as Faust's *alter ego*. A similar device had been used by the Moscow Art in its adaptation of *The Brothers Karamazov*: the actor Kachalov had played the dialogue between Ivan Karamazov and the Devil as if it were taking place inside Ivan's head, and for forty minutes he kept up a schizophrenic colloquy.

For Evreinov, who worshipped theatricality as the primal motivation in human life, such attempts were wrong-headed and belittled the stage. *The Fourth Wall* pits an older generation of veterans of the presentational theatre—the actor, the props-man, the assistant director, the prompter —against the young Turks, a Producer and a Director who intend to "change all that." By following the logic of naturalism to its utmost, *Faust* is stripped of its music, its lyrics, its spectacle, and turns into a crackpot experiment in archaeological solipsism. Evreinov juggles the jargon familiar to his audience: the "living through" or "emotional experience" (*perezhivaniya*) prescribed by Stanislavsky, and the dismissal of traditional theatrics as "mummery" and "Punch-and-Judy shows."

That kind of well-informed, well-heeled audience disappeared with the October Revolution. At first, the Revolution promised freedom to the arts, and satire flourished in a rudimentary way, as a propaganda tool used against reactionaries and for the promulgation of Soviet policy. In the poster-like primary colors of a political cartoon, it attacked White Guards, kulaks, emigrés and "ex-people" of all ideological stripe; the message had to be brought across to naive, inexperienced playgoers, so subtlety went out the window. One theatrical collective that called itself the Theatre of Revolutionary Satire significantly changed its name in 1920 to the Theatre of the Revolution and declared its task, and that of the theatre as a whole, to be one of political agitation and social utility. All artistry was subordinated to those goals. It became the earliest of the "Blue Blouse" troupes, Living Newspaper shows who used fairground techniques to bring the latest in revolutionary propaganda to outlying communities.

Of the comic drama of the immediate post-Revolutionary period, only Vladimir Mayakovsky's *Mystery-Bouffe* (*Misteriya-buff*, 1918, revised 1921) tries to invent a new form that answers to the needs of a new society. His one-dimensional mixture of circus attractions and Bolshevik indoctrination was soon transferred to the cinema, minus his colloquial verse; and the Factory of the Eccentric Actor carried on the grotesque tradition in films of the 1920s.

Stage satire did flourish again, for a brief but exciting time, during the period of the New Economic Policy. In 1921, the Soviet government, facing a crippled economy and expiring industry, decided to make concessions to private enterprise and restored agriculture and commerce to a form of capitalism. The policy, which lasted until 1928, was successful, but its side effects were controversial. The entrepreneurs and middlemen who leapt in to take advantage of the policy evoked an ambivalent response: these NEPmen, as they came to be known, alienated true socialists by their vulgarity. Legally, they were subject to a number of discriminatory regulations in education and civil rights, and when the policy was revoked, their property was confiscated and they themselves deported and exiled. Their relatives strove to efface their memory.

Yet, despite the tragic aspect of the NEPmen's activities, they were perfect foils for Bolshevik satire, safe targets to shoot at. Their sharp practices and shady deals were the very stuff of comedy, right in the tradition of Lesage's Turcaret, Balzac's Mercadet and Mark Twain's Colonel Sellers. In Boris Romashyov's The Whipped-Cream Cake (Vozdushniy pirog, 1924/25), Nikolay Erdman's Credentials (Mandat, usually misleadingly translated The Mandate, 1925) and Mikhail Bulgakov's Zoya's Flat (Zoykina kvartira, 1926), a spectacular swindle is conceived and partially carried out, only to be defeated in the end by the characters' own flaws and (shades of Fonvizin!) the intervention of the security police. The scam in The Whipped-Cream Cake is RAIN, acronym for the Russo-American Industrial Network, a profiteering export-import firm shadily associated with a piratical bank. In Credentials, a young ne'er-do-weel terrorizes his neighbors by claiming to be a Communist party member, while a group of "ex-people" mistakenly assume his cook to be the Grand Duchess Anastasia and hope to effect a restoration of the monarchy. Zoya's Flat, behind the front of a dress-designer's salon, is a maison de rendezvous that specializes in blackmail. Gogolian influence is abundant in the comedies of Romashyov and Erdman, particularly in the way the initial deception swells and burgeons until it explodes in the faces of its perpetrators. Bulgakov's satire seems more reminiscent of Sukhovo-Kobylin as the comedy takes on the sinister overtones of melodrama.

Oddly enough, many of the satires of the NEP era come to a climax during a social ritual. Credentials, as well as Mayakovsky's The Bedbug (Klop, 1929) feature hilarious weddings that degenerate into riots. Erdman's The Suicide (Samoubiitsa, 1928) stages a spectacular "going-away" party for its felon-de-se who then appears as a mourner at his own funeral. The comeuppance of the villain of The Whipped-Cream Cake occurs during a banquet, when the title item is brought on; and Yuriy Olesha's The Conspiracy of Feelings (Zagovor chuvstv, 1929) culminates at a soccer game. By using social rituals familiar to the audiences, dramatists found common ground for the mockery of bourgeois customs and attitudes. The practice also hearkens back to the traditions of

Greek New Comedy, with its invitation to the feast at the end, reintegrating the deviant characters and reconfirming a norm.

Ilya Ilf and Evgeny Petrov, best known as the authors of the picaresque novels of NEP-period skulduggery, *The Twelve Chairs* and *The Little Golden Calf*, had recourse to the same device in one of their rare plays, *The Power of Love* (or more literally, *Powerful Emotion—Silnoe chuvstvo*, 1933). This one-act comedy is a Sovieticization of Chekhov's "joke" *The Wedding* (*Svadba*, 1890). In that play, a pretentious petty-bourgeois wedding is in progress at a Moscow restaurant. The groom is an appraiser at a pawnshop who has married for a paltry dowry of featherbeds and lottery tickets; the in-laws are vulgarians who send a friend to hire a "general" to grace the board with his presence. The "general" turns out to be a deaf, garrulous retired naval captain, unconscious that he has been rented; when his recitation of shipboard orders gets too boring, the guests turn him out. His moment of realization that he is the subject of a "shabby trick" is the one humane flicker in an otherwise unrelenting caricature of philistinism and callous feeling. Chekhov's celebrated "objectivity" is hard to find here.

Ilf and Petrov update the action to the aftermath of the NEP period. In her communal flat, the bride is wedding a man as obnoxious as Chekhov's groom in order to secure roomier accommodations. To dress out the party, a foreigner, of the sort imported to '30s Moscow by Intourist, is essential; but the authors complicate Chekhov's situation by splitting the *quid pro quo* between an American victim of the depression looking for a job in Russia, and the bridegroom's father, who is on furlough from prison, but who the guests think is the favored inmate of a posh sanatorium. The laugh is on "parasites" who envy life in the West: jazz on the victrola, rejuvenating gland treatments, black marketeering, the juggling of union memberships to procure special treatment are symptoms of a malaise affecting Soviet society.

The offstage but brooding presence of the bride's first husband Lifshits, a Karaite (*i.e.*, a Caucasian Jew who rejects the Talmud) becomes a running gag that propels the action and rises to an apotheosis when he finally appears to abduct the bride. This stirring dénouement is made possible by the looser marital laws of the Soviet Union. And the guests' accelerating drunkenness testifies to the persistence of old Russian shortcomings in the modern age, even while it adds to the confusion.

The Power of Love closely resembles Bertolt Brecht's early one-act, *The Lower Middle Class Wedding* (*Die Kleinburgherische Hochzeit*, 1926), another assemblage of small-minded citizens for a domestic celebration. Brecht's play, however, is very much in the tradition of Hebbel: it tacitly condemns the family as a corrupt institution that stifles individual incentive. Sardonically, Brecht presents a pregnant bride and a stage metaphor of breakaway furniture. Ilf and Petrov, reflecting the communality of Russian life, convene a broader array of types; and the ghastliness of their picture is relieved by its high spirits. If Chekhov's

Wedding is a *grisaille* lithograph by Daumier, and Brecht's holiday-making burghers are savage caricatures out of Georg Grosz and *Simplicissimus*, then Ilf and Petrov's satiric crew might have stepped off the Russian equivalent of the Toonerville Trolley.

An ambiguously ironical celebration also concudes Isaak Babel's *Sundown* (*Zakat*, 1928), a play which cannot easily be categorized as a NEP comedy, even though it comes from that period. *Sundown* retrospects to the abuses of a bygone era and an exotic locale: the Odessa ghetto before the Revolution. The milieu is that of Babel's tales of Benya Krik the gangster (1927), and the satiric treatment is grander and more poetic than that of his contemporaries. Given a political interpretation, the play could be explained as a depiction of the ugliness and squalor of life on the eve of its redemption by the Bolsheviks; certainly, Maksim Gorky's *Yegor Bulychyov* trilogy explicitly fits that description, and even Naidyonov's pre-Revolutionary dramas of Jewish households match it closely. But Babel is a more figurative writer, for whom reality is only a point of departure.

The critic Pavel Markov, on seeing the first production at the Moscow Art Theatre, noted the play's "epic simplicity, terseness, calm and economy": it did not take sides. Mendel Krik's cruelty and his downfall both have a mythic grandeur: Kronos seeks to devour his children, but is castrated by his son Zeus. It is worthwhile to compare Babel's dramatic handling of the Krik overthrow with the story, "Sundown," that preceded it. (After being lost for forty years, the story was first published in a 1964 issue of *Literaturnaya gazeta*.) In the narrative, Mendel's harsh injustices are shown and dwelt upon; Nekhama is his malign accomplice. His aspirations are played down, and the action narrowed to his house and business. Benya, throughout the Odessa stories, is portrayed as a flamboyant Robin Hood of the ghetto, the life-force sporting a red bandanna.

The play readjusts these emphases. We are told of Mendel's violence and ferocity, but see very little of them; on the other hand, his rhapsodic evocation of the future, his tenacious will to seize life and hang on to it, are rendered in an admiring, almost ennobling light. Benya, however, is reduced in scale: the motive for his symbolic parricide is not so much survival of the fittest as the thirst for respectability. His motives and actions seem mean-spirited when contrasted with Mendel's; and even though Rabbi Ben-Zakharya in his curtain speech explains that the setting of Mendel's sun is the natural prelude to the rising of Benya's, the bare statement is unconvincing. Seen against the panorama of Odessa with its taverns, synagogues and stableyards, Benya's world of well-kept accounts, neat marriages and table manners has less appeal than the disorderly, ruthless but somehow titanic world of the old teamster Mendel, whose last name means "Shout." The world before the Revolution, implies Babel, was messy but vital. His satire operates not on a social but on a universal level: and the process of the passing of the generations is itself subjected to critical laughter.

Any kind of satire became increasingly endangered by the early 1930s. Mikhail Bulgakov's dramatic career is an object lesson in mindless censorship and wasted talent: *Zoya's Flat*, in which sexual and economic corruption were equated, caused a scandal and was soon withdrawn; and *The Purple Island* (*Bagroviy ostrov*, 1928), a motley sendup of theatrical censorship, was similarly short-lived. Only through the direct intervention of Stalin was Bulgakov allowed to make a living as dramaturg for the Moscow Art Theatre, a kind of literary maid-of-all-work, consigned to adapting classical novels and foreign plays. His dramatization of Gogol's *Dead Souls* (*Myortvie dushi*, 1932), a highly imaginative conspectus of Gogol's mind, was scrapped for a more slavish rendition of the book into *tableaux vivants*. He prepared a similar conflation of Molière's work as *Demented Jourdain* (*Poloumniy Zhurden*, 1932) and a four-act version of Cervantes's *Don Quixote* (*Don Kishot*, 1938), neither of which was performed in his lifetime. Of his original works, *A Cabal of Hypocrites* (*Kabala svyatosh*, 1930-36), a biographical play about Molière, which commented obliquely on the position of the artist in a hostile society, opened at the MAT but was banned after seven performances. *The Last Days* (*Poslednie dni*, 1943), a tragedy about Pushkin's death, another artist destroyed by a cruel totalitarian regime, was staged only posthumously. When Bulgakov himself died in 1940, he left behind some twenty dramas, only a few of which have even now been produced in the Soviet Union.

Bulgakov can hardly have expected *Ivan Vasilievich* (*Ivan Vasil'evich*, 1935-36) to be produced in his lifetime, and this freed his imagination from the constraints of censorship and contemporary stage convention. At first glance, it seems to lack the satiric punch of his NEP comedies, or even the humanitarian sentiments and lyrical effusions of his serious plays, like *Flight* (*Beg*, 1936). But themes dear to Bulgakov are subtly camouflaged in it. The mission of the scientist, here travestied as Engineer Timofeyev's quirky time machine, is continually thwarted, frustrated and exploited by outside forces. Bunsha's threat to report Timofeyev to the police; Miloslavsky's desire to convert the machine to burglarious ends; and Zina's incomprehension of the value of her husband's work are all sly metaphors for the sullying of the scientific ideal by interested agencies.

An early draft of the play, entitled *Bliss* (*Blazhenstvo*, 1934) uses many of the same characters—the inventor, named Reyn this time; the burglar, the building super, and a brief glimpse of Ivan the Terrible—but the time machine cast them into the future, and the joke was unnecesarily protracted for four acts. The people of the future were bland cousins of the technicians of 1959 in Mayakovsky's *Bedbug* and the Phosphorescent Woman in his *Bathhouse* (*Banya*, 1930). In the revised play, Bulgakov sent his time travelers back to sixteenth-century Muscovy in order to heighten the comic contrasts. Modern types like a suave actor turned housebreaker and a former aristocrat turned janitor are made to survive in the realm of Ivan the Terrible, while the awesome tsar has to cope with film directors, police informers and open marriages.

Moreover, the simultaneity of past and present—a theme Bulgakov explored more profoundly in his novel *The Master and Margarita*—is used to make a statement about power. Under the proper circumstances, such as the unabashed autocracy of a Renaissance court, Bunsha-Koretsky the *ci-devant* prince, now an officious building super, evolves into a self-indulgent tyrant. Like Chekhov's "man in a shell" who reduces everything he touches to triviality, Bunsha manages to diminish the responsibilities of power to the sating of his appetites. It is important to remember that by the 1930s Ivan the Terrible was being rehabilitated as a precursor of Stalin; the novels and plays of Aleksey Nikolaevich Tolstoy, for instance, display a forward-looking heroic tsar who easily defeats the machinations of the reactionary boyars. Bulgakov's comedy covertly suggests that, removed from their natural habitats, both Stalin and Ivan would be more than mildly ridiculous.

Much of the fun resides in the language. Bulgakov concocts an ersatz Old Slavonic for Ivan and his courtiers, whose quaintness jars with the brisk and up-to-date talk of the contemporary Muscovites. The Soviet Ivan Vasilievich speaks a stiffly formal garble of party clichés and pre-Revolutionary bureaucratese; Miloslavsky sprinkles his remarks with petty-bourgeois French, and Zina and Yakin palter in cinematic shop-talk. Bulgakov almost seems nostalgic for the mouth-filling oaths and colorful syntax of bygone Muscovy, when contrasted with the empty formulas of modern speech.

The dream framework is the least successful aspect of the comedy. *Bliss* had been subtitled "a dream of Engineer Reyn in four acts," and, although *Ivan Vasilievich* is simply called "a comedy," the nodding-off and reawakening of Timofeyev vitiate the farcical significance of the time-travel. It might be a sop to realism, in a forlorn hope that the play be staged; but compared to the unapologetic cross-fading of past and present in *The Master and Margarita*, Bulgakov's device seems timid and unadventurous.

A Theatre of Satire had been founded in Moscow in 1925, on the premises of the old Bat Cabaret; and after a period of playing revue sketches, it settled down to comedies of manners, like Kataev's *Squaring the Circle* (*Kvadratura kruga*, 1928) and Shvarkin's *Father Unknown* (*Chuzhiy rebyonok*, 1933), since true satire was scarce and out of favor. These domestic comedies, in increasingly milder doses, sustained the theatre until the early 1950s, for during that period, it was dangerous to engage in satire. The need for monolithic solidarity during the Five-Year Plans and the Great Patriotic War made comic criticism seem subversive. Fantasy and the grotesque had no place in the aesthetics of socialist realism, and moral militancy could safely be directed only at "enemies of the people." Such satire as was produced was ponderous and strident, aimed at such unmistakable targets as the Nazis and, later, American cold warriors. During the post-Stalinist thaw, however, and the Krushchyov regime, the Theatre of Satire once more lived up to its name. It staged new productions of Mayakovsky's comedies, dramatized Ilf and Petrov's novels, and dared to be topical by adapting for the stage Aleksandr Tvardovsky's anti-Stalinist poem, *Tyorkin in the Other World* (*Tyorkin v tom svete*) in which his soldier-hero discovers that *apparatchiks* preside even in Hell.

Far more important was the rediscovery by the Leningrad State Theatre of Comedy of the plays of Evgeny Shvarts. Its director Nikolay Akimov created brilliant productions of *The Shadow* (*Ten*, 1940) and *The Dragon* (*Drakon*, 1944), which established Shvarts as the greatest Russian dramatic satirist of the post-NEP age. Shvarts, who had begun as a children's writer, couched his very real, sagacious questions about corruption, power and individual responsibility in the deceptively parabolic form of fairy tales. *The Naked King* (*Goliy korol*, 1934), rather too light-hearted a spoof of Nazi racism, was banned during the time of the Hitler-Stalin pact; and, unlike his war propaganda, children's and film scripts, his masterpieces had to wait for his death in 1958 before they could be produced. *The Shadow*, taken from Hans Andersen's tale of the student whose shadow usurps his personality, is a lyrically evocative study of the loss of integrity; and *The Dragon*, accepted by the Soviets as another anti-Nazi fable, can as easily be applied to any society in which the people covenant to live under a falsely protective repression. Shvarts was an anomaly, and he has had no followers.

At present, the Russian drama dabbles in old-fashioned forms like the *vaudeville*, while its realistic drama makes muted criticism of time-servers and bureaucrats, perpetually the sanctioned target. Fantasy and the grotesque are to be seen in the staging of the classics, but rarely in new plays. Will Soviet censorship slacken enough to allow true, pungent satire to reach the audience avid for it? Vasily Aksyonov's "anti-alcoholic comedy," *Your Murderer* (*Tvoy ubiitsa*, 1965), a throw-back to the NEP style in its verbal exuberance, attack on commercialism and use of fantastic moralistic elements, got on to the stage and enjoyed a colorful, ribald production. The impulses do persist, but for now, prospects for a resurgence of powerful dramatic satire look dim indeed.

Laurence Senelick

The Milliner's Shop

A Comedy in Three Acts

(1806)

Ivan Krylov

Characters:

Sumburov (*Mr. Addlepate*)
Mrs. Sumburov, (*Mrs. Addlepate*), his wife
Liza (*Betsy*), his daughter by his first wife
Lestov (*Young Flattery*), her suitor
Masha (*Polly*)
Annushka (*Nancy*)
Madame Carié (*Mme Shoddy*), a Frenchwoman who owns the shop
Monsieur Tricher (*Mr. Cheat*)
Andrey (*Andrew*), Lestov's servant
Antropka (*Obadiah*), the Sumburovs' servant
Police officers and constables

The action takes place in a milliner's shop (in St. Petersburg).

ACT I

The stage represents the interior of a very elegant milliner's shop, filled with luxurious merchandise and goods in the latest styles. Lestov and Masha, who is seated, busy at her work.

LESTOV: Well, now! Tell me, Mashenka, have you been making money? Have you made your fortune without any help from me? Will you soon open your own millinery shop? A comely, sharp little minx like you should have been out of service long ago and her own mistress by now.

MASHA: Oh sir! I'm not well-born enough for that!

LESTOV: What do you mean? Just to keep a milliner's shop?

MASHA: You must be joking, surely? Here as elsewhere birth makes all the difference, and if your name isn't Madame La Broche or Madame Brochard . . .

LESTOV: Poor child! Haven't you the wherewithal to buy a French husband?

MASHA: I could do so easily enough. But would your sister give me my writ of emancipation?

LESTOV: Damn it all! I always forget that and think you are a freed woman. Masha, why didn't you fall to my share? My sister doesn't realize the treasure she owns. In my house you would have but a single order to carry out—reigning over me, my sweet!

MASHA: Oh, sir, do leave off! You're ruining everything I mend. Don't you know you are besmirching my good name?

LESTOV: Aha! Is it ever on display with your other wares?

MASHA: I see you're still the same rake you were before the last campaign.

LESTOV: Oh, no, no! You can't imagine how a single year has changed me.

I'm quite a different man.

MASHA: What? Don't you still squander your money?

LESTOV: Not the least little bit.

MASHA: Since when?

LESTOV: Since my pockets were emptied.

MASHA: What about gambling?

LESTOV: For shame!

MASHA: You really stopped gambling?

LESTOV: Completely! Except for cards, oh, and billiards every so often.

MASHA: What a reformation! But the love affairs and dallying must still go on as before?

LESTOV: Ah, Masha! Why did you remind me?

MASHA: Bah! What a long-drawn sigh! What a melancholic, mournful gaze! Are you play-acting for my benefit?

LESTOV: No; I am actually in love, madly, desperately in love!

MASHA: You in love? Madly, desperately? With how many, may I ask?

LESTOV: Giddy girl! A year ago, travelling with my regiment, we stopped at a prosperous village outside of Kursk. The lord of the manor invited me to dinner . . .

MASHA: Ah, sir, you can't imagine the fun when people from the sticks come in here, especially provincial fops and fashionplates. Seeing the elephant is nothing to it.

LESTOV: Then it's a pity you didn't meet my hosts. Mister Sumburov is an old fellow, a good man, it's true, but headstrong and passionately attached to all the old-fashioned Russian customs. He's happy only when he finds occasion to rail at either new fashions or foreigners. He's so eccentric that the slightest folly committed in his family torments him as if a near relation had been publicly hanged. Well, since there are about a score of females among his closest kin, you can imagine how many easy moments he has left! Mrs. Sumburov, his second wife . . .

MASHA: What! People have two wives in those parts?

LESTOV: Don't be silly! He's a moral man and started out as a widower.

MASHA: Aha! Well, what about his wife? . . .

LESTOV: She's a backwoods clothes-horse who has been going on twenty-nine for the last fifteen years. In addition, wilful, malicious, stingy, cunning and pigheaded. On the other hand, Liza, Mr. Sumburov's daughter by his first marriage . . .

MASHA: Your voice grows gentle. Your expression suddenly becomes tender . . . Ah, sir, this Liza is an enchantress! She's bewitched you!

LESTOV: She's lovely as an angel; charming, clever, every virtue, every perfection . . .

MASHA: Oh! Of course Nature despoiled all other women of their charms to bestow them on her alone.

LESTOV: I fell in love, confessed my love to her, and read my happiness in her face. If it depended on Liza's consent, things would have come to pass long ago . . .

MASHA: Tsk, tsk! Stop, sir!

LESTOV: What's the matter?

MASHA: Stop, stop! Catch your breath and begin categorically the second volume of your novel. The persecutions, partings, the thousand and one obstacles; please leave nothing out. Your little romance will make my work go more quickly.

LESTOV: You're most demanding, Masha! Then hear me out: I forgot to tell you: from the first word I had with Mister Sumburov I found that he and my late father had been old friends. They cherish such remembrances in the hinterlands and consequently I was received with open arms. The old man even observed the mutual love that grew between me and Liza without grumbling. I was honest with him and he already half agreed, when his wife, who had promised her stepdaughter to one of her kinsmen who had offered her a rich reward in return, spoiled the whole affair. And on the pretext that I wasn't rich enough, I was dismissed. I was in despair. By leaving Liza, I lost peace and happiness. It is now a year since I've had any word of her. All hope is gone and yet my passion keeps increasing.

MASHA: A whole year? Ah, that's beyond a joke. But what do you plan to do?

LESTOV: Go on loving and . . .

MASHA: Sighing, and despairing! . . . What a shame! At your age, with your good qualities, the best thing you can find to do with your time is weep it away. However, sir, if you absolutely must, come and do your moaning in our shop. A young man as sentimental as you is a novelty here, a source of wonder.

SCENE 2

Masha, Lestov, Mrs. Sumburov and Antrop.

MRS. SUMBUROV: (*Enters and hands her cape to Antrop, who stands gaping at the shop and doesn't take it.*) You gaby! Quit that gawking!

LESTOV: (*Aside.*) Mrs. Sumburov!

ANTROP: Sorry, m'lady, my eyes is racin' round!

MASHA: (*In an undertone.*) Ah! No doubt these guests are visiting from the backwoods.

LESTOV: (*In an undertone.*) What bliss!—Yes—I'm not mistaken . . .

MRS. SUMBUROV: Madame dearie! Lemme see what you've got that's good.

MASHA: We've got nothing but the best, madam! (*Aside.*) You, my chick, will pay us with curtsies, whatever we stick you with. (*Aloud.*) What would you like?

MRS. SUMBUROV: Oh, my goodness! . . . what does this mean? Antropka, you scoundrel, come over here.

ANTROPKA: Missus, jest look at the purty bonnets! the purty bonnets! The mayor's missus herself ain't got nothing like that.

MRS. SUMBUROV: Him and his carry-on! Didn't I order you, you nasty thing, to drive me to a French shop. Where have you taken me, you lousy freak?

MASHA: He is right, Madam. This is the leading French shop in the capital. You may inquire of anyone you please concerning our employer, Madame Carié! The loveliest, most renowned ladies of fashion have the honor of going bankrupt in our establishment.

MRS. SUMBUROV: Is that so? . . . Sorry, my pet! When I heard you speak Russian, I got worried. These brutes of mine can't understand a thing. It would be just like 'em to drive me to a Russian shop; but I need the finest of whatever you've got. It's for my step-daughter's trousseau.

LESTOV: (*To himself.*) Her trousseau? . . . What dreadful news! . . . They're marrying off Liza. I must learn everything and at any cost break off the match. (*To Mrs. Sumburov.*) Allow me, madam, to express my delight . . .

MRS. SUMBUROV: So far as I'm concerned, kind sir, I'm most delighted at your delight, although I don't know what you're so delighted about. (*Aside.*) Yes, that's Lestov.

LESTOV: (*To himself.*) Not one of your warmer welcomes. (*Aloud.*) Last year, during the far too short stay I made with my regiment on your estate . . .

MRS. SUMBUROV: Ah, sorry, kind sir!—I didn't recognize you. But it's no great wonder—practically the whole army tramped across our village. How are we supposed to remember everybody? (*To Masha.*) My pet, lemme see some of your finest linens and laces.

LESTOV: Allow me, madam, to come and pay you my respects.

MRS. SUMBUROV: What's the point, kind sir? We'll be leaving here soon. (*To Masha.*) Is it true, my pet, that they've taken to wearing sarafans around here?

MASHA: Here, madam, one is at liberty to dress as one chooses.

LESTOV: Of course, you haven't deigned to come by yourself?

MRS. SUMBUROV: (*To herself.*) He won't let up! (*To Lestov.*) I'm here with my husband, kind sir, with my husband. I don't like rushing into distant parts without Artamon Nikiforych. Who knows how long we'll be?

ANTROP: You're right there, m'lady. When you go fer a day, lay in bread for a week.

MRS. SUMBUROV: Who asked you to open your mouth? Shut up, animal!

ANTROP: Dern it all, I'm tuckered out with standin' on the footboard all day with my mouth shet, and m' bones feels broke all night long.

LESTOV: No doubt your charming step-daughter is with you?

MASHA: (*To herself.*) Poor fellow! He can't get wind of her!

MRS. SUMBUROV: Yes, sir! (*To Masha.*) I don't at all like your lace. Lemme see your tulle and chiffons.

LESTOV: Allow me to ask, madam, whose happiness have you arranged by this marriage?

MRS. SUMBUROV: That's a family affair, kind sir. It would be too long and boring for you to listen to. (*Aside.*) He'll drive me out of here. (*To Masha.*) I don't like none of it. I don't think you got anything nice, my chick. Have to go to another shop.

MASHA: (*Aside.*) Chick indeed! Ah, what a country bumpkin! She won't get out of here, I warrant you. (*Aloud.*) Take a look at these overdrapes, madam, we received them direct from Paris by the last boats.

MRS. SUMBUROV: From Paris?

LESTOV: Masha, for heaven's sake, get her out of here so I can, by means of her servant . . .

MASHA: Wait, wait, you'll see how we'll take her down a peg or two. Annushka! Annushka!

SCENE 3

Mrs. Sumburov, Lestov, Masha, Annushka, Antrop

ANNUSHKA: What would you like?

MASHA: Is the Countess Timova's gown ready yet? You know she'll need it for the court ball this evening.

ANNUSHKA: It will be ready today along with the gown for Lady-in-waiting Rosina.

MRS. SUMBUROV: What! You sew for ladies-in-waiting? Couldn't I take a look, my pet?

MASHA: (*To Annushka.*) Over there in the window, that box with the chiffon veils, send it to the Baroness Filinbach.* She complimented us highly on them.

MRS. SUMBUROV: (*Aside.*) A baroness pays them compliments! (*To Masha.*) Listen, my treasure. (*To herself.*) What to do now? I've annoyed her. She isn't even looking at me any more.

MASHA: (*To Annushka*) By the way, don't forget to tell Madame Carié that General Tupinsky's lady is presenting her daughters at court the day after tomorrow and has come three times to ask us to furnish the wardrobe.

MRS. SUMBUROV: (*Aside.*) Ah, what a blunder, what a blunder! (*To Masha.*) My treasure, my angel, I hope you won't refuse to do me the great favor of dressing me in the same style as your countesses, your princesses and your ladies-in-waiting. Money is no object.

MASHA: In that case, finery is no object. Such is the custom in our shop; ladies

---

*Baroness von Screech-owl.

ask what they like of us, and we, in return, take what we like from them.

MRS. SUMBUROV: My angel, just show me their clothes in the meantime, perhaps I'll get someone to make me up something similar. But where is your Madame? Would it be possible to see her? . . .

MASHA: Out of the question, madam! She's taking tea, and I dare not announce you.

MRS. SUMBUROV: Announce? My treasure, you only announce people to persons of importance.

MASHA: Indeed, madam! Anyone you need is always of importance.

MRS. SUMBUROV: Then let's see the finery, my pretty . . . lemme see the finery.

MASHA: Annushka, show the lady what we have that's deluxe . . . I will be with you in a moment.

SCENE 4

Masha, Lestov, Antrop.

LESTOV: Dear Masha, she hasn't changed a bit . . .

MASHA: Don't you give me any credit for shrewdness? I read her like a book.

LESTOV: Listen, agree to assist me diligently in my love. You know how fond my sister is of me. If you find means to win Liza for me . . . your freedom and three thousand rubles dowry . . . Well, is that tempting?

MASHA: Oh sir! Is it tempting! However, Madame Carié must be in on the plot. You're in her good graces, you come and go unannounced . . . Run to her; you know how easily her heart is vanquished by amorous sighs. I'm sure she'll let me assist you and so will all our shop . . . I'm sure your intentions are honorable.

LESTOV: Can you doubt it?

MASHA: The young lady loves you, so I practically guarantee success.

LESTOV: What? You have hope?

MASHA: Oh! she wouldn't be the first girl who's gone from our shop up the aisle.

LESTOV: Step into the other room, and I'll have a go at that fellow. Only, Masha, he looks so brutish.

MASHA: Never mind, never mind, shake out your pockets nice and easy. Money has won over better servants than he.

SCENE 5

Lestov and Antrop.

LESTOV: (*To himself.*) I must appear indifferent, lest he suspect the importance

I give this, and in the guise of a mere acquaintance . . . Yes, that's it.

ANTROP: Lordy, laddy, I reckon the tsar's palace ain't half so perty! No matter what y' look at, it's one wonder after another.

LESTOV: Friend, tell your young mistress that Lestov sends his respects and greatly wishes . . . I'm talking to you, friend!

ANTROP: Me, your honor? Don't git angry, if I talk out o' turn—this stuff, I reckon, comes from overseas?

LESTOV: (*To himself.*) What does he have to know that for? (*To Antrop.*) Yes, from overseas. I would like you to bear the compliments of Lestov . . .

ANTROP: And it's here our masters brings their money from so far off?

LESTOV: (*To himself.*) What a . . . (*To him.*) For heaven's sake, tell the young lady . . .

ANTROP: Don't git angry, master, if I talk out o' turn. Do they wear these doodads every day o' the year that they make so many?

LESTOV: (*To himself.*) Here's a new torment! (*To him.*) Listen, for god's sake, I greatly need you to tell . . .

ANTROP: Never mind that! I mean to say, we don't gussy ourselves up that way even on big holidays!

LESTOV: Oh torturer! Will you please do me the great favor of just two words . . .

ANTROP: Don't git angry, master, if I talk out o' turn, but what d'they wear on holidays?

LESTOV: (*To himself.*) There's nothing for it! Let's try a friendly tone and maybe I'll be able to get through to him. (*To Antrop.*) Here, my friend, they do not recognize the differences you do in the backwoods. Here people dress, drink, eat and live on weekdays as if every day were a holiday. There, I've told you what you want to know; listen to me in turn. I very much want your young lady to know . . .

ANTROP: What goin's-on, what goin's-on! But then, master, if Carnival falls on Lent, don't Christmas fall on Easter?

LESTOV: (*To himself.*) The devil take you and your observations! (*Aloud.*) I would like you to tell your young lady from Lestov that he . . .

ANTROP: Don't git angry, master, if I talk out o' turn . . .

LESTOV: Oh the barbarian! I think Satan himself set him to drive me mad.

SCENE 6

Masha, Lestov, Antrop.

ANTROP: (*On seeing Masha.*) Since they don't lemme open my mouth, it sure was lucky runnin' into this nice young lord. But now I gotta stand here agin like a dummy. I reckon this here's a jolly place to live, 'cause they don't keep you from talkin' to nobody.

MASHA: Well, sir, have you succeeded?

LESTOV: Have I? Look at the sweat pouring off me. This rascal has torn my soul out of my body, and I can do nothing . . .

MASHA: Leave him to me. I'm defter at this than you. Leave now and don't come back for two hours. Your darling will be here.

LESTOV: What! Is it possible? How kind you are, Masha. I really must kiss you again and again.

MASHA: Gently, sir, gently, leave something for your beloved. We shall see if you've got good taste. Go on now, to avert suspicion.

LESTOV: Mashenka, I promise . . .

MASHA: Oh! Promise nothing, sir. I've heard experienced men say it's very bad luck for those to whom the promises are made.

LESTOV: Goodbye then. I couldn't get anywhere with the mistress, I failed with the servant, so I'll go and box the ears of the coachmen.

SCENE 7

Mrs. Sumburov, Masha, Antrop.

MRS. SUMBUROV: It's all exquisite, my dear!

ANTROP: Ah! Missus! There you be now!

MRS. SUMBUROV: (*To Antrop.*) What is it now?

ANTROP: That there feller was the gennelman from last year, you remember . . . Yourself told us he was killed and our poor missy cried over it, but I see'd him so he must be alive.

MRS. SUMBUROV: Stop your lying and go to the carriage instead. You never open your mouth except to tell lies.

ANTROP: Well, I sort o' figgered they didn't kill him.

SCENE 8

Mrs. Sumburov, Masha.

MRS. SUMBUROV: Don't forget, my chick, tell your Madame I need a lot, an awful lot of finery and fabric in the latest style. I want to deck out my step-daughter like a little doll. She's the best match in our whole county. What's more, I'm marrying her to one of my own kinsmen. So, you see, I want to do myself proud.

MASHA: Please, bring her by. We'll take her measurements and our skills are bound to please.

MRS. SUMBUROV: Yes, yes, my pet, we'll come in person. I would have sent for you to come to us, but that husband of mine is so grumpy and narrowminded we'd never get anywhere. What can you do with him? He won't hear a word about French shops, French goods. Don't spread it around, but he even hates the French. All he'll have is Russian stuff. But what do we produce that's any good? If it wasn't for your Madames, God forgive me, we'd all be walking around in the nude.

MASHA: With your refined taste you ought to be a lady of fashion!

MRS. SUMBUROV: I am, my pet, I'm the leading landowner in our whole parish.

MASHA: Do you need anything for your son-in-law as well? Our shop has excellent haberdashery for men, and you have probably picked out your son-in-law with the same good taste as you have your clothes.

MRS. SUMBUROV: Can you doubt it, my dear! On his account I had to put up with all kinds of things from my hubby, but at last I got my way. My darling son-in-law, Mister Nedoshchetov,* is a sight for sore eyes; my pet, he's been to London, Paris and done the tour of Europe. What can you say, he's a cultured man, and so thrifty that he lives in the country for economy's sake. You know, he does everything the way foreigners do it. He sows and reaps according to the German almanac. But honestly, our land is so idiotic that when he needed summer, bingo! as if for spite, autumn showed up and everything was a total loss! . . . So, my angel, I'll be back, for I still have urgent need of you!

MASHA: How so, madam?

MRS. SUMBUROV: Couldn't you lend me some little patterns? I'll set every wench in the house to sewing and I'll be dressed in the latest fashions by the time I leave.

MASHA: Cart fashion models a thousand miles away? Ee, madam!

MRS. SUMBUROV: What a nuisance! Well, at least, you can knock yourself out sewing it for us. I'm really afraid my hubby will find out, God help us! Then there'll be a hullaballoo to wake the saints above!

SCENE 9

Mrs. Sumburov, Sumburov, Masha.

SUMBUROV: Oho, my lady wife! Very nice indeed! Whatever I say is so much wind! In my heart I felt you couldn't resist doing something silly! Why have you chosen to visit this place?

MRS. SUMBUROV: For shame, Paw, at least in front of people!

SUMBUROV: People? What people? No, only leeches who suck your blood, swindle you, bankrupt you and, when they've made off with your money, laugh in your face.

MASHA: Judging by his manners, it seems your dear hubby is not a courtier.

---

*Mr. Impecunious.

MRS. SUMBUROV: Ee! All right, dearie . . . you only rave about Russian stuff. I'm following the advice of people who know as much as you; my niece Neshchetova . . .*

SUMBUROV: Almost her entire estate and her husband's she's poured down the drain.

MRS. SUMBUROV: My sister-in-law Khoprova . . .**

SUMBUROV: She too is starving with half her estate left.

MRS. SUMBUROV: My brother is a clever man . . .

SUMBUROV: Your brother the clever man has signed so many promissory notes and I.O.U.'s to these shops that the clever man will soon have to live on his cleverness alone.

MRS. SUMBUROV: Ee, dearie, that's enough of your Russian notions. Anyway, you know that Sudbin and Tagaev, your brothers-in-law, are sensible men, men of position, and they say . . .

SUMBUROV: Oh, they've dinned their balderdash into my ears already. All they do is boast that nothing they own is of Russian-make, that everything's ordered from England or France. I'll bet they'll soon import bladders filled with English wind; and you're hankering for me to follow in their footsteps! No, no, nothing doing. I give you my word that no French soul will ever see a kopek of mine.

MRS. SUMBUROV: Well, but foreigners have such taste . . .

SUMBUROV: Yes, a decided taste for our money. Do you really think that without them we'd be as naked as jaybirds?

MRS. SUMBUROV: Ee, watch your language! Do you want us to dress like our grandmothers and scare the wits out of people?

SUMBUROV: That's enough of your blather, wife. If our grandmothers had frightened people away, there wouldn't be anybody on earth today. A good-looking woman is fine enough without the help of French frippery. What does she need it for?

MASHA: To keep from being ridiculous . . .

SUMBUROV: Ridiculous? In whose eyes? Giddy-pates' and flibbertigibbets'? There's a great sin for you!

MASHA: It's no sin, sir, but in a big city, it's worse than any sin.

MRS. SUMBUROV: That makes sense, dearie. We answer for our sins only to God, but if you're ridiculous, you can't show yourself anywhere.

SUMBUROV: You're spouting hogwash, my love. You'll see how I'll deck out Lizanka in stuff from Russian shops . . . Confound it, I forgot I left her waiting for me in the carriage.

MASHA: Ah, if only Lestov had seen her!

MRS. SUMBUROV: What, in the carrage!

---

*Impecunious.

**Grabby.

SUMBUROV: Yes, here at the door. As I was riding by with her, I spotted Antropka and came in just to drag you out of this sinkhole. Well, let's be off.

MRS. SUMBUROV: Just let me see a little bit more.

SUMBUROV: Not the tip of a ribbon, not the tiniest needle, and I advise you
not to toddle off to such places in future, unless you want a good . . . you
understand me. *I* don't chase after fashions, do I? And as a man of the old
Russian breed, I prefer my wife to obey me. Antropka, the mistress's cape!

SCENE 10

*The same and Antropka, drunk. Antropka hands Mrs. Sumburov the cape, which she puts
on very slowly.*

SUMBUROV: So! You regret the parting! No turning back. March, madam,
march! (*To Antrop.*) What are you standing there for, you booby? Go open
the door!

ANTROP: Which one, sir?

SUMBUROV: Hey, you're drunk!

MRS. SUMBUROV: When did he have the time?

ANTROP: 'Scuse me, sir, but a old friend wanted to treat me and Senka to
some vodka and pointed out a tavern, so, y'know, it woulda been a shame
to turn 'im down.

SUMBUROV: You have friends and acquaintances everywhere, you do. Where
is Senka?

ANTROP: He'll be done soon, sir!

MASHA: (*Aside.*) Our young lover is behind this!

MRS. SUMBUROV: Them drunkards! You can't let 'em out of your sight for a
moment. Suppose it was that good-for-nothing Lestov?

SUMBUROV: March, madam, march! And how are we going to manage two
carriages with one footman! . . . Very thoughtful of those loafers!

ANTROP: 'S'all right, master sir, I'll stand behind both carriages. Senka can
git along on foot.

SCENE 11

Masha and Sumburov.

MASHA: Please come back soon. (*To herself.*) Well, it's bad for Lestov: that
damned yokel has upset all our plans.

SUMBUROV: Eh! Hold on, sweetheart! You look Russian to me.

MASHA: Ah, sir, unfortunately!

SUMBUROV: Unfortunately? You mean fortunately, don't you?

MASHA: How so?

SUMBUROV: It just occurred to me . . . well, I haven't any time now! But another time will come. Have to think it over, goodbye.

MASHA: What does he want? What's he talking about, I'd like to know? These yahoos are like Tatars, it's not easy to catch their drift. I'll go and arrange this business with Madame Carié.

END OF ACT I

ACT II

SCENE 1

Masha and Andrey.

MASHA: (*Reading a letter.*) "I have been to the Sumburovs'." That was efficient!—"The old gent greeted me with open arms and begged me, as the son of his dear friend, to visit him more often." Lucky boy! "But his accursed wife spoiled it all; she told him I had got his servants drunk and had spoken with Liza."—Ah! That did it, my friend!—"Sumburov lost his temper, destroyed any hope of my winning Liza and kicked me out with threats and curses. I am in despair . . ." (*To Andrey.*) Where is your master now?

ANDREY: He's gone home and is lying on his bed in sorrow.

MASHA: That's all right, sorrow isn't fatal. Bah! there's more. "I will demand satisfaction from my rival." Very nice! "Then I'll fight Sumburov . . ." Better yet! "And finally I'll blow my brains out." How original! "Can you think up anything better? Come and advise me." That's the most sensible thing of all.

ANDREY: He's waiting for an answer!

MASHA: Tell him, most politely: you, sir, have lost your wits. Goodbye!

SCENE 2

Masha, alone.

MASHA: He's good, he's kind, but all the same he's fooling, just like a nobleman!

SCENE 3

Masha and Monsieur Tricher.

TRICHER: Ah! *Bonjour, ma chère* Mashenka! 'Ow are you, my anzhel?

MASHA: Bah, Monsieur Tricher! What a lucky day! I'm running into all my old acquaintances. I've just seen one who's left the army, but you, Monsieur Tricher, have probably not been chasing glory the six months you've been away?

TRICHER: Oh no, no! I go for vhat eez profeet, soleed . . . een short, cash.

MASHA: Why then have you stopped selling us pomade. We always paid well, I think. The Lord knows why you got angry with us!

TRICHER: Oh! I no more deal in ze pomade, *ma chère enfant*, I am no more ze peddlair, but a respectable and well-to-do marshant.

MASHA: Congratulations, Monsieur Tricher, congratulations. Have you found buried treasure or what?

TRICHER: Trezhair? . . . I not compre'end vot means zis. No, I 'ave found a sharming *seigneur*, a young lord greedee for ze money. I teached 'im ze beezneez and *enfin*, ze young man eez cleaned out, veree cleaned out—and Monsieur Tricher 'as clammed to ze top of ze tree.

MASHA: I think, Monsieur Tricher, for such a lovely swindle, you should be swinging from that tree.

TRICHER: Oh, I 'ope so, I 'ope so. Eez Madame Carié een 'er room?

MASHA: She is. What do you want of her?

TRICHER: A beautifool *affaire*. I know from a reliable source zat you 'ave received goods on wheech zey forgot to poot ze customs stamp. You cotch my dreeft?

MASHA: What do you mean? You're talking rubbish.

TRICHER: Vot, vot? Rubbidge?

MASHA: It means nonsense.

TRICHER: Aha, not nonsanse, but 'orse sanse! I know exactlee whan zey came and where zey poot ze goods. *Eh bien!* I 'ave a 'undred tousand rubles in I.O.Me's from a reech zhentleman een Koorsk, named Monsieur Nedoshitu, and seence I need money *ou bien* marchandise,—I vant to make a *proposition* to Madame Carié, to tak zees I.O.Me's as securité. I 'ope my old fran from Franch soil, Madame Carié, weel do me zees flavor.

MASHA: (*Aside.*) Nedoshchetov? Nedoshchetov! . . . Ah, that's Liza's fiancé! Wonderful! We'll wave this I.O.U. at Sumburov and maybe it will cool his desire to wed his daughter to him. (*To Tricher.*) Monsieur Tricher, I have some advice for you.

TRICHER: Advice, my beautifool?

MASHA: I know someone . . . (*To herself.*) Bah! That's it! Sumburov's our man! . . . oh! here he comes now—right on cue. (*Aloud.*) Wait here, Monsieur Tricher, you'll thank me for it!

TRICHER: Wiz plaizhoor, darlang!

SCENE 4

Masha, Tricher and Sumburov.

MASHA: (*Low, about Sumburov.*) Is he bewitched? He's muttering to himself!

SUMBOROV: Yes! Suppose this girl were to consent to become a maid to my wife or daughter . . . She could dress them like Chinamen and I wouldn't care : . . but at least my money would be in Christian hands.

MASHA: (*To Tricher.*) This is a gentleman from Kursk, he's wealthy and will gladly buy those I.O.U.'s from you.

TRICHER: Excellant! (*To Sumburov.*) Monsieur . . .

SUMBUROV: Your servant! (*To Masha.*) My dear, I should like to have a couple of words with you.

MASHA: (*Aside.*) With me? I don't get it!

SUMBUROV: (*Aside.*) No, she's dressed like a lady and stares like one too . . . I'm embarrassed to tell her . . .

TRICHER: Monsieur, do you spik Franch?

SUMBUROV: Who me, Moosoo? If I wanted to settle in France, the first thing I'd do is learn French, and those who come here would be well advised to learn *our* language. As it is, I wasn't prepared for such a welcome guest,—the cheeky fellow!

TRICHER: (*To Masha.*) *Ma chère* Mashenka, zis gentleman eet sims, eez a leetle beet booreesh.

SUMBUROV: (*To Masha.*) I'd like to employ you, my pet . . . (*Aside.*) She'll never consent.

MASHA: (*To herself.*) Employ me? . . . Does he mean . . . ? No, that's impossible!

TRICHER: I mak bold to suzhest a beezneez, your 'ighness! . . .

SUMBUROV: (*To Tricher.*) I am *not* high! (*To himself.*) Plague take this Frenchman! (*To Masha.*) How might I, my beauty, have a heart-to-heart chat with you?

MASHA: (*To herself.*) Heart-to-heart? No, no, that's not what his face says.

TRICHER: (*To Sumburov.*) I wood lak, my dear Monsieur . . .

SUMBUROV: (*Rushing at him.*) Well! Spit it out! What do you want?

TRICHER: Ay! ay! *mon cher* Monsieur, vhy such angair? I ask of you nussing, except to propose zat you buy zees I.O.Me signed by a young *seigneur* of your province, Monsieur Nedoshitu.

MASHA: (*To herself.*) The stone is flung, but will it hit its mark?

SUMBUROV: What? what? Nedoshchetov? Is he mixed up in their hanky-panky too? Oh, wife! You've estranged me from Lestov, I hope we weren't mistaken! (*To Tricher.*) What I.O.U's?

TRICHER: Oh, monsieur! I know ze laws of *politesse* and do not vant to eenterupture you.

SUMBUROV: Moosoo Frenchy, I can see you aren't expert at talking *or* shutting up at the right time. Show them to me. (*To himself.*) I.O.U's made out to loan sharks; but I never heard anything that bad about Lestov. (*To Tricher.*) Well, what about those I.O.U.'s?

TRICHER: Oh, eet's a bagatelle, a mere bagatelle for a reech zhentleman lak Monsieur Nedoshitu.

SUMBUROV: True enough, I thought it would be unimportant—we consider him to be very frugal.

TRICHER: Oh, zees money was gone for sharitable vorks. (*He hands him the I.O.U.*)

SUMBUROV: What! Twenty!—thirty!—fifty thousand rubles! A pretty kind of frugality! Here! When did he squander all this money?

TRICHER: *Oh, pardonnez-moi,* Monsieur deed sqvandair nussing, Monsieur bought many sings: ze Dutch cows and calves, ze Eengleesh rams and ze Spanish lambs for eez farm.

SUMBUROV: There's dirty work somewhere. I never saw any of that at his place.

TRICHER: No dirty vurk! A 'arsh climate! And zen you see, 'alf pereeshed and ze ozer 'alf died. But I am sure zat Monsieur Nedoshitu got zair 'ides most correctlee.

SUMBUROV: Hides? For breeding! (*To himself.*) A pretty kind of frugality! The more I think about it, the more I regret Lestov, and his father was a good friend of mine. Lestov of course is a scapegrace who got my servants drunk so he could talk to Liza. That's low and underhanded! But in the long run it's better than handing out I.O.U's for a hundred thousand rubles. And to whom? . . .

TRICHER: Eez Monsieur agreeable?

SUMBUROV: Ask my footman for the address where we're staying and come to me in half an hour. (*Aside.*) I want more detailed information.

TRICHER: Your servant! I weel zhust see Madame Carié for one minoot . . .

MASHA: What for?

TRICHER: Oh, my beautifool! Een ze beeg ceeties zair eez more zan wan Monsieur Nedoshitu. I 'ave many ozer I.O.Me's.

SCENE 5

Sumburov and Masha.

MASHA: (*To herself.*) The old gent is meditating? I think we're in for a windfall.

SUMBUROV: Yes! I ought to consult my wife. I don't want to be my daughter's undoing. These money-lenders know how to pick our young men clean and it looks like they've sunk their claws awfully deep into Nedoshchetov!

MASHA: No doubt you're pondering those I.O.U's?

SUMBUROV: Just so. The man is one of my close relations. But let's drop that. It's not a hanging offense, it can be remedied. He acted foolishly! A good lesson for the future! Who doesn't learn from experience? He did go overboard; but let's drop it for now. (*To Masha.*) Just listen: you look like a decent sort of girl. I like you a lot . . .

MASHA: (*Aside.*) Oho! The dirty old man! Here comes the punchline! (*To Sumburov.*) Sir, I am very glad . . .

SUMBUROV: Tell me, my love, what would you take as an annual salary?

MASHA: (*To herself.*) A salary! He certainly does things on the up and up. (*To him.*) How can you think. . . ?

SUMBUROV: (*To himself.*) I knew she wouldn't consent! (*To Masha.*) Listen, my pretty, instead of working here for the whole town, why don't you agree to come to my house where you'd have very little work. I wouldn't wear you out, I promise you . . . Why are you staring at me so strangely? Have I offended you?

MASHA: (*Aside.*) He must have gone mad . . .

SUMBUROV: Think it over carefully, my girl. You're so witty, so dainty, so ladylike that I advise you not to stay in such an exposed spot where any rapscallion . . .

MASHA: How can you, sir, with a wife and daughter? . . .

SUMBUROV: Well, they're the reason that I need you. What can I do if fashions have turned their heads?

MASHA: (*To herself.*) So that's what it's all about. Poor old man! I've slandered you unjustly!

(*Mrs. Sumburov enters.*)

SUMBUROV: I'll let you think it over, my chick. Honestly, I'll give you a big salary, plenty to eat and wear, and at my house you'll be in clover.

SCENE 6

Sumburov, Mrs. Sumburov, and Masha.

MRS. SUMBUROV: (*Aside.*) Lovely! My darling hubby, now I see why he chases me out of French shops.

MASHA: (*To herself.*) No! I shan't refuse, so that I can lure them here somehow. (*To him.*) I'll have to think it over, sir! . . .

SUMBUROV: Think it over, think it over! I'll reward you as well as your Madame can and find you a husband. Aha! There's your little ears blushing pink! (*Takes her by the hand.*) Let's think about the handsome dowry.

MRS. SUMBUROV: (*Coming between them.*) A handsome dowry! Need to think it over! . . . Oh you old ninny! What do you think you're up to? What's on your mind?

SUMBUROV: Leave off, leave off! (*To himself.*) What the devil's come over her?

MRS. SUMBUROV: What's this, you renegade—cast off your living wife, you reprobate! And I'm supposed to stand for it? No, no, I'm going to scream so all decent people will come a-running and see . . .

SUMBUROV: (*To himself.*) She'll cause a scandal, and that'll be the end! (*To her.*) Listen to me, you nitwit!

MRS. SUMBUROV: I listened to you all right! . . . To my face you pretend you can't stand French shops, you curse and swear at them. But it seems when I'm away you hum a different tune!

MASHA: (*To herself.*) We must turn this to our advantage! . . . (*To Mrs. Sumburov.*) You see, madam, how sometimes innocence itself falls prey to slander! Well, what if there was reason to thank the gentleman instead of scolding him!

SUMBUROV: Of course there's reason!

MRS. SUMBUROV: (*To Masha.*) That's as may be—but it's you who'll thank him, my chick, not me! Didn't I hear what he said about the dowry?

MASHA: Of course! the dowry, madam, for his daughter!

SUMBUROV: What?

MRS. SUMBUROV: Lizanka's?

MASHA: Yes! He was planning a pleasant surprise for you and had already picked out a large quantity of superb merchandise especially for you.

MRS. SUMBUROV: For me?

SUMBUROV: (*To Masha.*) What? What are you talking about?

MASHA: (*Low to Sumburov.*) Please contradict me if you're not afraid of bickering and a scandal.

SUMBUROV: (*To himself.*) A scandal? She's right! It's the best way to avoid it.

MRS. SUMBUROV: (*To Masha.*) Can it be? . . . But no, I can't believe it!

MASHA: You'll believe it shortly. Girls! Someone come in here and bring those two pieces of embroidered muslin and give them to the gentleman's servant.

SUMBUROV: (*To Masha.*) I seem to recall there was only one piece . . .

MASHA: (*To Sumburov.*) A fine thing! You've forgotten . . . (*To one of the girls.*) Take that lace and those two baskets of flowers and set them carefully in the carriage!

MRS. SUMBUROV: My precious! I never would have believed it . . .

SUMBUROV: (*To himself.*) Neither would I. (*To Masha.*) Do you want my head on a platter or what, damn you?

MASHA: (*To Mrs. Sumburov.*) One can see that the gentleman loves you madly, madam! (*To one of the girls.*) Take care you don't break this porcelain luncheon service. You see, madam, such artistry! Such taste! And all for you!

MRS. SUMBUROVA: (*To Sumburov.*) My priceless one! Why aren't you happy? Am I right, you can never find such wares in Russian stalls?

MASHA: Of course not, madam! What do they have that's good? There's nothing to buy there!

SUMBUROV: (*To Masha.*) You brazen trull! I'd like to buy a rope in one of 'em and choke the life out of you!

MRS. SUMBUROVA: What, what did he say?

MASHA: (*To Sumburov.*) Oh, so sorry, sir! (*To Mrs. Sumburov.*) He was pleased to order me to measure you and your stepdaughter for more expensive gowns!

SUMBUROV: What? What? When did I say that? You didn't hear well. Come a little closer. Listen, my chick, you'll make me lose my temper in the end . . .

MASHA: Threats! Oh, that's a sign of weakness. Who's keeping you from speaking for yourself? When it comes to words we'll see which of us goes under.

MRS. SUMBUROV: Now what? What are you on about over there? Is it some new whim of his?

MASHA: He is so impatient! . . . He's pleased to complain that the young lady, your step-daughter, isn't here. He wants her measured right away!

SUMBUROV: (*To his wife.*) Never mind, my love, we'll come back with Lizanka some other time. (*To himself.*) If only I can lure her out of here. (*To Masha.*) There, you rogue, you're hoist on your own petard.

MRS. SUMBUROV: (*To her husband.*) No, no, my angel! Lizanka can be here in a trice. When I saw your footman at the door, I wanted to find out what you were doing in here, that's all! These shenanigans of yours never entered my mind! I left Lizanka with her auntie. They merely wanted to take a turn in the lane, and they'll be here any minute. I had a sort of presentiment that told me you'd come to your senses.

MASHA: And it's about time too! I'll go and announce you to Madame Carié at once. (*Aside.*) To tell her that the girl is here and send for Lestov. (*To Mrs. Sumburov.*) Madame Carié will strive to serve you. (*To Sumburov.*) Well, sir! Who's hoist on whose petard now?

SUMBUROV: (*Aside.*) What torment! But I must be patient, lest something worse happen. (*To Masha.*) You're a fine one, you slut! I think the devil himself must have sent me here! (*Masha exits.*)

SCENE 7

Sumburov, Mrs. Sumburov, Mme. Carié, M. Tricher.

MME. CARIÉ: *Non, non, Monsieur.*

TRICHER: I weel not spik Franch, I weesh zat Monsieur et Madame learn of your eengratitude.

MRS. SUMBUROV: (*To Mme. Carié.*) I'm here, Madame dearie . . .

MME. CARIÉ: (*To Tricher.*) *Et vous osez* . . .

TRICHER: I weel not spik Franch! Monsieur, pliz leesten to me. Madame 'ere knows me veree eenteematelee. I need money, a mere peetance. I geeve I.O.Me's as securite. But Madame eez so eegnorante, so rude she weel not trust me.

MME. CARIÉ: *Eh bien!* I do not trus'! I 'ave no money for ev'ry vagabond.

TRICHER: Vagabond! . . . Vagabond yourself, you not-for-nussing wooman! You 'ave forget ze time ven you run barefoot in ze streets of Paris and now you are all puff up like ze great ladee!

MME. CARIÉ: And you, Monsieur, remembair also zat een Paris?

TRICHER: *Allons, soyez discrète!*

MME. CARIÉ: Ah! now I am ze one zat don't spik Franch. You forget, Monsieur, zat een Paris you peecked ze pockettes, *et* for long time, Monsieur, you leeved undair ze breedges . . . But Monsieur eez treeky, Monsieur got out of Paris . . . *Le scélérat!*

MRS. SUMBUROV: I'm here, my dear . . .

TRICHER: Remembair, Madame, 'ow, sanks to my *récommendation,* you was 'ired by a riche Russeean family as governess for to titch ze young girl 'ow to be'ave. Even zo Madame, for 'er good be'avior, paid some veesits to ze Salpétrière lockup.

MME. CARIÉ: Veeshus pairson! I vas innocente! I 'ad powerfool enemies!

TRICHER: Yes! Yes! Your eennocence always got een trouble veez ze Paris police.

MME. CARIÉ: Et Monsieur remembair 'ow aftair I got 'im a place as tootor een a riche 'ouse, 'e vas so eegnorant and so vulgair zat 'e tootored no ze noble sheeldren but ze good dog! Ze veellain!

TRICHER: Deesgustang *créature,* vait ze moment. I know ze good vay to mak you beggair and tramp as evair vas een Russeean family.

MME. CARIE: *Comment?*

TRICHER: No vords een Franch. I vant Monsieur to 'ear 'ow you are ze not-for-nussing, vulgair wooman, 'ow you are ze treekstair and deal een contraband. Eh-heh? So, now you are become so quiette, zees means I am right! (*To Sumburov.*) Monsieur, I leave 'ere and go to your quartairs, to wait you zere. I 'ave eemportant beezneez to communiqué to you.

SUMBUROV: (*To Tricher.*) Go on, go on! (*To his wife.*) Come along, wife, I too have something important to say!

MRS. SUMBUROV: At least wait for Lizanka!

SUMBUROV: What have you got to do with her?

TRICHER: *Adieu!* You veel 'ear from me soon, you not-for-nussing!

MME. CARIÉ: Traître!

SCENE 8

Sumburov, Mrs. Sumburov, Mme. Carié.

SUMBUROV: Come along, missus, let's go. I've got something important to talk over with you.

MRS. SUMBUROV: Hold on; here comes Lizanka . . . Give me time to take her measurements.

SUMBUROV: I need an extra dose of patience! But for Heaven's sake, hurry it up. Oh, that hussy Masha, if I could only . . .

SCENE 9

Mrs. Sumburov, Sumburov, Liza, Mme. Carié.

LIZA: Still here, Daddy? I was afraid I'd be late, but auntie was so tired that we barely dragged this far. She left me and went home . . .

MME. CARIÉ: Madame do not spik Franch?

MRS. SUMBUROV: Sorry, no, my love! You see, dearie, how my folks brought me up. I'm ashamed to show my face before wellbred people. And you, you've raised your daughter the same way.

SUMBUROV: I brought her up to be a good wife, a good housekeeper and a good mother, and not to gabble like a magpie. I've had time to see lots of your lady-friends here, fine ones. "It's shameful not to learn music, shameful not to know how to dance, shameful not to chatter away in French." But there's no shame, ladies, in . . . it was on the tip of my tongue, but that's enough, I'm discreet.

MME. CARIÉ: For sure you are from ze deestant proveences?

SUMBUROV: Why? Is it so wonderful to think here as I do?

MRS. SUMBUROV: Madame dearie, my step-daughter and me need lots of gowns . . .

SUMBUROV: Slow down, wife, take it easy. Order a gown apiece; that'll be plenty. Do you want to walk off with the whole shop or what?

MME. CARIÉ: Plizz come, Madame, I myself weel shooz ze good fabrique and all you 'ave to do eez pay.

MRS. SUMBUROV: Fine, my angel! Did you hear, my love? She'll choose it herself, the sweet thing! Lizanka, you stay here a bit.

MME. CARIÉ: Mashenka! Mashenka!

SCENE 10

The same and Masha.

MME. CARIÉ: Be so good to stay wiz Mademoiselle. I go to shooz ze goods for Madame.

SUMBUROV: If you don't go with her, she's liable to carry off the whole shop. Let's go, Liza, what have you to do here?

MASHA: What a good idea! Come along, come along, madam, inside you will see the loveliest, most expensive things, and I'll help you make a selection . . .

SUMBUROV: No, no, just stay here! I'll go by myself. This scoundrel would be glad to ruin me. (*He exits.*)

SCENE 11

Liza, Masha, Mme. Carié

MME. CARIÉ: *Ma chère enfant,* you are about to see ze young zhentleman 'oo adores you.

LIZA: My heart is beating so loudly.

MME. CARIÉ: Fear nussing, Mademoiselle, Madame Carié knows 'er beezneez and weel know 'ow to kip ze old man een ze back room. Mashenka, don't forget to tell Monsieur Lestov zat my shop eez reesking 'er *réputation* for ees *rendez-vous* weez zees sharming mam'sel and zat 'e veel be gratefool for zees service een 'ard cash.

MASHA: Go on, go on, I won't forget.

SCENE 12

Liza, Masha, Lestov.

LESTOV: Liza, my beloved! Tell me once more that you love me.

LIZA: How can you doubt it? I have been brought up in the country, far from the big cities.

MASHA: That'll do, that'll do, leave your sweet nothings till the wedding. You'll have plenty of time then, if you haven't lost the urge. We'd better figure out how to overcome the obstacles.

LIZA: What am I supposed to do! Won't the promise I've given you suffice: to marry no one but you or die a virgin!

MASHA: No, no, that's not quite what we had in mind. It must be all or nothing. Right, sir?

LESTOV: Oh, absolutely. Without you I cannot be happy; my life would be too burdensome. Either you must be mine or . . .

MASHA: Or he will live on until he dies. So have pity, Miss . . .

LESTOV: Consent to go with me to my sister's. Her estate is only a few miles away. There we can be wed and thereafter no one can part us.

LIZA: Heavens! What are you suggesting?

MASHA: Why, where's the great calamity, miss! An elopement! How many plays, how many novels end that way? Yes, and in fact so many girls are abducted you can't count them. And so many more would love to be abducted but aren't!

LIZA: What are you asking of me?

LESTOV: You must, if only to raise my hopes somewhat.

LIZA: Cruel stepmother! You will be the cause . . .

LESTOV: I ask only a word . . . You keep silent? . . . Then farewell forever.

LIZA: Stop! (*She drops into an armchair.*) Lestov, how wretched I am!

LESTOV: Masha, she's losing consciousness!

MASHA: Of course! You see, everything's just as it should be . . . (*Sumburov appears.*)

LESTOV: (*Throws himself on his knees.*) Liza! Liza my beloved! What shall I do? Masha! Liza!

MASHA: I'll go get some smelling salts. Ee, have you gone crazy! Can it be, sir, that you've never seen anyone faint before?

SCENE 13

Sumburov, Masha, Liza, Lestov, then Mrs. Sumburov.

SUMBUROV: What! What! What does this mean? On his knees before my daughter! In a shop! In the busiest part of the city! Right in broad daylight! O disgrace! O ignominy! The impudent creatures!

LIZA: Daddy!

LESTOV: A fresh disaster!

SUMBUROV: You shameless hussy! You deserve to be strangled on the spot . . .

MRS. SUMBUROV: What a racket! What a to-do! What's going on in here?

SUMBUROV: Come closer, wife, look, admire your handiwork! We owe this all to you! If it weren't for your hellish mania for loitering in all these damned shops . . .

MRS. SUMBUROV: But what's going on!

SUMBUROV: What's going on is that I found His Lordship here on his knees before my daughter! Now do you understand, you birdbrain! What a shame for our whole family! . . . on his knees in a public place . . .

MRS. SUMBUROV: Well, dearie, you were always the first to take his part. You've only got what you deserve! But you, sir, how dared you?

SUMBUROV: (*Imitating her.*) "But you, sir, how dared you?" Why not dare, since he's come across an idiot. Just come here once too often and eventually he'll dare something with you too.

LESTOV: Pardon me, sir, my passion . . .

SUMBUROV: No, no, sir, I shall never pardon such a disgrace. How could you! . . . And I! I was already predisposed to like you. Your first gift to me was to entice my servants to a tavern so you could stay and chat with my daughter, without regard for my name, without considering what passersby might say when they saw a girl alone in a carriage and no one with her but a young rake. What must they have thought of her and her parents! Well, I might have forgiven even that. I would have put it down to your youth, your rashness, I would have made allowances, recalling my friendship with your father . . . but you, you bribed these scoundrels to lend you a hand . . .

MASHA: Ee, sir . . .

SUMBUROV: Shut up, shut up, my chick, I'm not so blind nor such a booby . . . You bribed these scoundrels to fool us and arrange a tryst. You have considered neither the honor nor the good name of your father's friend,— and in front of this brainless slut, to my shame and so everyone can see, great and small, on foot or on horseback! . . . No, no, we are no longer acquainted.

LESTOV: I implore you . . .

SUMBUROV: I won't hear another word!

LESTOV: I swear . . .

SUMBUROV: Forget you ever knew my family. Forget too, if you can, that I was your father's friend. Otherwise, your conscience will give you no peace after the way you've behaved. Let's go, missus!

LESTOV: Then neither my pleas nor my promise to make amends . . .

SUMBUROV: I couldn't care less.

LESTOV: Then farewell, sir, and expect the worst from my despair!

SUMBUROV: The impudence! Look, wife, that's your French shops for you! That's your French knowhow! They knew how to make a laughing stock of you. Oh the shame! Oh the scandal! There's never been anything like it in the Sumburov family since the world began! Out of here! Quick, out of this hell hole! (*Mrs. Sumburov exits.*)

MASHA: Is it our fault then?

SUMBUROV: As for you, my chick, go and find your Madame and tell her she's a baggage and so are you; that for her respectable dealings she deserves to be in a reformatory and so do you; and that I hope the earth swallows her up, damn her, and her shop, and you with 'em! (*He pushes Masha out of the way and leaves.*)

END OF ACT II

ACT III

SCENE 1

Lestov, Masha and Annushka.

LESTOV: An excellent idea, Andrey!—Listen here, Masha!

MASHA: That damned Frenchman! Have you hidden everything that ought to be, Annushka?

ANNUSHKA: Clean away. We left out only those things the police can wonder about, but nothing they can latch on to.

LESTOV: What's going on around here? Spit on all that, Masha, and praise my scheme instead.—Andrey!

MASHA: Wait a minute; and let's start by holding council. Can't you see I have something else on my mind! What about the bronzes?

ANNUSHKA: In the loft.

LESTOV: What devil's tricks are these? Why are you hauling all those bronze gods and goddesses upstairs?

MASHA: It's nothing, sir, nothing at all. They've suffered a slight accident which compels them to flee to the loft to avoid the police.

LESTOV: What rumor have you heard? This is absurd, Masha. With powerful friends, you have nothing to fear. Listen to me instead . . .

MASHA: Oh! Just a minute . . . What about the lace?

ANNUSHKA: I hid it in a place known only to me, and naturally *I* won't show the way to the police.

MASHA: Well, go inside a while and keep a close eye on things.

SCENE 2

Masha, Lestov, then Andrey.

LESTOV: But what's the meaning of all this commotion?

MASHA: An attack on our innocence. There's a certain French good-for-nothing, a certain Tricher, who threatened to denounce us for keeping contraband.

LESTOV: Do you have any in fact?

MASHA: Certainly not. But, even though our house is in order, a little precaution in cases like this isn't a crime.

LESTOV: Tricher! Tricher! Who in the world is this Tricher?

MASHA: About two years ago he was a peddler, and then he became a valet and called himself Dupré. Since then, he's made his fortune and turned into Monsieur Tricher.

LESTOV: Dupré! Ah! That's the rascal who served me as valet, then robbed me blind and vanished.

MASHA: Well, he's the one, damn him, who's threatening our shop.

LESTOV: Rubbish! I'll cool him down whenever I please. First listen to what I've cooked up . . . Andrey! Where the devil has he got to?

ANDREY: What's wanted, sir?

LESTOV: Run as fast as you can and quickly find out where the Sumburov woman is and tell the lady very secretly, so that nobody knows . . . (*He whispers.*) Fly like an arrow!

ANDREY: I'm flying, sir!

LESTOV: Andrey!

ANDREY: What's wanted, sir?

LESTOV: You realize you mustn't call yourself my servant, but pretend to be someone from this shop.

ANDREY: I get you, sir!

LESTOV: Go on.—Andrey!

ANDREY: Here, sir.

LESTOV: Be sure the old man in particular doesn't catch sight of you—by no means.

ANDREY: I know, sir!

LESTOV: Andrey!

ANDREY: What now, sir!

LESTOV: Diligence and caution!

ANDREY: Very good, sir!

LESTOV: Andrey!

ANDREY: Now what!

LESTOV: Listen: either five rubles in your fist and permission to drink without stint for two whole days, or else a warm reception from the soldiers.

Understand? Farewell!

Masha, Lestov.

LESTOV: Well, Masha, the ambassador is on his way. Now let us conspire.

MASHA: But is his mission a good one? Are you sure?

LESTOV: Here's vanity for you! Unless you've dreamed up the plan yourself, it can't be any good!

MASHA: Here's vanity for you! Since the gentleman dreamed up the plan himself, it has to be good! Let's take a look at this good idea.

LESTOV: Well, of course, it's not too bad. Listen with both ears and be amazed by my inventive genius. I sent Andrey to Mrs. Sumburov to tell her on behalf of Madame Carié that you have at this moment contraband frills and furbelows that she can buy for a song. All she has to do is come here, a little later this evening. What do you think? Will it tempt her?

MASHA: There's no problem about her coming. Well, what then?

LESTOV: She'll come, bringing Liza, unbeknownst to the old man. You will take her into the next room. Liza knows that we have no other recourse but elopement after this morning's scandal. She'll have to consent.

MASHA: And what if Mrs. Sumburov comes without her step-daughter.

LESTOV: Without her step-daughter?—That never occurred to me. Well, then I use all means of winning Mrs. Sumburov to my cause—tears, prayers . . .

MASHA: And what if she isn't won over? There'd be nobody to elope with!

LESTOV: Then I'll elope with *her!*

MASHA: Ha, ha, ha. Marvellous idea! Planning to open a freak show?

LESTOV: No, really. Joking aside, I'll take her out of town to my sister's estate. Then I'll speed to the Sumburovs with parlay of a truce, and if it works, I'll effect an exchange of prisoners and carry off the charming Liza.

MASHA: Charming indeed! Now listen to me: the step-mother will either not come at all or come alone. To win her over is impossible, and to carry away the old bag through the whole town is fine in a novel, but not in real life. Now what do you think: wouldn't it have been better to ask advice before sending off Andrey?

LESTOV: Wretched girl! You've disillusioned me and just at the wrong time. At least I was happy in my imagination. Why wouldn't you talk to me when I asked you for advice?

MASHA: It's every man for himself, sir. Now that I am provided for, I can think up something for you. Only the more I think up, the more I'm convinced that your mission was at the wrong time to the wrong place.

LESTOV: Perhaps you're right, Masha. But Andrey is far off by now. What can you concoct to keep his mission from being a total loss?

MASHA: The only good that might come of it is the ability to insinuate myself into Mrs. Sumburov's confidence, and that'll take time.

LESTOV: Time! You've gone mad!

MASHA: You would prefer, sir, to have your novel end on Page One. Such impatience! True, it does give me an idea . . . Yes, yes, if Mrs. Sumburov comes, excellent! I must confess, we women, even little girls, are craftier than the cleverest man.

SCENE 4

Lestov, Masha, Annushka.

ANNUSHKA: Madame Carié sent me to tell you that Tricher and the police officers will be here at any moment. Is everything squared away?

MASHA: I believe we're ready to receive our beloved guests. Ah! Good heavens! I completely forgot about that cupboard. For heaven's sake, quick, help me to clear it out . . .

ANNUSHKA: Someone's coming!

MASHA: It's Sumburov! Get out, get out. Ah! What a disaster. The devil must have sent him here at this hour!

SCENE 5

Masha, Sumburov.

MASHA: Bah, sir, is it you? Quite an unexpected call!

SUMBUROV: Yes, my sweet. I hope though that it'll be my last. I came to settle up accounts for all the folderol I've been saddled with, thanks to you.

MASHA: Dear me! The bill isn't drawn up yet and Madame Carié is not here. My goodness, sir, have we been rushing you?

SUMBUROV: No, no. I want to put an end to this as soon as possible once and for all. Until then my soul won't rest easy. I'll pay you off and then I won't have a care, except to avoid looking at your side of the street, if I can.

MASHA: Isn't there plenty of time tomorrow?

SUMBUROV: What do you mean, tomorrow? Come here again! God forbid!

MASHA: Actually, sir, *we* haven't the time right now. We'll send you the bill.

SUMBUROV: Hell and damnation! Don't you understand I don't want to see your shop or anybody from your shop . . . it looks as if everything here is topsy-turvy!

MASHA: I must admit, sir, that Madame has not yet made a list of your purchases. She's gone out and it'll be a long while . . .

SUMBUROV: I'm ready to spend the night here, so long as I can call it quits with you. But, my chick, why so panicky? . . . Am I disturbing you, by chance?

MASHA: In what way, sir?

SUMBUROV: How do *I* know? You've got so many kinds of business. And if the Frenchman Tricher was telling me the truth . . .

MASHA: He's a scoundrel! Oh, that miserable Tricher!

SUMBUROV: Ha, ha! I'd like to see someone give you a good lesson, otherwise your shops would soon get rich in all sorts of underhanded ways. Be still, be still! Tricher's preparing a fine surprise for you.

MASHA: We aren't afraid of him.

SUMBUROV: That's your affair! Mine is my bill! I demand my bill!

MASHA: Allow me, perhaps I can find it in the other room. Oh! The confounded old man! (*Aside.*) If only I could get him out of here!

SCENE 6

Sumburov, alone.

SUMBUROV: Yes! She's very frantic about something. The Frenchman apparently told me the truth; they deal in contraband merchandise. If only they were caught in the act, we'd be revenged on all the vicious trades they practice here. I'll bet that reckless mothers who brought their daughters to these blessed shops have more cause for weeping than I do. And the poor husbands . . . Oh! Little do they know of all that's bought and sold here.

SCENE 7

Sumburov and Masha.

MASHA: What rotten luck! She hasn't returned yet!

SUMBUROV: What about my bill? Do I really have to spend the night here? I don't think you would appreciate a guest like me, especially now.

MASHA: I'm very sorry to make you wait so long, but it's impossible to draw up the bill in Madame's absence. If you'd consent to . . .

SUMBUROV: I consent to wait here until tomorrow. You see this pocketbook? It weighs more to me than forty pounds of lead, because I know it holds your money. (*He throws the pocketbook on the table.*)

MASHA: I protest, we're very busy just now.

SUMBUROV: So! Evidently the Frenchman's threats weren't airy nothings! Tell truth: are there some little items that slipped by the customs?

MASHA: No, sir. We run a respectable business.

SUMBUROV: And a hardworking one . . . See: all the Russian shops are closed by now; but you lot, you don't want the nights to go by without making a profit. And certain kinds of merchandise are more profitable than others! Tricher told me everything!

MASHA: Tricher! He was never one of our confidants!

SUMBUROV: Well and what if he knows from reliable people where the goods come from and where they're kept, suppose he heard it from the men who shipped them and stored them . . . For example, isn't there a cupboard in this room where something is hidden? Well! Why have you suddenly grown so quiet? . . .

MASHA: Really, I'm pained for my employer's sake . . . Your suspicions . . . there are the same goods in this room as in the others.

SUMBUROV: Oh, no, these are more lucrative, for there are goods and goods. Ha, ha, ha! How delighted, how delighted I'd be to see some uninvited guests drop in on you while I'm here!

SCENE 8

Masha, Sumburov, Antrop.

ANTROP: Master, sir, things is bad!

SUMBUROV: Well! what is it? did you smash up the carriage?

ANTROP: How d'ye figger that, sir! 'Tain't that at all! . . . things is mighty bad!

SUMBUROV: Damn it all! What is it then? The horses have bolted with the coachman or what?

ANTROP: No, sir, 'tain't that neither, but it's powerful bad! . . . Our young mistress . . .

SUMBUROV: My daughter! What's happened to her?

ANTROP: Things is bad, master, and I see'd clear jest how bad things is!

SUMBUROV: Nincompoop! Will you speak or must I . . .

ANTROP: Jest a minute, sir, jest a minute! . . . if you keep a-interruptin', I'll jest git more and more mixed up. Listen to this here: I'm a-settin' on the front steps when all of a sudden up drives this carriage and from inside there's a squeaky voice callin', "Antrop! Antrop! is that you?" I was, y'know, suspicious, and I figgered somebody was in that carriage. So, "What d'ye want?" sez I. "Is Daddy in the shop? Are you with him or what?"

SUMBUROV: My daughter!

ANTROP: Jest what I suspicioned, master, it musta been young Missie.

SUMBUROV: Well, was my wife with her?

ANTROP: That's where things is bad, master, Missus weren't there. That officer from way back as stayed with us in the country with his regiment—he was there. He stuck his head outta the carriage winder—I reconnized him in the lamp-light—and sez he, "Greet your master for me and tell him he was the one who forced me to this." To what? The Lord alone knows, yer honor! Then he sez to Miss, "Let's drive somewheres else darlin' to hire you a maid," and then they whips up the horses and off they go! That's when I figgered out that things is bad . . . I reckon Missie run off with him.

SUMBUROV: O the disgrace! O the scandal! That wretch! But why didn't you raise a hue and cry at once?

ANTROP: That's up to you, sir, who's stoppin' us? Let's go in the street and shout fer help. The two on us'll shout louder as a team.

SUMBUROV: Is my carriage there?—O the impudent chit!

ANTROP: Sure 'tis, sir, I figgered you wouldn't stick around here, so I told the coachman to git back on the box.

SUMBUROV: I'll rush home, see if I can pick up their trail, and discover in what direction they're to be followed . . . Hurry to our lodgings and send riders out at full speed.

ANTROP: Right you are, sir, I figgered shank's mare wouldn't be good enough now!

SCENE 9

Masha, Lestov, and then Annushka.

LESTOV: Masha, Masha! Are you alone here?

MASHA: All alone. The old man fell for it hook, line and sinker, and has gone home to track you down. See! In his excitement he forgot his hat, his stick and his pocketbook! My, how plump it is! It must have got fat on the backwater estates. Annushka, empty out this cupboard.

LESTOV: Ha, ha, ha! I played my part to perfection and Annushka performed like an angel! Such a meek, such a squeaky little voice! Poor Antrop, when he heard her calling his name and asking after Daddy, thought sure she was his young mistress. We spoke our fond farewells, whipped up the horses, turned down a side street . . . and came in by the back door. Well! Is my report satisfactory, ma'am?

MASHA: Couldn't be better!—If you only knew what's going through my mind now . . . Tell me, has Andrey returned?

LESTOV: Long ago. Mrs. Sumburov wanted to come at once, but what further need have we of the old witch? That really was a silly blunder of mine before . . .

MASHA: Oh! If you only knew how this blunder may have a happy ending!

LESTOV: How?

MASHA: Just a moment, just a moment. Let me mull it over. (*To Annushka.*) Lock these boxes in your trunk. (*Aside.*) I've got it! (*To Annushka.*) You can leave the gowns in the other room . . . wait a minute. (*Aside.*) The old man is just what we need. (*To Annushka.*) Carry these items to Madame and make sure they're put in some out-of-the-way place. Even though we're innocent, the further we are from troublemakers, the easier we can rest. (*Aside.*) Nothing's more likely, if only we succeed in wangling him back here . . .

LESTOV: You seem restless, Masha. Are you developing a fever?

MASHA: Yes, yes! But this fever will be to *my* profit, not the doctor's. Now, sir, leave here and don't come back until Madame Carié has returned. Then run around the building and enter by the street-door.

LESTOV: If I understand any of this . . .

MASHA: Go on, clear out . . . ssh, someone's coming! . . . Be sure and keep your word if we win the bride!

LESTOV: If you doubt it, here's a kiss as security.

MASHA: Foo, what a maniac! Watch him like a hawk and he still waylays you!

SCENE 10

Masha, alone.

MASHA: Well, Masha, your freedom and three thousand rubles dowry—it's a pretty prospect! Knuckle down, my love, you're only missing one trivial item: a husband! Bah! That is truly trivial; in this day and age you can always find a bridegroom if you've got a good dowry!

SCENE 11

Masha, Mrs. Sumburov, then Sumburov.

MRS. SUMBUROV: Well, I've made my peace with you, my chick, though I must avow, the recent incident . . .

MASHA: Believe me, madam, I had nothing to do with it. You know what a flutter we were in: carrry this over here, put that over there, it didn't occur to me to keep an eye on that rapscallion. We told him straight out never to set foot in our shop again! And really, heaven alone knows what you must think of us,—why, madam, actually we lead the well-regulated life of a nun here.

MRS. SUMBUROV: Let's get down to business, my pet! Close the shop so that no one I know can see me and bring it to my husband's ears . . .

MASHA: The door is closed. Fear nothing.

MRS. SUMBUROV: I've already sent my carriage and my footman twenty yards down the street; although, truly, it's very dark in the courtyard. But all the same, God forfend that my old man ever learn of it . . . He'll never let me hear the end of it. Listen, my pet, you told me you had certain goods . . .

MASHA: Superb goods, madam, and you can have them for a song. We're afraid they might attract attention here in the city, but since you are going to the hinterlands you can wear them in good health. Wouldn't you like them for your step-daughter?

MRS. SUMBUROV: No, no, my dear. I really mustn't thwart my old man in everything . . . Back in the provinces we'll make her up some lovely gown . . . However just put aside the most and the best for me. I can already see them elegant ladies of ours busting with envy when they catch sight of me at balls and outings, the peacock of peacocks, and I hope they eat their hearts out. (*Someone knocks.*) Someone's at the door. See who it is, my pet, and if possible keep 'em out.

MASHA: My God, it's your husband!

MRS. SUMBUROV: My husband! Ah! I'm lost! Whatever shall I do!

MASHA: What a racket, what pounding! I think they're trying to break the door down.

MRS. SUMBUROV: My precious! My angel! Can't I hide somewhere? For pity's sake, before he gets in here, I'll go in the next room!

MASHA: Ah! What a calamity! The door is locked from the other side, and there's nobody in there. We'll have to send for the key.

A VOICE: Open up! Open up!

MRS. SUMBUROV: What, all the way round and back here again! God forbid! I'm ruined, my precious, if you don't take pity on me! . . . Spare me the disgrace . . . The devil must have sent me here!

MASHA: (*Opening the cupboard.*) Ah! Here's a way. Get inside this. I'll put the key in my pocket and you shall wait out the storm.

MRS. SUMBUROV: Fine, fine, my dear. But do send him away as soon as ever you can. What a sin! What a sin! (*She climbs into the cupboard.*)

SCENE 12

Masha, Sumburov, and Liza.

SUMBUROV: What a stupid thing to do! Where's my pocketbook?

MASHA: Here it is, sir. Intact.

SUMBUROV: Most praiseworthy! Really, what with all the shenanigans around here, I'd be right in applying to you the proverb that tar,—tar . . .

MASHA: You mean, a spoonful of tar mars a barrelful of honey?

SUMBUROV: No, no! A barrelful of tar mars a spoonful of honey! That's what could describe you lot and your shop. However, I was quite absent-minded just now . . . there's my hat too, and my stick. A damned clever plot! Even now I can't quite make it all out. (*To Liza.*) You drive up to the door in the carriage with Lestov; he orders Antropka . . . What the hell is all this nonsense! It must be the after-effects of his hangover.

LIZA: How could you think such a thing of me, Daddy?

SUMBUROV: I don't think anything. Nevertheless, I'd do right not to leave you alone in the house now. Where did my wife skip off to? Well, all right, I'll settle up my bill; and then . . . straight home . . . I absolutely insist on paying my bill right now.

SCENE 13

Sumburov, Liza, Masha, Tricher, Police Officer, followed by Constables.

TRICHER: Ah, Monsieur, I am delightfool to find you 'ere. Now see yourself eef I 'ave lied. Monsieur Officer, pliz to follow me eento ze ozer room for to find beeg beezneez.

MASHA: (*Aside.*) Yes, yes! go on—if it took you a year, you'd still be in the woods!

SUMBUROV: Are you absolutely sure, Moosoo? They seem to be greeting you very calmly.

TRICHER: O no, no! Regard zees cup-board, plizz to see eet, Monsieur, it 'olds mush fine marchandises. Zees I vas told by ze pipple 'oo 'eed eet 'ere. Zhust wait a leetle, you veel see een a sudden zat I am right.

SCENE 14

Sumburov, Masha, and Liza.

SUMBUROV: Well, my beauty, you see I wasn't telling you a load of poppy-cock about that Frenchman. The hound didn't waste his time! Now we'll see how you get out of this . . . Aha! My lady doxies, here's an end to your holiday-making. You won't cheat and bankrupt any more plain people like us; you won't run a pretty little trade in contraband merchandise, you won't set up any more trysts in your infernal shop. You're getting what you deserve!

MASHA: Oh sir! You can see I'm calm. Truly this social call doesn't frighten us. But why are you so down on our shop? There are at least a hundred that stock the same goods we do.

SUMBUROV: No, my love! Don't be so modest. You can't easily meet with such ladylike goods as what's inside this cupboard.

MASHA: What sort of goods are in there?

SUMBUROV: I know it all, my pretty! Whisper in my ear, is there a customs stamp on their bottom? We'll soon see.

MASHA: Will you indeed! And by what right?

SUMBUROV: Don't get so flustered, my love—I probably won't touch it, even with my fingertips! But there will be men in uniform, functionaries, who will ever so gently and discreetly rummage a bit and inspect a bit.

MASHA: There's nothing to inspect.

SUMBUROV: Nothing to inspect? Brazen hussy! I won't budge till I see with my own eyes how you wriggle out of this. It's a pity my wife isn't here, I should have brought her along to observe her good friends. She would have seen how respectable they all are!

SCENE 15

Masha, Sumburov, Tricher, Mme. Carié, Officer and Constables.

TRICHER: Your excellance, please carry on ze searsh. Zees eez not ze end, I'm sartain . . .

MME. CARIÉ: 'E mus' be zhoking! Vairy zhoking! To suspect a decente personne like Madame Carié!

MASHA: You offend us.

OFFICER: Don't get upset, my dear! If we find nothing, you're in no danger . . .

MME. CARIÉ: Ah! Good 'eavens! Good 'eavens! Vat a nastee beezneez! . . . c'est vous . . .

MASHA: Don't worry.

TRICHER: I know not ze Fransh tong. Pliz, Madame, spik ze Russeean. I vant zat all ze world deezcovair vat kind rogue you are. Monsieur Officer, proceed wiz your *perquisition.*

OFFICER: Trust me, I know my business! (*Looks around.*)

SUMBUROV: Mind you don't forget the cupboard.

OFFICER: I find nothing suspicious here.

SUMBUROV: Oh, there's more to follow . . . Wait a bit.

SCENE 16

Sumburov, Liza, Tricher, Mme. Carié, Masha, Police, Lestov.

LESTOV: My! What a distinguished gathering! Your servant. Who are all these people?

SUMBUROV: It's nothing, sir; just a friendly visit from the police to our good friends. Rejoice; they've found contraband here. No wonder this place has grown so rich so quickly!

LESTOV: What! They actually found some!

SUMBUROV: Well, if they haven't found any yet, they soon will and as near as can be. Wait a bit, see what will emerge!

LESTOV: What does this mean, Masha?

MASHA: (*Whispers to him.*) Well! What do you say to that?

LESTOV: I think the Devil himself inspired you.

OFFICER: I've found nothing anywhere!

TRICHER: Monsieur, be so kind to look een zees cup-board . . . Ay! Lestoo!
 . . . Nevair mind. *Allons, Tricher, de l'audace!*

SUMBUROV: Yes! Yes! That's where the valuable treasure is kept. Ah! What
 a pity my wife isn't here! I would have paid dear to have her here. She's
 their perpetual champion. What a face she'd pull if she saw them now!

OFFICER: Be good enough to have this cupboard opened.

MME. CARIÉ: Mashenka, vair eez ze key to zees cup-board?

MASHA: Here it is; but I protest . . .

SUMBUROV: (*Takes the key from her.*) Hand it over, give us that precious key,
 my chick. Isn't your conscience clear? Will this key disclose only legal property? Charming! Somehow I get the impression you aren't overjoyed to
 let this little key out of your keeping. Madame, my love! Today you did me
 a nice favor which deserves repayment at my own hands. Well, you'll get
 your wages from my own hands, for I personally will open this precious little cupboard. Yes, yes; let's see these curios of yours. Ha, ha, ha! Samples
 of some sort? What a pity if we don't find any stamps on them! (*He heads for
 the cup-board.*)

MASHA: (*Stopping him.*) Stop, sir.

SUMBUROV: Fiddlesticks, what's there to stop for? Let's see the curios you've
 got inside! What far-off climes have they come from? Ha, ha, ha!

MASHA: (*Whispers to Sumburov.*) Stop, I tell you. Do you know what you are
 about to do?

SUMBUROV: How's that? You've lost your mind, impudence!

MASHA: You'll find . . .

SUMBUROV: I'll find . . .

MASHA: I'll tell you what you'll find . . .

SUMBUROV: I'll tell *you* what I'll find—contraband.

MASHA: As I was saying, what you'll find is—your wife . . .

SUMBUROV: What, what did you say? . . .how's that? . . .

MASHA: Your wife, I said! Just look through those panes of glass, if you don't
 believe me.

SUMBUROV: Oof! Am I getting shortsighted? . . . No, that's her in the flesh!
 O the villainess! that's lovely merchandise, that is! There's contraband for
 you!

MASHA: Well, why don't you open it, sir?

SUMBUROV: What lunacy! Oh the hussy!

OFFICER: My good sir, I can't wait much longer.

SUMBUROV: For heaven's sake, show a little patience, I'm going out of my
 mind! O shame! O scandal! Sir, couldn't we put it off until tomorrow?

TRICHER: Why tomorrow? *Mais que diable,* you are all so confuse. Geeve to me
 ze key, eef you plizz, me, I veel open eet.

SUMBUROV: The key? I'll knock you down before you lay hands on it, you heretic! O the godforsaken trollop!

OFFICER: The key, if you please.

SUMBUROV: Key? What key? What do you want of me? Do I have a key?

MASHA: Ee, sir, pull yourself together. You have it in your hand.

SUMBUROV: Ah! Too true. I wish I could swallow it and choke to escape such shame! O the wretched female! I think Satan himself stuck you in that cupboard to disgrace me.

LESTOV: (*Whispers to Sumburov.*) Sir, I know your dilemma.

SUMBUROV: Hush! For heaven's sake, keep still if you know it! Who else knows it? Ah! The whole town already knows of my disgrace, my shame! Lestov my friend, help me! Get me out of this ghastly mess!

LESTOV: You can imagine what a scandal there'll be if they pull your wife out of that cupboard.

SUMBUROV: Hush! Quiet, for heaven's sake! O you she-outlaw!

LESTOV: And they will draw up an official report of it for the authorities.

SUMBUROV: And they'll print it in the papers? . . . I'm a dead man!

LESTOV: I can get you out of all this; but I beg you, remember your friendship with my father. Remember I've given you no reason to persecute me, for your daughter reciprocates my love.

SUMBUROV: I understand, I understand. So you'll get me out of this fix? Good. You shameless woman, this will be your first punishment! You didn't want Lestov, very well, I'm delighted to have the chance of dumping that spendthrift of yours, that Nedoshchetov. Daughter, come here. Give me your hand—here is your husband-to-be.

LIZA: Ah, what bliss! Daddy, to whom do I owe such a change?

SUMBUROV: My confounded wife.

LIZA: Ah! I'm ready to bow at her feet! Where is Momma?

SUMBUROV: Hush, hush. What does it matter where she is? Mind your own business.

TRICHER: *Eh bien,* Monsieur, veel you 'and over zat key? I veel not geeve up, not *moi*!

LESTOV: Dupré, don't you recognize me?

TRICHER: Monsieur muss be mistake. I 'ave not ze honor of Monsieur's acqvaintance. I am no Dupré, my name eez Monsieur Tricher.

LESTOV: Wonderful! Only don't forget, Dupré or Monsieur Tricher, that I can have you punished for all the knavery you committed in my employ three years ago when you were my valet. We can still find at the police station the affidavit concerning your absconding.

TRICHER: Ah, Monsieur! In ze name of 'eaven, do not ruine me and my *réputation*. For t'ree year I 'ave been a honest man and a reech marshant. I veel do vatévair you desire.

LESTOV: Then, right this minute . . . (*He whispers.*)

TRICHER: A peety! a grat peety! but for me your weesh eez 'oly! (*He goes and whispers to the Officer.*)

OFFICER: What! All of a sudden you withdraw your accusation and admit your error and Madame Carié's innocence?

TRICHER: True, Monsieur Officer, I am mush to blemm and Madame Carié eez innosance 'erself. I spoke not ze truce.

MME. CARIÉ: Ah! I demande to prove my innosance and punish zees scondrelle Tricher!

LESTOV: Never mind, you won't have reason to regret it.

MME. CARIÉ: (*To Tricher.*) Eh bien, veeked man, I forgeeve you.

OFFICER: Then I have nothing more to do here. I advise you to be more circumspect in future about your allegations. Your servant! (*He leaves.*)

LESTOV: And you get out, too, Tricher. I've forgotten everything, don't worry. Goodbye!

TRICHER: Ze daveel tak me eef I compre'end ze list leetle sing! . . . *Serviteur*, vat a defeet! A locky sing I vas able to escape! (*He exits.*)

LESTOV: (*To Mme. Carié.*) And you, Madame, return to your room, I'll settle accounts with you later.

MME. CARIÉ: I am sartain zat Monsieur eez ze honorable man. *Bon soir*!

SCENE 17

Masha, Liza, Sumburov, Mrs. Sumburov, Lestov.

MASHA: Well! Now, sir, open the beneficent cupboard, but for heaven's sake, don't lose your temper. The poor lady has already had enough of a fright.

SUMBUROV: (*Opens the cupboard.*) Shameless creature! Godforsaken female! You've had me drawn and quartered! What diabolic power plumped you in there?

MASHA: Rest easy, madam. All has turned out for the best.

SUMBUROV: (*Pulling her out.*) Well, clamber out of there, you wretch! Say, have you decided to spend the rest of your life in there?

MRS. SUMBUROV: Ah! Artamon Nikiforych, dear heart! I sinned, abandoned woman that I am!

SUMBUROV: What, what do you mean by that, you miscreant!

MRS. SUMBUROV: It was the foul fiend who tempted me to hide from you . . .

SUMBUROV: Well and then what?

MRS. SUMBUROV: I was tantalized by a bargain. I hadn't even the time to see any of the stuff when you pleased to show up.

SUMBUROV: Oof! That's a load off! 'Pon my word, I thought it was the devil knows what kind of hanky-panky! Shameless, brainless woman! Thanks to you, I was on the brink of ruination. Well, my chick, in return, behold your son-in-law. Willy nilly, you'll accept him and treat him kindly and find another wife for your kinsman, that spendthrift.

MRS. SUMBUROV: What! My God! Oh, miserable creature that I am! Is it true, dear heart?

SUMBUROV: Indeed it is! Liza, kiss your betrothed! Now you see that my resolve is sincere. Would I allow my daughter to kiss anyone but her intended?

LIZA: Daddy, you bring me back to life!

LESTOV: How can I express my gratitude? Liza, dear Liza! What bliss! (*Softly to Masha.*) Masha, I owe you much. I also hope to reward you amply. My sister loves and respects me. Come to me two days from now for your emancipation and the three thousand rubles I promised you.

MASHA: What good fortune! Another two or three weddings like this and even Masha will become a somebody.

MRS. SUMBUROV: I don't know where I am. My head's in a whirl.

SUMBUROV: You ain't heard nothing yet, you wretch! But all right! May God forgive you! Let there be a general truce between us. Only on one condition: from now on you will never come within a mile of a French shop.

END

The Headstrong Turk,
or,
Is It Nice to Be a Grandson?

A Naturalistic-Conversational Play

(1863)

Kozma Prutkov*

---

*From the explanation of this dramatic work, published in *The Contemporary* No. IV, 1864 (in the section "Chronicle"), it appears that only a fragment of this work by Kozma Prutkov has survived. It was discovered in a portfolio belonging to the deceased, with the inscription "*Collection of unfinished pieces (d'inachevé) No. 1,*" stamped on it in gilt. Judging from a certain trait, Kozma Prutkov has depicted himself by the name of "A Well-Known Writer" in the Prologue.

(Author's Note)

Characters

A Well-Known Writer
Ivan Semyonovich
Ivan Semyonovich's Valet

PROLOGUE

The stage represents an open space, with a mound in the middle. The sun is rising from behind the mound.

THE WELL-KNOWN WRITER: (*Enters wearing a peaked cap and a voluminous cape and carrying an open parasol, with a hefty tome under one arm. He steps down to the forestage and closes his parasol.*) The ascendancy of this diurnal luminary marks the advent of a solemn day for me and my colleague. My colleague and I intend today to present a *new species of dramatic presentation.* We concur in designating as dramatic presentations those spectacles which take place on stage, and, in particular, in St. Petersburg at the Bolshoy (called for no good reason "The Stone Theatre"), the Alexandra, the Mikhailov, and the circus; and in Moscow at the Bolshoy and the Maly.

Plays can be subdivided into a number of categories, such as comedies, tragedies, dramas, operas, pantomimes, vaudevilles and ring-round-the-rosy folk dances.

My colleague and I have devoted our whole lives and all our adulthood to the invention of a new species of dramatic presentation. My colleague and I have decided to call it, after much lengthy deliberation,—I might even say, suffering!—a "naturalistic-conversational play."—Our creation is entitled: *The Headstrong Turk, Or, Is It Nice To Be a Grandson?* (*He walks up on to the mound.*) God grant that this production be received with the same purity and candor with which we offer it to the public! It is time we Russians commemorated the shift to the second half of the nineteenth century with a *new word* in our literature! This *new word*, so long awaited by all, will be uttered today by myself and my colleague! . . . Need we repeat that we have devoted our whole lives and our adulthood to it?! . . . Moreover, for its sake, I have turned down an advantageous match between my daughter and the merchant Gromov in order to bestow her on my colleague.

So, on with the play! . . . God grant, say I, that it be received with the same spiritual purity and heartfelt candor with which my colleagues and I present it to our public! (*He steps down from the mound, opens the parasol over himself and leaves the stage.*)

IVAN SEMYONOVICH: (*In one of our civil service uniforms, after standing in conceal-ment the whole time, steps down to the forestage, holding a fiddle and casting glances to either side.*) The merchant Gromov's daughter is after me . . . I've got lots of children, not counting the ones from my first marriage and the uninten-tional ones. But that's neither here nor there!—The author has left. The tendered performance is about to begin. I have to play the overture. Here is the music written in our era for the ballad "Mother dear, don't sew for me a scarlet sarafan." (*He throws the sheet music on the ground in front of him and prepares to play the fiddle. His valet hands him something on a salver.*) Don't need it. I always do without it.

(*The Valet exits. Ivan Semyonovich plays, but nothing can be heard. After a brief space of time the curtain goes up.*)

THE HEADSTRONG TURK, OR, IS IT NICE TO BE A GRANDSON?

CHARACTERS

Milovidov (*Mr. Prettyman*)
Prince Batog-Batyev (*Prince Batter-Bang*)
Kutilo-Zavaldaysky (*Mr. Boozer-Junkpile*)
Liebenthal
Mme. Razorvaki, a widow (*The Widow Hullaballopolis*)
Ivan Semyonych

(*The action takes place in St. Petersburg, in Mme. Razorvaki's drawing-room. She is pouring tea. Everyone is seated.*)

MILOVIDOV: (*Speaks in a velvety basso, rhythmically, pompously, authoritatively.*) And so, our Ivan Semyonych is no more! . . . All his pleasant qualities have vanished along with him!

KUTILO-ZAVALDAYSKY: (*With a sigh.*) How many peasants and acres of arable land did he have?

MILOVIDOV: His principal estate was the village of Bobtail, but I don't recall whether it's in Astrakhan or Arkhangelsk gubernia. According to the last census, his peasants numbered 550. At least that's what the Civil Bureau

Assessor Ivan Petrovich Firdin told me when we last spoke.

PRINCE BATOG-BATYEV: (*With his cheek bound up. He speaks in a whisper and whistles through his front teeth.*) Firdin? . . . Which Firdin? Surely not the one who was wounded in a duel by Cavalry Captain Kavtyryov?

LIEBENTHAL: (*Speaks rapidly, for the most part pretentiously and irritably.*) No, not Kavtyryov! Kavtyryov is my brother-in-law. What actually happened to him was this; he wasn't killed in a duel, he simply fell off his horse, leading it on a tether around the gazebo on Mytlev's villa. As a result he also dislocated his ring-finger, on which he wore a cast-iron signet, with the Chapyzhnikov family crest.

KUTILO-ZAVALDAYSKY: I don't care for cast-iron signet-rings. I prefer cornelians or smoky topazes.

PRINCE BATOG-BATYEV: Excuse me, but you're mistaken! . . . Cornelians and topazes, particularly smoky ones, as you quite accurately put it, are two entirely different appelations! . . . And you mustn't confuse them with malachite, excavated so tastefully by his excellency Mr. Demidov; indeed, I may even state before the world at large and my conscience that he received in recognition of this a certificate from the very hand of Parliament, bearing the English seal.

MME. RAZORVAKI: (*Speaks loudly, positively, in a fruity voice.*) Speaking of Demidov! . . . Is it true that he bequeathed his entire fortune to Lamartine?

(*A pause.*)

MILOVIDOV: (*In exactly the same voice and tone as before.*) And so, our Ivan Semyonych is no more! . . . All his pleasant qualities have vanished along with him! . . . He had, I venture to say, only one shortcoming: he was firmly convinced that a man with natural talent could play the fiddle without using rosin. I'll relate an incident that befell him.—On his nameday—as I recall now, the 21st of October—he invited some dignitaries in . . . It was some o'clock or other. Lots of noise. People came in. People mingled. People sat on sofas . . . Drank tea . . . Everyone was waiting . . . "Fetch me that case!" says Ivan Semyonych. The case is brought in. Ivan Semyonych takes out the fiddle, rolls up his sleeves and turns up the right hem of his dress uniform. The vice-governor condescends to wait. Ivan Semyonych's faithful valet brings him the rosin on a salver.—"Don't need it!" says he, "I always do without rosin." He unrolls all sorts of popular sheet music; he waves his bow . . . Everyone is holding his breath anxiously. The self-sufficient deceased strokes the strings—nothing! . . . He strokes a second time—nothing! . . . A third time,—absolutely nothing! By the fourth stroke—alas!—his career was dashed to pieces, despite the fact that he had married the daughter of Gromov, a merchant of the First Guild! . . . The offended governor stood up and raising his arms towards the ceiling, said, "I don't need you," says he. "I don't care for pigheaded subordinates. You imagined just now that you could play without rosin; it's highly likely that you'll want to write reports without ink! I don't know how to read such reports, and what's more, I won't sign them, so help me God, I won't."

(*A pause.*)

KUTILO-ZAVALDAYSKY: Have you heard that the price of wheat has soared phenomenally in Tambov gubernia?

(*A pause.*)

MME. RAZORVAKI: (*Loudly and fruitily.*) Speaking of Tambov! . . . How many miles is it from Moscow to Ryazan and back?
LIEBENTHAL: (*Rapid-fire.*) I can tell you the direction one way without even checking in the almanac, but back again—that I don't know.

(*Everyone turns aside in the same direction and snorts facetiously through his nose.*)

LIEBENTHAL: (*Offended.*) I mean it! . . . After all, there are so many days from Christmas to Easter, and that many more from Easter to Christmas, but not as many as from Christmas to Easter. Consequently . . .

(*Everyone turns aside in the other direction and snorts facetiously through his nose. A pause.*)

MILOVIDOV: (*In the same tone.*) And so, our Ivan Semyonych is no more! . . . All his pleasant qualities have vanished along with him! . . .
PRINCE BATOG-BATYEV: (*Whispering and whistling through his teeth.*) I knew him! . . . We roved together through the mountains of the East and shared the grief of exile as friends. What a land is the East! . . . Imagine: mountains to the right of you, mountains to the left of you, mountains straight ahead of you; but behind, as you can picture to yourselves, the putrid West turns dark blue! . . . At last with loathing you climb to the top of the highest mountain . . . some sharp-pointed Sumbek or other. There's no way your mare can stand upright on this mossy peak: only propped up against the mountain under her saddle-girth, she can spin round on this mountain-top as on her axis, all four of her legs dangling in the air together! And then, when you and she turn back, you perceive that you have arrived in the easternmost region, for the East lies before you and on either side. But the West? . . . perhaps you think it's still visible, like some dot, barely moving

in the distance?

MME. RAZORVAKI: (*Loudly, fruitily and banging her fist on the table.*) Of course!

PRINCE BATOG-BATYEV: Wrong! The East is even behind you! . . . To make a long story short, everywhere and every place nothing but endless East!

MME. RAZORVAKI: (*As before.*) Speaking of the East . . . I'll tell you about my dream.

EVERYONE: (*Rushing to kiss her hand.*) Tell us, tell us!

MME. RAZORVAKI: (*In a drawling, raconteuring tone, retaining her loud and fruity voice.*) I saw, right smack in the middle . . .

MILOVIDOV: (*Stops her with a respectful, well-meaning hand gesture.*) Having cherished a proper esteem for you from some time back, I beseech you . . . on behalf of all your guests . . . to keep mum about this dream.

EVERYONE: Why so? Why so? (*They vie with one another to kiss her hand.*)

MILOVIDOV: (*Intercepts them pompously, rhythmically, raising his voice a bit.*) And so, our Ivan Semyonych is no more! . . . All his pleasant qualities have vanished along with him! . . . You knew that he lived in comfort, but he wanted to appear richer than he was in actual fact . . .

MME. RAZORVAKI: (*Loudly, in amazement.*) Did he really have a velvet chair?!

MILOVIDOV: No . . . he didn't care for velvet. And even on his own belly he wore a flannel triangle shaped like a kind of mustard-plaster.

PRINCE BATOG-BATYEV: I also keep a mustard-plaster there. And besides that, I like to wear an incision to drain pus on my right arm, Hispanic fly on my left arm, rope in my ears, creosote in my mouth, and a tape to keep the discharges flowing at the nape of my neck.

EVERYONE: (*Except Milovidov; to him.*) Show us, show us!

PRINCE BATOG-BATYEV: I'd love to, but not until after tea.

MILOVIDOV: (*Raising his voice again.*) All his pleasant qualities have vanished along with him! . . . When Ivan Semyonych gave dinner parties and invited dignitaries, he loved to entertain in the most refined manner. The root-vegetables floating in the soup were cut to resemble all the medals adorning the chests of the guests . . . Around the pies, instead of the usual sort of flapdoodle, were strewn fried Chinese and domestic teas! The pies were topped with brushes, and sometimes with plumes! . . . The bones in the chops were of ivory and wrapped in curl-papers, on which each person could read out his particular rank, personality, biography and age—with his compliments! . . . Peacock's tails were invariably stuck in the roast chickens. The asparagus was always strung on a wire, while the peas were threaded on silken strands. The poached fish was served up in rosewater! The pastries were all laid out in envelopes sealed with the government imprint of each guest's department! The necks of the bottles were tied with good-conduct ribbons and embellished with tokens of impeccable service; while the champagne was served enswathed in imported foulards! . . . I don't know why but they never served jam . . . At the end of the meal Ivan

Semyonych's faithful valet sprinkled everyone with eau-de-lavande! . . .
That's the way he lived! And what happened? Rosin, rosin ruined him and
laid him in the grave! He is no more and all his pleasant qualities have
vanished along with him . . .

(*Suddenly the hall door opens and Ivan Semyonych enters with a solemn countenance
and a pleasant smile.*)

EVERYONE: (*Terrified.*) Ah! . . . Ivan Semyonych! . . . Ivan Semyonych!
IVAN SEMYONYCH: (*Smiling and clicking his heels in all directions.*)
    Friends dear to my heart,
    There's no call to start
        If at once at your part-
        Y I take my place
    With a smile on my face.

(*He turns sternly to Milovidov and Mme. Razorvaki.*)

    Danilo, you're wrong after all! . . .
    This dame's a lying knave.
    Though rosin prompted my downfall,
    It led not to the grave!
EVERYONE: (*Joyously leaping up from their seats and clustering round Ivan Semyonych.*)
    Ivan Semyonych! . . . How's this? . . . Are you alive?!
IVAN SEMYONYCH: (*Triumphantly.*) Alive, alive, I tell you! . . . I will say fur-
    ther! (*He turns to Mme. Razorvaki.*) You have a grandson of Turkish extrac-
    tion! I shall tell you forthwith how I came to make this important discovery.
EVERYONE: (*Impatiently.*) Tell us, Ivan Semyonych! . . . Tell us! . . .

(*They sit down around the table.—Ivan Semyonych settles his chair next to Mme.
Razorvaki, who is perceptibly perturbed by the awaited disclosure.—Everyone
thrusts his head forward, towards Ivan Semyonych in curiosity.—Ivan Semyonych
clears his throat.—A pause.*)
. . . .
. . . .
Here, regrettably, the manuscript breaks off, and one can barely conjecture
whether Kozma Prutkov ever completed this highly remarkable work of his.

END

The Fourth Wall

A Buffoonery in Two Parts

(1915)

Nikolay Evreinov

Characters:

Faust
Marguerite
Mephistopheles
The Producer of the Theatre, who is also its Chief Director
The Director
The Assistant Director
The Propsman
The Prompter
The Theatre Watchman
A Street Urchin
People

PART ONE

A corner in Faust's study in an ultra-naturalistic staging. Not one single detail is omitted! And everything is real. At right a window; in front of it Faust's worktable. At left a medieval bed wherein, beneath a medieval coverlet, there sleeps, in a medieval nightcap, the actor who plays the role of Faust. Near the bed is a medieval washbasin. Under the bed is a medieval "convenience." At the rise of the curtain the stage is dark. In the orchestra pit the musicians are gathering and lazily tuning their instruments.

ASSISTANT DIRECTOR: (*A grouchy old theatre rat, runs on stage in a flurry, looks at his watch and shouts at the electrician's booth.*) Let's have some light! . . . Hey, where the hell are you, damn it?! . . . Eleven o'clock and there's not hide nor hair of him! (*To Faust.*) Ivan Potapych! (*Rouses Faust.*) Ivan Potapych! . . . It's eleven! . . . I'm here already! I've got my furcoat off! The orchestra's already in place! . . . The prompter's already in his box!

FAUST: Haaw? . . . What? . . . What time is it? (*He stretches. At the window a spotlight blazes into "daylight," and the footlights follow suit.*)

ASSISTANT DIRECTOR: It's been eleven o'clock now for the last fifteen minutes! (*To the electrician.*) That spotlight of yours is blinking again! How many times do I have to call it to your attention?! Where did you ever see daylight flicker like that?! Tell me! . . .

WATCHMAN: (*Brings Faust a glass of tea and a roll and the "Petersburg Gazette." To the Assistant Director.*) Pal Palych is asking for you.

ASSISTANT DIRECTOR: (*To Faust.*) Ivan Potapych! Explain this! Explain what you're doing, letting them bring you breakfast! The whole orchestra is assembled! (*Mauling Faust about.*) Will you wake up, for Chrissake! Do I have to drag you out by the feet? What can I do with you? . . . Bloody hell!

What a dog's life! (*He runs off right.*)

WATCHMAN: (*To Faust.*) Tea's gettin' cold.

(*From the orchestra comes a bang on the kettledrum and a guffaw.*)

FAUST: (*Shudders and slips his legs over the side of the bed.*) Bastard! . . . (*Puts on a medieval dressing-gown and slippers, bites off a piece of roll and almost drinks off the tea at one gulp.*) I want a wash! . . .

WATCHMAN: Right away, sir! (*Lays the newspaper on the bed and brings over the pitcher of water.*)

FAUST: Honest to God, I'll go back to the provinces . . . This isn't a job, it's penal servitude, daily penance, flaying alive! . . . (*He washes, assisted by the Watchman.*) I'm not young any more . . . I can't cope . . . It's all very well, their naturalism and all this "truth!" . . . What with the rats around this place you don't get to sleep before three . . . (*Gargles and tests his voice.*) No consideration, it's incredible . . . To think they used to handle me with kid gloves back in the provinces! . . . (*He wipes himself off with a medieval towel!* . . . *Backstage we can hear the Director clapping his hands and calling, "Places, chorus! Look sharp! . . . Take your places! . . ." We hear the rumbling of a hundred voices—an effect achieved by means of the lower notes of the organ—and the stamping of feet. The Conductor appears behind his podium. Faust puts on a beard attached with tapes, adjusts his nightcap before the mirror and avidly peruses the newspaper. The Watchman carries away the slopbucket and the tea glass.*)

DIRECTOR: (*Clean-shaven, wearing eyeglasses and with a leonine head of hair, he looks like a proper young scholar; he carries the score of "Faust" and is jotting notes in a notebook; enters left with the words.*) Let's begin, ladies and gentlemen, let us begin! (*On noticing Faust's newspaper.*) Ivan Potapych! . . . What's going on here! (*Takes the paper away from him.*) This is really childish! . . .

FAUST: (*Embarrassed.*) Good morning! . . .

DIRECTOR: (*Nodding to him.*) Aren't you ashamed! . . . Do we have to keep a governess looking after you at all times?

FAUST: I just wanted to find out if that review had . . . (*Bites off a piece of roll.*)

DIRECTOR: Faust! And suddenly he's got a twentieth-century newspaper in his hands. How does that fit in! . . .

FAUST: Well, I just . . .

DIRECTOR: You should be ashamed of yourself, my friend! The management reserves the stage for you after performances only so that you can live yourself into the role, live it through!

FAUST: (*Chewing over the roll.*) You're all wrong,—I do live it through, I live Faust all night through, and all morning too.

DIRECTOR: With the "Petersburg Gazette" in his hands! . . . Maybe it helps you to chew through a hunk of roll, but Faust, excuse me, is no breakfast roll!—it's sixteenth century, my boy! If you don't meld with the role of

"Faust," don't live your way into it as your own individual, innate role, I tell you straight out—don't expect it to be a success and don't come crying to me if someone else is cast in your part! Excuse me, but we're not here to slap together a comedy! . . . Our work is far too serious! This is no puppet-show!

FAUST: What did I do that was so wrong?

DIRECTOR: How can you even ask? Hasn't it sunk in yet why we put up this whole complex set of Faust's study every night, why we make you sleep on this set, wear Faust's costume all the time, his makeup, why, in short, we're giving you the possibility of breathing, as easily as you please, the atmosphere of a medieval scholastic?! . . . How can you fail to understand that the entire purpose of our production is to present a true-to-life, do you follow me, truuue-tooo-liiife Faust, to the nth degree!

FAUST: I'm giving as much as I can.

DIRECTOR: (*Unrolling an old-fashioned manuscript on the table.*) Is that so!—you haven't even unrolled this alchemical treatise on homunculi! . . .

FAUST: I overslept a bit today . . . I got to sleep late . . . There are so many rats running around here . . .

DIRECTOR: (*Sarcastically.*) Ah, now it's the rats' fault! . . .

FAUST: The long and the short of it is, Karl Antonych, alchemy, chemistry, cosmography, they just aren't up my alley! . . . It's no secret, I flunked the course in high school and then I went on the stage . . . And now I'm too old to start!

(*The Propsman, who is even older than Faust, brings in a chalice and puts it on the table.*)

DIRECTOR: (*To the Propsman.*) Is the poison real?

PROPSMAN: Strychnine mixed with prussic acid.

DIRECTOR: Good. (*Propsman exits. To Faust.*) You see how far we go with details to give the actor the proper mood!—(*Sniffs the contents of the chalice.*) Real poison!—one sip and you'll be down among the dead men.

FAUST: (*Takes the poisoned chalice with trembling hand and sings.*) "Ah, thou, oh chalice of my forefathers! Thou wert wont to be full! Wherefore, wherefore dost thou tremble? Wherefore dost thy hand tremble so" . . . (*Fearfully he shoves away the chalice.*) I am beginning to tremble, damn it! . . . Is this really real poison?

DIRECTOR: (*Proudly.*) We have no truck with fakes.

PRODUCER: (*Who is also the Chief Director, a young man with a full beard, tall and imposing, although he makes an attempt to seem unpretentious, enters accompanied by the Assistant Director, and greets the Conductor.*) Good morning, Maestro! (*To the musicians, who stand up at his appearance.*) Good morning, gentlemen! . . . (*The Watchman, who has come in behind the Producer, places two chairs on the right side of the stage, close to the footlights, and leaves. The Producer sniffs around eagerly, then smiles.*) Smells like someone's been living here . . . Good . . . Feels real . . . Not a stage setting, but a lived-in dwelling! . . . That's how it should be . . . Although it's a shame there's not a greater stench of chemicals! . . . After all, it is an alchemist's laboratory!

DIRECTOR: (*To the Assistant.*) More chemical smells!

ASSISTANT DIRECTOR: Right away, sir. (*Jots a note in the notebook.*) Add chemical nuisance . . .

PRODUCER: (*To Faust.*) How's it coming? Living into it? . . . (*Adjusts Faust's beard.*) Do you find it easy to experience Faust here?

FAUST: I do my best . . . (*Slips the remainder of the roll on to the table.*)

PRODUCER: Today I'll come up with something new . . . Along the lines of realism . . . Yesterday things were still a little murky . . . Lying in wait for today . . . Well now, let's begin! . . . (*He claps his hands—the Director runs up.*) Take it from the allegretto chorus, A major, page 9! . . . (*To the Conductor.*) Entrance tempo, maestro!

(*The orchestra plays the requisite music.*)

CHORUS: (*Offstage.*)
    Ah! . . .
    Why asleep, fair maiden?
    Welcome in the day!
    Soon the sun will gladden
    Heaven with its ray.
    Hark, the cocks are crowing
    Loudly to the morn,
    Heaven's vault is glowing
    As the light is born.
    Posies now are breaking
    Into buds of May,
    All the world is waking
    To love and joy today . . .

FAUST: (*Who has accompanied the words of the chorus with dramatic action, worked out in great detail, runs over to the window with improbable tragicality.*)
    Joyous impulse, thou art so insensate!
    Be still!
    Begone from me, oh life! oh life!

PRODUCER: (*Seated at right, with the Director.*) Sing with your back! . . . Your back! . . . Forget about the audience! . . .

FAUST: (*Takes the chalice and turns his back full upon the audience.*)
    Ah thou, oh chalice of my forefathers!
    Thou wert wont to be full!

Wherefore, oh wherefore dost thou tremble? . . .
Wherefore does thy hand tremble so? . . .
PRODUCER: (*To Director.*) Now that's what I call realism! . . .
DIRECTOR: (*Flattered.*) Half strychnine, half prussic acid.
PRODUCER: (*Shaking his head in approval.*) You can tell.
CHORUS: (*Offstage.*)
> The meadows with their beauty beckon,
> Over them are widely strewn
> Lovely patterns you can reckon,
> Made of fragrant, wondrous blooms.
> Everything is full of magic,
> All things tempt us, charm our eyes,
> Everything is full of . . .

PRODUCER: (*Clapping his hands.*) Sorry! . . . Shhh . . . (*Everyone falls silent. He walks to the window.*) Ladies and gentlemen of the chorus! . . . For heaven's sake, forget that this is an opera! . . . Sing the way you sing in real life! . . . After all, this is a chorus of German burghers, farmers, peasants! . . . Cut out all that Italian stuff!—It's got no business here! Give me more vulgarity, simplicity, naturalness! . . . Have you ever heard bargehaulers singing along the Volga? . . . That's what I'm after! . . . These people are just the same as bargehaulers, only—German. (*Claps his hands and returns to his seat.*) From the top!

(*The chorus repeats.*)

PRODUCER: (*Stopping chorus and orchestra.*) Appreciably better. But still far, far from ideal. (*To the Director.*) Call some special rehearsals! Explain to the chorus again what truth in art is all about!
DIRECTOR: Right you are. (*Makes a note of it.*)
PRODUCER: (*To Conductor and Faust.*) Allegro agitato, please! "What is God to me!" . . .

(*The Orchestra supplies the desired introduction.*)

FAUST: (*Sings, lying in weariness upon the bed.*)
> What is God to me!
> He rewards neither faith nor love! . . .
> He will not give me back my youth.

(*He puts his feet on the floor and sings, sitting on the bed, straining with all the reality of a bilious, irritated little old man, while the Producer, Conductor and Director by gestures, stamping and all other means possible try to extract from Faust the maximum naturalistic annoyance.*)
> I curse you, earthly joys,

And I curse the fetters of my earthbound prison!
I curse my corporeal, ailing and imperfect form.
I curse all dreams of love!
What are life and fame to me?
What to me are hope and bliss?
I curse them too!
My patience is at an end . . .
Oh Satan! . . . Come to me!

(*From a trapdoor Mephistopheles appears, costumed according to our latest historical research.*)

MEPHISTOPHELES: (*Sings.*)
  Here I am!
  Wherefore do you wonder? . . .
  I heard thine appeal at once.
  So I appear, sword at my side! . . .
  A feather in my cap! . . .
  A broad mantle at my back! . . .
  And money in my purse.
  Have I not all that's needful! . . .
PRODUCER: (*Clapping his hands.*) Sorry! . . . (*Everything stops.*) Good morning, Semyon Andreyevich! (*Exchanges greetings with Mephistopheles.*) I didn't see you earlier. Don't get angry, dear boy, but I've got to eliminate this aria of yours.
MEPHISTOPHELES: What for? Why?
PRODUCER: Don't get excited, sweetheart! It has absolutely nothing to do with your performance, but the fact is . . .
MEPHISTOPHELES: Is what? . . . What am I doing wrong?
PRODUCER: It has nothing at all to do with you. It's much more serious. Mephistopheles, as I was reading in Eckermann yesterday, is only one aspect of Faust himself. Understand?
MEPHISTOPHELES: So what?
PRODUCER: So, for Goethe Mephistopheles is the same person as Faust, but a Faust who's negative, compromised, earthbound in the vilest sense of the word. Mephistopheles is to Faust's tragedy what the devil is to Ivan Karamazov's!
MEPHISTOPHELES: (*Reeling.*) You can't mean . . .
PRODUCER: My dear fellow! Truth above all! . . . If the Moscow Art Theatre had no compunction in rejecting the devil as a separate character, then we, the producers of a realistic opera, should have done so long ago.
MEPHISTOPHELES: You must be joking!
PRODUCER: Certainly not. In "The Brothers Karamazov," Kachalov com-

bined both the devil and Ivan in his own person, and in our "Faust," Ivan Potapych (*points to Faust*) will combine in his own person both Mephistopheles and Faust! . . .

FAUST: Pa . . . pa . . . pa . . . pa?

PRODUCER: What do you mean, pa-pa, pa-pa?

FAUST: Part's too low! . . . Mephistopheles is a basso, but . . . but . . . I'm a tenor.

PRODUCER: Don't be silly!—sing it an octave higher and have done with it. I've thought of everything!

DIRECTOR: This had occurred to me as well. After all, what have we got here! . . . A work of realism, living characters, true-to-life images and all of a sudden an element of fantasy! . . . A bogeyman from a fairy tale! . . . The devil! . . . A goblin to scare children with! . . .

MEPHISTOPHELES: (*Nonplussed.*) I . . . I . . . I can't find the words . . . I . . . have to speak frankly . . .

PRODUCER: (*Ever so sweetly and reasonably.*) For heaven's sake, Semyon Andreyevich, if there's anything you're unhappy about, put off your remarks to some other time! I'll be entirely at your disposal after the rehearsal! But right now, dear chap, we're rehearsing! Show a little tact! You're an artist and should recognize how precious every hour of our creative work is. (*Mephistopheles staggers into the wings with an agonized look on his face. To Faust and the Conductor.*) Gentlemen, take it from Mephistopheles's entrance.

MEPHISTOPHELES: (*Turning around.*) What? . . .

PRODUCER: No, no! . . . We'll get on without you! (*Mephistopheles exits.*) Ivan Potapych! If you please!

FAUST: I, you see . . . I haven't learned Mephistopheles's part!

PRODUCER: Can it be that after the 138th consecutive rehearsal you don't hear the part ringing in your ears? . . .

FAUST: But what sort of acting should I do in the meantime?

PRODUCER: The same as before. Pretend that you are listening to somebody else! Imagine that Mephistopheles is your inner voice! . . . a voice from within!

FAUST: And sing to myself in this voice?

PRODUCER: Why, of course! . . . but from within! (*Claps his hands. To the Conductor.*) Moderato! Entrance of Mephistopheles!

FAUST: (*Sings as Mephistopheles, acts as himself.*)
Here I am!
Wherefore do you wonder?
I heard thine appeal at once!
So I appear, sword at my side! . . .

PRODUCER: (*Explaining to those around him.*) That's a symbol!

FAUST: "A feather in my cap."

PRODUCER: (*As before.*) Another symbol.

FAUST: "A broad mantle at my back! . . .
      And money in my purse.
      Have I not all that's needful!"

PRODUCER: Splendid! . . . From now on the problem of interpreting Mephistopheles on the stage is to be considered solved! . . . Without all those antinaturalistic appearances from trapdoors, colored flares and the rest of the mummery, which is unworthy of a serious theatre, of the true motto, "Everything as it is in real life." (*Presses Faust's hand.*) You must agree that this way is better, cleverer, nobler?

FAUST: (*Melted by the praise.*) Yes, of course, it's more original this way, much more original . . . although I really . . .

PRODUCER: Nonsense, nonsense! Don't be modest! Naturally you're still a little shaky in your lines, but that's not what makes it so powerful! (*To the Conductor.*) Have them transpose Mephistopheles's part for Faust! . . . (*To the Director.*) Begin special rehearsals for this scene! (*To the Conductor.*) Now shall we go straight to the vision of Marguerite?

(*The orchestra plays the necessary music. At left, the form of Marguerite at the spinning wheel begins to glow through the wall.*)

FAUST: (*As Mephistopheles in a spooky, coarse-grained voice.*) "How now? How dost thou like her?" (*As himself, tenorishly saccharine.*) "I am thine!" . . .

PRODUCER: (*Clapping his hands.*) Bravo! . . . (*The orchestra stops playing.*) You can feel at once that a duet is being sung. (*To those around him.*) Am I right? . . . the illusion is complete! and totally plausible as well. Why this didn't occur to me sooner, I can't figure out. But this is what we're after!—And right after such plausibility comes the totally fabulous, I mean non-naturalistic vision of Marguerite! True, science does acknowledge hallucinatory states, but we can hardly grant them to Doctor Faust, that sober intellect, tempered in the furnace of positivism, and it's not night time either, it's early in the morning! . . . What's your opinion, gentlemen? . . . Looking at it this way, I think that if we have to have "A Vision of Marguerite" . . . the most suitable place for her would be somewhere out the window.

MARGUERITE: What do you mean, "out the window"?

PRODUCER: Just that. Faust sees Marguerite out the window.

MARGUERITE: But this scene is called "the scene with the spinning wheel."

PRODUCER: So what if it is! Let Marguerite pass by the window with a spinning wheel!—as if she's just bought it at the market, is taking it home and stops a while to admire her new acquisition right in front of the house where Faust lives.

DIRECTOR: Absolutely true to life. Maybe even Martha can go with her to lend a housewifely air to the whole scene.

PRODUCER: Martha certainly can. Even more realistic!

DIRECTOR: I'll call her! (*He runs off right.*)

PRODUCER: (*To Marguerite.*) Please come over here, Alisa Petrovna! Just for a second! (*Marguerite leaves her place. To Faust and the Assistant Director.*) I've just this minute noticed the entire lack of harmony in her costume! . . . A regular fancy-dress ball gown! (*To Marguerite, who has come downstage in her traditional, lovely costume.*) Such dissonance, Alisa Petrovna! . . .

MARGUERITE: What do you mean, dissonance?

PRODUCER: Your costume. Clashes with the whole production.

MARGUERITE: It's made from the designer's sketch . . . You approved it yourself . . .

PRODUCER: I know. (*Looks her over.*) It won't do at all . . . We need something else. And besides, you're too refined in general!—Unconvincing! Marguerite is lower middle-class! More than that, she's a village lassie! A footsoldier's sister. Lives with a procuress! . . . and in the rough and ready age of the Landsknechts at that. The makeup and the rest ought to be totally different. We have to make the audience feel that this kind of Gretchen wolfs down herrings, tail and all, her hands are covered with callouses from spinning, she's practically a beggar, earns her crust of bread by hard labor, runs to the market in the mornings in bare feet. Otherwise who would believe in your Marguerite!

MARTHA: (*Leaning out the window.*) You want me?

PRODUCER: Yes, yes! (*To Marguerite.*) Under the window please! (*Marguerite goes to the other side of the stage and stands under the window with Martha. The Producer groups both of them in a pose, examining the spinning wheel, and returns to his place. To the Conductor.*) Take it from where we left off! (*The Orchestra proceeds.*)

FAUST: (*As Mephistopheles, offering himself, from left hand to right, the chalice of poison.*)

> "Take thou this chalice!
> Now no death, no poison is in't,
> But joy of life—but drink of it!
> No death lurks there! No poison's there!
> Youth lies there and love!"

(*Speaks.*) How can I drink it, if it's real poison?

PRODUCER: Pretend to be drinking it! . . .

FAUST: (*As himself, timorously.*)

> "I drink! . . .
> I drink!"

(*With great caution he "pretends" to drink. The Director runs offstage and gestures to Marguerite and Martha to come on. They cross slowly, arms around one another's waists, to the left.*)

> "I drink!

       I drink for thy sake, divine image.''
  (*Mephistopheles's voice.*) Well!
  (*His own voice.*) Shall I behold her?
  (*Mephistopheles' voice.*) Thou shalt!
  (*His own voice.*) Soon will't be?
  (*Mephistopheles's voice.*) This very day!
  (*His own voice.*) Oh rapture!
  (*Mephistopheles's voice.*) Let us begone.
  (*His own voice.*) Let us begone.
  (*Speaks.*) Now what?
PRODUCER: How do you mean?
FAUST: Now I have a duet with Mephistopheles.
PRODUCER: Sing it as Faust! (*To the Conductor.*) Have the cellos come in as
    Mephistopheles's voice! Reorchestrate it!

(*The Conductor bows in agreement and, without stopping the orchestra, proceeds.*)

FAUST: ''I want the love, I want pleasure
        That in kisses and caresses alone do burn,
        I want, as in bygone days of love and passion,
        To sup my fill of ardent young embraces.
        O thou, bring youth back to my life!
        Return to me my erstwhile ecstasies!''
PRODUCER: (*During the singing spurs him on, together with the Director.*) Give
    us your back! More back! Forget about the audience! . . . More naturally!
    . . . More naturally still! . . . (*After the words, ''My erstwhile ecstasies,''* the
    Producer claps his hands, stopping the orchestra and the singer. To the Director.) It's
    all in verse.
DIRECTOR: What?
PRODUCER: It's in verse, I said.
DIRECTOR: We adapted it as much as we could.
PRODUCER: But all the same you can feel the verse, the rhyme, the metre—
    in short, verse! Have you ever heard of a thing called verse?
DIRECTOR: Good God, stop talking to me like a child—as if I didn't know it
    myself.
PRODUCER: Then we'll have to try and turn it into prose. After all, this isn't
    ''Vampuka,''* it's a realistic opera! What's verse doing in it, I ask you! If
    we can't manage to make it sound as trivial as everyday conversation, who
    would believe that this is life and not a stage production!
DIRECTOR: (*Making a note.*) Fine. I'll adapt it all over again.

---

*''Vampuka'' was an immensely popular parody of grand opera staged some years before by
''The Crooked Mirror.'' (Translator's note)

PRODUCER: (*To the Conductor.*) Go on!

FAUST: Pardon me. I wanted to ask how you're going to handle my transformation from Faust into a young man? You promised to explain it to me several days ago, but in the meantime . . .

PRODUCER: (*Breaking in.*) Transformation? . . . What transformation?

FAUST: The one into a young man! In the play, after Faust drinks the potion, he becomes young!

PRODUCER: (*Roars with laughter.*) Ha, ha, ha! . . . Good lord, Ivan Potapych, when are you going to scrap that childish notion of Faust! . . . It's a wonder you're not nauseated by these pocket operatic miracles! . . . Do be serious! . . . For the last time, look at Faust not as a mountebank, but as a psychologist! For the last time, understand that Faust is rejuvenated *spiritually*! Can't you understand? Spiritually, not physically. Why, where would we be if, in our realistic production of *Faust*, interpreted soberly, we went in for such infantile stunts as the instant transformation of a gray-haired old man into a raven-haired young man! . . . Is that the way you think of Faust's rejuvenation? Can't you live without the masquerade of sky-blue tights, a hat with an ostrich plume and the rest of the trumpery?

FAUST: Then what, am I to remain in my nightcap like this?

PRODUCER: I assert that a nightcap is more worthy of Doctor Faust than a duncecap!

DIRECTOR: (*To Faust, amicably taking him by the skirt of his dressing-gown.*) You're an odd duck, Ivan Potapych! It's no secret that when we asked you to play Faust, we had in mind not so much your voice as your age.

FAUST: My age?

DIRECTOR: Why, of course! . . . Faust is an elderly man and, therefore, the best person to portray him on stage would be an elderly man like himself.

FAUST: But I . . . I'm not all that old!

DIRECTOR: You're just the age. And you have the proper voice—a croaking, cracking, creaking voice . . .

FAUST: I've got a little cold today.

DIRECTOR: For heaven's sake, don't get well, otherwise you'll spoil our whole production. You should be exactly as you are now throughout the entire opera! . . . What's more, I would personally prefer it, if, in the interests of realism, you rasped, croaked, hacked and coughed, blew your nose a good deal more—to put it briefly, it would make Faust's old age seem all the more naturalistic.

PRODUCER: (*To Faust, from a great height, upholding the Director's opinion.*) Certainly if an old man won't act on stage as an old man with all the infirmities appertaining to an old man, where is the realism in the acting, I ask you!

DIRECTOR: I even considered, in the interests of realism, releasing a sort of smell of old age into the audience! . . . Yes, yes! to fumigate the auditorium with some kind of mixture that would give off an odor of mustiness, snuff, mothballs and a lot more! . . . So that the audience will actually sense the nearness of Faust! . . . Old fellows always give off a smell! . . .

ASSISTANT DIRECTOR: (*Offended on behalf of his venerable age-group.*) What do you mean, they give off a smell?

DIRECTOR: For heaven's sake I didn't mean you!

ASSISTANT DIRECTOR: Then be so good as to explain what you *did* mean!

PRODUCER: Drop it, gentlemen, we'll straighten this out later! There's no time now for squabbling. (*To the Conductor and Faust.*) Let's go over the Faust-Mephistopheles duet again! "I want love." (*To Faust.*) If you please! In the new interpretation!

FAUST: You mean, with a frog in my throat?

PRODUCER: That's right!

FAUST: But it'll ruin my voice.

PRODUCER: Be so kind as to obey the director's instructions!

FAUST: The director won't get me a new voice!

PRODUCER: You refuse? . . . Very well. In that case don't complain if you're docked a month's salary! . . .

FAUST: For what?

PRODUCER: For refusing to carry out the director's instructions! Clause 171 in your contract.

FAUST: But I was hired to sing, not to croak!

PRODUCER: You were hired to act. Would you rather *act* the role of Faust or pay two thousand rubles for breach of contract?—Clause 183!

FAUST: But if I can't manage it, what then?

PRODUCER: Why, then we shall rehearse until such time as you can!

FAUST: (*Having thought it over.*) No, I'd better give it a try right now! . . . My voice is dear to me.

PRODUCER: It's about time! (*He claps to the Conductor. The orchestra plays the introduction.*)

FAUST: (*Sings in a very decrepit voice.*)
    "I want the love, I want pleasure
    That in kisses and caresses," etc.

(*During his rendition the Producer and the Director gesture to him with the inspired phrases, "Cough," "Blow your nose," "Clear your throat," "Hack a bit," "Good," "Expectorate," "That's it! That's it!" and so forth. The aria stops short because Faust begins to cough in actual fact, spraying saliva about.*)

FAUST: Ugh! . . . Give me some water! . . . (*The Assistant Director rushes to give him the chalice of poison. Faust, infuriated, shoos it away with the back of his hand.*) You can go to hell!

DIRECTOR: (*Calming him.*) It's mere inexperience! It'll pass presently . . . Has it passed? . . . There, you see! Nothing to it! . . .

FAUST: (*Gasping for breath.*) I was choking there for a minute.

PRODUCER: But the realism was of the fullest! The "old man" you gave us was a sight for sore eyes!

DIRECTOR: However, don't make this gesture! (*Shows him.*) That's pure Vampuka. For heaven's sake don't vampukicize—and then the illusion will be total.

ASSISTANT DIRECTOR: (*Walking over, with fear and trembling, to the Producer and the Director.*) Beg pardon, gentlemen, might I offer a piece of advice concerning the realism?

PRODUCER: (*Pompously.*) Any sensible advice will be received with thanks.

DIRECTOR: (*Equally pompously.*) Say on! We're listening!

PRODUCER: Don't be shy!

ASSISTANT DIRECTOR: (*Hesitantly.*) Of course I'm just an ordinary sort of man, I don't know anything about the more advanced directorial skills, and yet it struck me . . .

PRODUCER: Yes?

ASSISTANT DIRECTOR: Please don't get angry now! . . . I mean this to be helpful . . . well, after a good deal of cogitation, so to speak . . .

PRODUCER: Get to the point!

ASSISTANT DIRECTOR: It struck me that if the opera is to achieve total realism, half-measures aren't enough, but . . .

DIRECTOR: Finish what you have to say.

ASSISTANT DIRECTOR: When did you ever hear a man in real life not talk—forgive me—but sing instead! . . .

DIRECTOR: (*Taken aback; after a pause.*) Yes, but this is an opera!

PRODUCER: (*To Director.*) Not an opera, but a music-drama, if you want to be precise! In the first place. And in the second place . . . hm . . . do you know this very same thing just occurred to me!

DIRECTOR: Yes, but what can we do about it?

ASSISTANT DIRECTOR: Make it talking to music!

DIRECTOR: What do you mean "talking?"

ASSISTANT DIRECTOR: The same as we do in real life. Then the audience will both understand it and find it natural!

PRODUCER: (*Mulling it over a bit.*) I see, I see what you mean . . .

ASSISTANT DIRECTOR: Simply have everything spoken . . .

PRODUCER: Everything and everyone! . . . that's quite a brain you've got!

ASSISTANT DIRECTOR: (*This shaft is aimed at the Director.*) I don't know what sort of brain it is, but at least it doesn't give off a smell! . . .

PRODUCER: That'll do! . . . If you insist on thinking he was referring to you! What more did you have to add?

ASSISTANT DIRECTOR: Well, if they're going to talk instead of sing, they ought to talk in German, not Russian.

PRODUCER: Why's that?

ASSISTANT DIRECTOR: Well, after all it's taking place in Germany, and Faust is simply a German!

PRODUCER: (*After a pause of gleeful meditation.*) Goddam it! You're a Columbus, a regular Columbus! . . . Why didn't I think of it sooner! (*To the Director.*) What's your opinion?

DIRECTOR: Obviously, you can't deny that Faust is a German, but . . . but in that case, if we're going to be consistent, I mean, if we're going all out for historical authenticity—our Faust ought to speak a Middle High German dialect.

PRODUCER: Absolutely! We'll translate "Faust" into Middle High German! . . . Naturalism is naturalism.

FAUST: (*Timidly.*) I ought to inform the management that not only don't I know Middle High German, but I can't get my tongue around any kind of German.

PRODUCER: (*Profoundly, earnestly, thoughtfully.*) Yes, that is a fundamental difficulty . . . We might postpone the production for another two years, while you learn German like a native, live in Germany . . .

ASSISTANT DIRECTOR: Gentlemen, allow me to extricate you from your difficulty! . . .

PRODUCER: Please do!

ASSISTANT PRODUCER: There's no reason for Ivan Potapych to go to Germany, because from the naturalistic standpoint, from one end of the opera to the other he doesn't have to sing,—sorry—*say* more than a few words.

PRODUCER: ⎫
DIRECTOR: ⎬ What do you mean?
FAUST: ⎭

ASSISTANT DIRECTOR: Just this. In the part of Faust the greater bulk of the monologues and conversations are with Mephistopheles. Well, who holds long conversations with himself?—Only a lunatic. Marguerite does at the end of the opera, but that proves my point: the girl's gone out of her mind, so she can talk to herself to her heart's content! But Faust—where does the author say that he's out of his wits! . . .

PRODUCER: Goddamit! . . . that's the barefaced truth! (*To the Director.*) What's your opinion?

DIRECTOR: (*Embarrassed.*) In real life only madmen talk to themselves and Faust *isn't* a madman—I knew all this long ago.

PRODUCER: (*To the Director.*) Then why didn't you say something all this time! . . . 138 rehearsals go by and not a peep out of you!

FAUST: Excuse me, I'm beginning to lose track of all this . . . I've got a terrific headache . . . Do you mean, I don't quite follow, in Act I, for instance, I'm not supposed to sing *or* talk? . . .

PRODUCER: Didn't you just hear our latest decision!

FAUST: (*His hand to his forehead.*) Do you mean you don't need me now? . . .

PRODUCER: What do you mean, don't need you?! . . . What about the inner feeling! the mime! the acting! Faust is on stage the entire act! Who's going to perform in your place?

FAUST: Then it's pantomime? Standing there tongue-tied like a dummy? . . .

PRODUCER: (*Severely.*) Ivan Potapych, remember Clause 14 of your contract! . . .

FAUST: (*Terrified.*) What did I say that was so bad! . . . I just don't understand what I'm supposed to do on stage!

PRODUCER: (*Dogmatically.*) Live through the role to music. (*To the Conductor.*) Take Act I from the top! We'll re-rehearse it without wasting any more time!

(*The orchestra plays.*)

ASSISTANT DIRECTOR: (*To the Producer.*) Sorry! One other thing!

PRODUCER: (*To the Conductor.,*) Just a second! . . . Sshhh . . .

ASSISTANT DIRECTOR: The way I see it, if you want to achieve total lifelike-ness in an opera, I mean—naturalism, you'd better set limits to the music!

PRODUCER: (*Dumbfounded.*) What do you mean? You must be joking! . . .

ASSISTANT DIRECTOR: By no means. Good grief, sir! A man wants to take poison, he's tired of living—do you want music playing during this! What's consistent about that! Where's your naturalism then?

DIRECTOR: Yes, but this is an opera!

PRODUCER: (*Correcting him.*) A music-*drama*.

DIRECTOR: Exactly so, a *music*-drama! But you want to do away with the music altogether.

ASSISTANT DIRECTOR: (*Condescendingly.*) Altogether? . . . No, what for? Somewhere backstage,—the play does say it's carnival time!! There's a lit-tle band playing and a choir singing, why not, sir! There's nothing against it! Maybe you can take some of the themes from "Faust" itself. But if it's to be as natural as in real life, sir, you can't have a full orchestra coming in and playing a symphony in front of the stage! Why, there's a man up there saying his last farewell to life!

PRODUCER: (*Nervously pacing.*) That's perfectly true . . . Perfectly true . . . It's really daring! . . . awfully daring! I'm even a bit afraid we'd be somewhat . . . ridiculed in the papers over it, caricatures would appear,—"an opera minus music," they'd call it, the cabarets would make us a laughingstock and so on, but . . . the principle of truth in art is superior to it all! As the saying goes, "If you fear wolves, keep out of the woods." (*Stops in front of the Conductor. Nervously.*) Maestro! . . . You are free for the present . . . And so is the orchestra! . . . We have to work something out on this . . . I'm afraid it will take some time . . . and . . . in short, goodbye for the time being.

Don't be angry! . . . I'll give you all your instructions tomorrow.

(*The Conductor and the orchestra leave their seats.*)

PROPSMAN: (*Has appeared on stage. To the Producer.*) Will you be needing me any more? Things look fine and dandy on the props side, so . . . Time for dinner . . .

PRODUCER: Hold on, dear chap. (*The Propsman remains on stage until the end of the act.*) Ivan Potapych, let's try and re-rehearse your duet with Mephistopheles in the new staging!

FAUST: (*Crumbling to bits.*) You mean, the duet with myself? . . . without an orchestra? or singing? or words? Just plain mime?

PRODUCER: Exactly so.

FAUST: (*His hand on his forehead.*) I don't know if I can any more! . . . my head's spinning round something awful . . .

PRODUCER: Come now, none of your whims! . . . Pull yourself together! (*Faust adopts a pose.*)

PROMPTER: (*A tiny little old man with a tiny little bald head, and bespectacled, leans out of his box.*) Maybe you can let me go get something to eat while you're . . . Since you're doing it without words now, I . . .

PRODUCER: (*Interrupting.*) Prompt the action! . . . Remind him what comes next in the mime! . . . (*The Prompter, groaning, flops back into his box.*) Only, for heaven's sake, not so much face to the audience! . . . Don't forget that right here (*he draws a line parallel to the footlights*) we're assuming a fourth wall.

ASSISTANT DIRECTOR: (*Definitely in mockery.*) Excuse me, but why not give us the fourth wall itself, for the sake of verisimilitude?

PRODUCER: How do you mean?

ASSISTANT DIRECTOR: Like so—put up a real fourth wall, and be done with it.

DIRECTOR: But that way we'll close off both the singer and the set!

ASSISTANT DIRECTOR: It's up to you. My job is only to point out that there are no such rooms in real life, rooms that dispense with a fourth wall! . . . If it's Faust's study, then it ought to follow the rules! Otherwise it makes no sense! A man is withdrawing from society, he wants to take poison in private, and there's an audience standing by, looking on, criticizing—basically *extraneous*. And why is it extraneous? Because no fourth wall has been put up—there's no way to hide things from prying eyes—you end up "slapping together a farce" as far as most decent people are concerned. It turns into a Punch-and-Judy show.

PRODUCER: (*Nervously pacing the stage.*) Good grief, this gets tougher every minute! . . .

ASSISTANT DIRECTOR: Forgive me for pointing out the Gospel truth!

PRODUCER: Who the hell knows! Why I didn't think of this earlier I can't imagine! . . .

DIRECTOR: Well, I had an inkling of it before! . . .

PRODUCER: Then why did you keep silent all this time!

DIRECTOR: (*Practically in hysterics.*) Because you kept clamping the lid on me! You kept my hands tied! You practically accuse me of wanting to be original, of wanting to contradict you! You want to hog all the glory for yourself! . . . That's why I've been as dumb as a post! . . .

PRODUCER: (*Waves him away, flairs his nostrils and turns to the Assistant Director with an imperiously beseeching gesture.*) Put up a fourth wall! (*To the Propsman.*) Put up a fourth wall! (*To the Director.*) Put up a fourth wall!

FAUST: Is this what I get for living here, living-through here, spending my nights here on stage with rats?! . . . As a final reward, I'm to be shut off from the audience?

DIRECTOR: (*Pompously.*) No wall, dear chap, can conceal truthful inner feeling from an audience. You just try and live it through and let us take care of the rest.

ASSISTANT DIRECTOR: (*Consoling Faust.*) In the first place, excuse me, your frantic nose-blowing, coughing and so forth, sir, will be distinctly heard from a window, because (*turning to the Producer*) you might build a window in Faust's study so the audience can see him through it . . .

PRODUCER: (*Overjoyed.*) That goes without saying . . . There will be a window here. (*He points to the imaginary wall downstage.*) Right at this point . . .

FAUST: (*Interrupting.*) Ah, so there'll be a window? . . .

ASSISTANT DIRECTOR: But of course!

FAUST: And I can appear in it?

ASSISTANT DIRECTOR: As much as you like!

FAUST: (*Laboriously imagining it.*) Aha . . . I get it now . . . The window is here . . . I am here . . . the audience is over there . . . (*Puts his hand on his forehead.*) Ugh, my head's spinning round . . . (*To the Producer.*) Let me go, for heaven's sake . . . I can't understand anything anymore . . .

PRODUCER: Go ahead, go ahead! . . . (*Saying goodbye to Faust.*) I am more pleased with today than with anything that's come before. From now on we can consider the most important problems of the theatre as solved! (*Faust exits.*) A fourth wall! . . . This is a veritable Columbus's egg! . . . Simple, clever and natural all at once. (*Dreamily.*) A fourth wall! . . . It marks the dawn of a new theatre!—A theatre free of lies, compromises, and the cheap mummery that is unworthy of pure art! . . . (*To the Director.*) Let's go! . . . We have to draw up a ground-plan immediately, one that applies to a fourth wall! . . . I'm coming up with such ideas . . . such ideas that . . . I won't leave one stone standing from our original staging!—That was pure "Vampuka," no matter what you say. (*Squeezes the Assistant Director's hand and kisses him on both cheeks.*) Thank you! . . . I am eternally obliged to you . . .

ASSISTANT DIRECTOR: (*Modestly.*) A tiny little bonus to my salary, if you'd do me the favor . . . Five measly rubles or so . . . comes in handy, a hat for the wife, laundry, the trolley . . .

PRODUCER: Positively. I consider it an obligation.

(*Clasps his hand tightly and exits with the Director. The Assistant Director, after accompanying the big shots out with obsequious bowing and scraping as far as the wings, turns back to the puzzled Propsman and explodes into soundless laughter. The Prompter pops out of his box; he systematically shoves his eyeglasses up on to his forehead, pulls from his pocket a sausage, a roll, some hardboiled eggs and a twist of paper containing salt, and settles in to have a bite at Faust's worktable.*)

PROPSMAN: (*To the Assistant Director.*) What are you so cheery about?

PROMPTER: (*Sniggering in approval.*) Well, you've got them to take the plunge!

ASSISTANT DIRECTOR: (*Continuing to laugh.*) But those idiots took it all for solid gold! . . .

PROMPTER: Yes, that's some prank you played on them! No doubt about it! . . . I was almost scared to death on the spot—they'll catch on to him, I was thinking.

ASSISTANT DIRECTOR: (*Still laughing.*) Not them! . . . They never had a glimmer! Their ideas were getting ahead of their brains! "You're a Columbus," they say! Ha, ha, ha . . . A Columbus! . . . (*Plants himself next to the Prompter, with his own lunch.*)

PROMPTER: (*Eating heartily.*) Yes . . . there's plenty of dimwits on God's green earth, but *naturalists* like them, you won't find in a month of Sundays . . .

PROPSMAN: But I jest come in . . . didn't know nothin' . . . What's up, thinks I, our Kuzma Ivanych is gone off his chump! . . .

PROMPTER: (*Correcting him.*) Columbus Ivanych, you mean! . . . (*He laughs, slapping the Assistant Director on the back.*)

PROPSMAN: So I figger, somethin's up! . . . From where I'm standin', you'd think it was the Chief was layin' down the law. (*Plants himself down and decorously pulls a sandwich from his pocket.*)

ASSISTANT DIRECTOR: Why not? Don't you think in a case like this I can be every bit as good as the Chief? As much as you like! Easy as pie! . . . If this were only *real* art, where there's imagination and beauty and what-have-you, genuine creativity—but that, if you please, isn't good enough for us. Now, making everything the way it is in life, an ersatz imitation, authentic naturalism—well, let's have a helping! . . . Any fool can do that! . . . What kind of art is that! . . .

PROMPTER: (*Chewing.*) But what if it's a subject from history?

ASSISTANT DIRECTOR: And what are illustrated books for? . . . Nowadays they take photographs of every archaeological artifact and publish it in a book! . . . That shouldn't stop you! . . . Better learn how to read.

PROPSMAN: You asked for a bonus, you scallywag! . . .

ASSISTANT DIRECTOR: And why not!—You think I'm going to teach them for nothing! . . .

PROMPTER: Columbus Ivanych, that's what you are! . . .

ASSISTANT DIRECTOR: (*To the Propsman, seriously, taking up the neglected "poisoned chalice."*) You didn't really and truly put strychnine and prussic acid in this, did you? . . . What if somebody made a mistake and . . . Keep that in mind, my boy!

PROPSMAN: You think I'm dead drunk or somethin'! . . . I ain't riskin' my neck.—This here's a tonic for the stomach! . . . Doctor prescribed it for my wife:—it tones her up.

ASSISTANT DIRECTOR: (*Pulling a bottle out of the Propsman's pocket.*) Is this the tonic? . . .

PROPSMAN: Careful with that!—it's strychnine!

ASSISTANT DIRECTOR: (*Uncorks the bottle and sniffs the contents.*) It's very potent strychnine, you've got to admit! . . . You keep this for atmosphere too? (*They all guffaw.*) Well, let's drink our troubles away! (*They clink glasses.*) Maybe our little day really *is* done! . . . They're debasing us to "non-theatre!" . . . It's downhill all the way! (*They drink.*)

PROMPTER: (*Sings.*) "That was in the golden age . . ."

(*The Propsman joins in, the Assistant Director weeps quietly.*)

A STAGEHAND: (*Coming in after a pause.*) Should I let down the curtain?

ASSISTANT DIRECTOR: Hey, did you just wake up! . . . We've been done for a long time! . . . Do you think we're putting on a show here or what? You can see the rehearsal's over, so let down the curtain! (*The Stagehand exits.*) How many times do I have to tell him! . . .

PROPSMAN: (*Taking charge of the bottle and slapping it.*) Maybe they're gonna re-rehearse again! . . .

PROMPTER: (*Bursts into a sardonic laugh along with the Assistant Director.*) Maybe so! . . . That's another story! . . . (*The Propsman pours, his hand wobbling with laughter.*) To the health of our Columbus! . . . (*They all eat and drink.*)

CURTAIN

PART TWO

The musicians of the orchestra, all in white tie and tails, ceremoniously take their places before an auditorium lit like a gala. For a brief span, the carefully tuned instruments produce music; then the Conductor appears, bows to the audience and the orchestra, pompously sits in his seat and imposes silence. The Director appears before the curtain. He is in evening dress, with white gloves, impeccably shaven and coiffed, and beaming with complacency.

DIRECTOR: (*Bowing to the audience in several directions.*) Kind ladies and gentlemen! Before the overture to the immortal opera "Faust" commences, the management considers it fitting, nay more—indispensable—to draw the audience's attention to the historic date of tonight's premiere, which celebrates a conclusive victory for realism in the art of the theatre. Today marks the 2600th anniversary of the founding of the ancient Greek theatre, the 715th anniversary of the founding of the Western European theatre, and the 159th anniversary of the founding of our Russian national theatre. Add up these figures and you will see that over the course of 3473 years, the greatest minds in the theatrical world have been vainly striving to discover the "elixir of life"—if I may be fanciful—for verisimilitude on stage. But such is the fate of all remarkable discoveries!—they compel us fatefully to wait for them, century upon century! . . . One need merely recall how much time preceded the discovery of America, to realize that the discovery of the absolute in theatrical verisimilitude would need somewhat more time. Be that as it may, the one important thing is: there is now an end to the search, and this very day, this truly remarkable day, all who have hitherto sickened for truth in the theatre will at last receive the long-awaited cure. Today's premiere—and I am here on behalf of the management to inform you of it, proud that the allotted mission has fallen to me—today's premiere, ladies and gentlemen, is the total liquidation of old-fashioned, conventional art, steeped through and through with falsity! Today's premiere is a triumphal victory for unadorned truth in the theatre. Today's premiere is the greatest event in the universal history of dramatic art—an event, the scope of whose originality can be measured only by the production itself, which comprised this event. Regard it with the esteem it in all fairness deserves. But, whatever your opinion, the management is happy solely in its awareness of having done its duty!—the duty of preferring, all in all, the truth of sober reality on stage, to tricks of theatrical deceit.

(He exits. The orchestra plays the overture to "Faust," during which time the first curtain rises, revealing a second, on which Truth is depicted, tearing apart a wig in front of a mirror and trampling a heap of masks beneath her feet; Truth is represented as an unattractive, elderly woman, devoid of any kind of adornment. On either side of her are sewn laurel wreaths, with the inscriptions (on one) "Amicus Cato, sed magis amica Veritas," (on the other) "Eat salt and bread, But let Truth be said." At the conclusion of the overture an unendurable silence ensues, during which the Conductor leaves his place and the second curtain rises.

On stage, almost at the footlights themselves, towers the notorious fourth wall. It is constructed with all the realism of the stonemason's art and observes all the archaeological findings relating to German architecture of the late Middle Ages. The half-light of early morning. The stage is empty. In one of the windows on the second story we can see the flickering light of an oil lamp; judging by the two or three retorts, globe and skull visible on the window-sill, it is the window to Doctor Faust's study. As a matter of fact, his dishevelled shadow flashes by! Then, at last, his characteristic old man's cough is heard! . . . As if in response to it, somewhere far, far away, the bell of the townhall rings out, tolling five o'clock in the morning. The light gradually grows brighter. At the right we can hear the drunken singing of the guild artisans to a theme from the first chorus in "Faust.")

> "Die Schaefer putzte sich zum Tanz
> Mit bunter Jacke, Band und Kranz,
> Schmuck war er angezogen.
> Schon um die Linde war es voll
> Und alles tantzte schon wie toll."

(From right to left passes a band of youths who have been up all night carousing, while one of them plays a Dutch chorus on a fiddle.)

> "Es drueckte haftig sich heran,

Da stiesz er an ein Maedchen an
Mit seinem Ellenbogen;
Die friche Dirne kehrt' sich um
Und sagte: Nun, das find ich dumm.''

(*The roisterers stagger off left. Faust pops his head out of the window, wags it after the departing youths and, shedding a tear for the memories of youth that well up in his soul, he loudly blows his nose. From the right comes the sound of street-sweeping. Faust, having turned his head to the right, hides. In the open window on the third story appears an unattractive female figure, howling at the top of her lungs and scratching herself. A scruffy ragamuffin runs in at left and stops before the wall with an unequivocal intention. At that moment, the woman, noticing him from above and coming to some decision, disappears. A sweeper who shows up at right with the cry ''Aber Donnerwetter, willst du Ruten kriegen,'' runs at the urchin, waving his broom at him. The urchin, emitting an ''Ow,'' rushes to escape the blow, which lands on the wall, while the sweeper trips and falls. The woman above pours on him the slops she had meant for the scruffy ragamuffin. The sweeper, shaking himself off like a poodle, lifts his head and roars, ''Verfluchte Sau! So musz denn doch die Hexe dran! . . .'' while the urchin with a shriek of laughter, escapes left. The sweeper, crying ''Halt, dummer Jung,'' runs out after the urchin. A few typical German villagers from the provinces cross the stage. The auditorium is filled with the stench of salt fish, onions and pork.*)

CHORUS OF DRUNKARDS: (*Offstage left, to the tune ''The meadows with their beauty beckon''.*)
    ''Ach wie und wo ich mich vergnuege,
     Ach mag es immerhin geschehn,
     Ach laszt mich liegen, wo ich liege,
     Ach denn ich mag nicht laenger stehn.''

(*Marguerite and Martha appear right. Both in dresses made of ticking. Marguerite, barefoot, holds a spinning wheel. They stop just in front of the window to the study of Faust, who, having heard Marguerite's lickerishly vulgar laugh, reappears in the window, but this time holding the poisoned chalice.*)

MARGUERITE: (*Admiring the spinning wheel.*) Ach, Gott! mag das meine Mutter sein!

MARTHA: O, du glueckliche Kreatur! . . .

MARGUERITE: Ach, seh Sie nur! Ach, schau Sie nur! . . .

MARTHA: Geht! Ist schon Zeit! . . .

MARGUERITE: (*Slowly exiting left with Martha, sings, playing the spinning wheel.*)
    ''Es war ein Koenig in Thule,
     Gar treu bis an das Grab,
     Dem Sterbend seine Buhle

Einen goldenen Becher gab . . .
Es ging ihm nicht darueber'' etc.

(*The music of a carnival is heard at right.*)

FAUST: (*Turning to the audience.*) I can't stand any more of this! . . . Ladies, and gentlemen, you are my witnesses! . . . (*He drains the chalice of poison dry and, staggering, disappears.*)

(*A tumult on stage. Voices are heard: "What's happening?," "What's going on?," "Did you hear that?," "Let down the curtain," "Hold on," "Where's the director?," "Doctor," "What's come over him?" and so on. The curtain is rapidly let down. The Assistant Director, just the slightest bit tipsy, appears before the curtain.*)

ASSISTANT DIRECTOR: (*Bows to the audience and clears his throat.*) Ladies and gentlemen, owing to the stark raving madness of the performer who plays Faust, the rest of the opera cannot proceed . . . (*Steals a glance at the notes, concealed in his hand.*) Which fact I bring to the attention of the most esteemed audience.

(*He bows and exits.*)

END

The Power of Love

A Vaudeville in One Act

(1933)

Ilya Ilf

&

Evgeny Petrov

Characters

Stan Markhotsky, the bridegroom
Aleksandr W. Markhotsky, his father
Nata Markhotskaya-Lifshits, the bride
Lifshits, Nata's first husband
Rita, her sister
Mama
Chulanov, a young dude
Bernardov, a member of the Civic Committee of Writers
Spravchenko, a doctor, specializing in donkey-gland treatments
Comrade Chekhov ⎫
Comrade Tolstoy ⎪
Seguedilla Markovna ⎬ Guests
A Young Man ⎪
Some Girls ⎭
Mister Peep, a well-dressed foreigner

A one-room flat in Moscow. Preparations for a wedding feast are under way. Mama and Rita are fussing about the table.

RITA: There's definitely not enough vodka. Three bottles for fifteen people! How can you call that living, Mama!

MAMA: Rita, not everybody drinks!

RITA: Practically everybody, Mama! Bernardov drinks, Chulanov drinks. Seguedilla Markovna drinks, the Doctor probably drinks too . . .

MAMA: You think the Doctor will come? I just can't get over it. Curing people with such an indecent treatment, with those horrid donkey-glands . . .

RITA: Cut it out, Mama! Nowadays they inject 'em into everybody! Which means, the Doctor obviously drinks. Comrade Tolstoy and Comrade Chekhov drink like fish. Stan drinks . . .

MAMA: (*Horrified.*) Stan drinks!

RITA: Like he's got a hollow leg!

MAMA: Gracious, Rita, what an expression! Really, I find this a dreadful piece of news—Stan drinks! Such a respectable, mild-mannered young man!

RITA: If I'd been in Nata's shoes, I never would have married a second time. Lifshits was a big improvement over Stan!

MAMA: Yes, but Lifshits is practically a Jew, Rita dear,—he's a Karaite!

RITA: Mama, you've got to look at things from the proper angle. A Karaite is practically a Turk, a Turk is practically a Persian, a Persian is practically a Greek, a Greek is practically an Odessan, and an Odessan is practically a citizen of Moscow!

MAMA: I've got nothing against Greeks, but Stan has a big room!

RITA: It's pretty aggravating, just the same! Picking out a husband on account of his room!

MAMA: But what a room!

RITA: But what a husband . . . No, there's positively not enough vodka! If I ever get married, it'll only be to a foreigner, so I can go abroad with him! How I'd love to live in a bourgeois society again, in a bungalow on the bayshore, with foreigners! . . . By the way, the foreigner drinks too, most likely! It'll be a crying shame! Not enough drink, not enough booze!

MAMA: Good grief, where did you pick up such language?! Booze indeed! . . . Coming from such a sweet young girl!

CHULANOV: (*Runs in, without saying a word tosses Mama a fish and hurries over to the telephone. During his speech he pulls assorted food packages and bottles out of his pocket. Part of his remarks is addressed into the receiver, the other part to Rita.*) Operator! (*He declaims.*) "Operator, 'twas inscribed on his buckler with his blood . . ." Rita, I'm a mastermind . . . B one zero eleven . . . Yes, across the river . . . Here are the eggplants. This is Georgian wine from the private . . . Hello! Can I speak to Mister Peep? . . . Rita, this Peep is an A-number one foreigner! Only arrived yesterday . . . First-class baked beans. Got 'em through pull . . . Hello! Mister Peep! . . . What? . . . Where did he go? . . . Excuse me, but I'd already made arrangements with him . . . This is downright gall! (*He hangs up the receiver.*)

RITA: What happened?

CHULANOV: (*In a sepulchral voice.*) Total disaster! Mister Peep's been kidnapped. Just at the last minute he was dragged off to a party at the Popovs. You know those Popovs?

RITA: (*In a glacial tone.*) Meaning, the foreigner won't be coming?

CHULANOV: For Heaven's sake . . .

RITA: Then clear out of here.

CHULANOV: Let me explain! I keep telling you, now is not the season, it's not the season! There's an inadequate number of tourists. For Heaven's sake, there's a shortage of foreigners! If you'd asked me two weeks ago, I could have brought you as many as you like. Then there was a whole boatload of 'em. Four hundred peace commissioners. Thick as pickles in a jar! All in tuxedos, black on white! But there's none left now. I even stopped by the National Hotel, the doorman there is a pal of mine, and he said the same thing: there's none left. Better I should have brought you Utesov. I've got a pal who's like *that* with Utesov. He talks to him. Do you realize what that would be like? Utesov at a wedding! (*Hums meekly.*) "And no-o-w, and no-o-ow . . . And no-o-ow that night is nigh . . ."

RITA: And now that you haven't brought a foreigner, I'm no longer on speaking terms with you!

CHULANOV: (*Having considered this a moment.*) I love you, Rita!

RITA: Make yourself scarce!

CHULANOV: But this is nothing but red tape, pure bureaucracy. I'll register a complaint!

RITA: Who to? Cupid? Anyway I . . . I'm not going to marry anyone but a foreigner!

CHULANOV: How about me?

RITA: You're no foreigner.

CHULANOV: So what am I, in your opinion—some yokel from back of beyond? If you were to make a thorough investigation, you'd find I'm a foreigner too. (*Getting up steam.*) What have I got in common with the Soviet government? Regard me as a representative of capitalist society.

RITA: Some representative! Can't even do a favor for his girlfriend.

CHULANOV: (*Snatches up his cap.*) For your sake I'll attempt anything! Look, I offer myself as a sacrifice! Laugh, clown, laugh . . . You'll get your foreigner!

RITA: What about a Victrola?

CHULANOV: Bernardov's bringing it. I'll do it all, and then I'll hang myself. Men die for love. (*He exits. In the doorway.*) Looks to me like there's not enough vodka! (*He exits.*)

MAMA: There's no reason to treat him like that. He's quite a respectable young man.

RITA: With you everybody's respectable . . . There's plenty of wine, but there is absolutely not enough vodka!

MAMA: What can be keeping Nata and Stan? It's high time they were back . . .

CHULANOV: (*Entering.*) Citizens, Lifshits is waiting on the staircase!

RITA: Lifshits?

CHULANOV: Right, Izzy Lifshits, the first husband. Waiting on the staircase black as black can be.

MAMA: Oh dear, that's all I needed! What's going to happen? Stan and Nata will be coming back from the registry office any minute, and if they bump into him . . . This is awful! . . . How does he look?

CHULANOV: I just told you. He's waiting there white as white can be . . .

MAMA: He'll kill her! (*Wrings her hands.*) He's a Karaite, all Karaites are jealous by nature . . .

RITA: That's right. Karaites are practically Turks, Turks are practically Moors, and Moors, you know yourself . . .

(*The doorbell rings.*)

CHULANOV: That's him!

MAMA: We've got to do something. Say something to him.

RITA: Chulanov, honey, go out on the stairs, try to influence him . . .

(*The doorbell rings shrilly.*)

CHULANOV: You think it's worth the trouble? What am I supposed to say to him? I'm no public speaker, no Maxim Gorky . . .

RITA: Ye-es . . . You're far from being a public speaker.

CHULANOV: (*In a lachrymose voice.*) If I were a soldier, it would be a different story. But I'm a civilian, a pacifist. This is a job for the police—combatting outbreaks of jealousy and other varieties of day-to-day delinquency. (*He looks at Rita.*) Fine. Laugh, clown, laugh! I'm off. (*Crosses to the door, solemnly.*) Farewell! (*A loud knock on the door. Chulanov leaps away from it.*)

RITA: Don't open the door! (*The bell rings.*) No, better open up! Persuade him.

CHULANOV: Better you open up. And I'll persuade him afterwards.

RITA: (*Contemptuously.*) Some foreigner! (*She opens the door.*)

BERNARDOV: (*Enters with a Victrola.*) Citizens, Lifshits is waiting on the staircase!

MAMA: Practically Othello!

BERNARDOV: (*After a cursory glance at the table.*) Citizens, there's not enough vodka!

RITA: Hold on, what did he say?

BERNARDOV: He said he had come for Nata.

MAMA: The nerve! Did you explain to him that Nata's marrying Stan?

BERNARDOV: I explained. But he says he doesn't give a damn.

RITA: What did you say to that?

BERNARDOV: Nothing, of course. After all, I'm only a guest. I told him it was a nuisance—a wedding going on and all. But he said he'd show the lot of them!

MAMA: He said *that*?

BERNARDOV: That's what he said. I was beginning to fear for my Victrola.

(*A ruckus begins on the other side of the door. We hear an ever increasing noise of fighting and indistinct voices.*)

CHULANOV: Listen, Rita honey, I'll run over and get a foreigner. Ever so quietly, through the back door! (*He exits rapidly.*)

(*The door is flung open, and Stan flies into the room, followed by Nata. Nata's hat is on crooked. Stan is somewhat rumpled.*)

MAMA: What happened? Did he insult you?

NATA: Worse!

MAMA: Did he hit you?

NATA: Ach, Mommy dear . . . (*Weeps.*) Worse!

MAMA: What did he do to you, the louse!

NATA: He kissed me!

STAN: Nothing less than behaving like a thug! (*He adjusts his suit.*) I regret I didn't kick him down the stairs! Guys like that should be fined!

RITA: (*To Stan.*) Well, never mind. I'm so glad everything turned out all right, you can't imagine! . . .

STAN: (*Offended.*) Why can't I imagine it? Haven't I got any imagination? Or maybe I'm an idiot?

RITA: Of course not, you don't understand.

STAN: Why don't I understand? You mean I'm a dope—is that what you're driving at?

RITA: You must be joking.

STAN: (*Getting even more offended.*) When was I joking? I wasn't joking. Everyone here can bear witness.

RITA: Fooey, why did you bother getting married, if you've got such a touchy personality?

STAN: (*Primly.*) I got married in order to regulate the matter of sex.

RITA: What a dope. (*Exits.*) No, only to a foreigner. Only to a foreigner! . . .

(*Enter Doctor Spravchenko.*)

NATA: Good evening, Doctor. I'm so glad to see you!

DOCTOR: What's the matter with that young man waiting on the staircase?

NATA: This is getting insufferable!

STAN: He's waiting for me to kick him down the stairs.

DOCTOR: Well, sir, permit me to congratulate you on your lawful . . .

(*Enter Comrade Tolstoy and Comrade Chekhov.*)

TOLSTOY: Hey, ain't there going to be a wedding today?

CHEKHOV: You called it off?

STAN: Don't be silly!

TOLSTOY: But Lifshits just told us the wedding was off.

CHEKHOV: He's waiting out there on the staircase.

STAN: Smart-aleck scum!

TOLSTOY AND CHEKHOV: In that case, may we congratulate you . . . Natalya Viktorovna . . . (*Smack, smack.*) Stanislav Aleksandrovich . . . Dear Mama (*Smack, smack.*) It's a good thing you didn't call it off . . . Is that all the vodka there is? It ain't enough . . .

(*Enter Seguedilla Markovna, two girls and a young man.*)

SEGUEDILLA MARKOVNA: Nata darling! (*They kiss one another.*) Lifshits asked me to give you this note. He's out there on the staircase. (*Says hello to the other guests.*)

STAN: (*Snatches the note from Nata, reads it and tears it into shreds.*) So, he's waiting for me to kick him down the stairs.

NATA: (*To Stan.*) You can't conceive the extent to which he loves me.

STAN: Why can't I conceive it? What am I, a degenerate?

NATA: (*To the Doctor.*) Is it true, Doctor, that you literally work miracles?

DOCTOR: Literally—no, but on the whole, so to speak, different things happen.

NATA: (*Wiping away tears.*) Tell me, Doctor, do you earn much money by gold conversion?

DOCTOR: Gold conversion, n—no . . . but on the whole . . .

SEGUEDILLA MARKOVNA: Doctor, I'd like to get a donkey-gland injection too. May I?

DOCTOR: You? On the whole, no, but in general . . . maybe.

BERNARDOV: Say, Doc, take me, for instance, a member of the Civic Committee of Writers. I'd like to find out what influence the injection has, if I may use the expression, on the specific nature of creative effort? Would it improve the quality of a writer's productivity?

DOCTOR: Quality? N—no. Quantity? Yes, indeed.

(*Chulanov appears from the back entrance, stops in the doorway.*)

CHULANOV: (*Mysteriously.*) Rita!

RITA: (*Walks over to him.*) Well, did you get a foreigner?

(*Noise on the staircase.*)

CHULANOV: What's that?

RITA: That's Lifshits. What about the foreigner?

CHULANOV: (*Disconcerted.*) I've got one. I left him in the kitchen.

RITA: How stupid! That's embarrassing. Fetch him in here right away!

CHULANOV: But I've got to warn you first . . . Even though he's a foreigner, you see, he's not a European . . .

RITA: Who is he then?

CHULANOV: (*Hedging.*) Well—a diplomat. He's very fond of white women.

RITA: (*Delighted.*) A Jap?

CHULANOV: (*Stammering.*) A Jap.

RITA: From the embassy?

CHULANOV: Yes, from the embassy, more or less. His duties are equivalent to those of a commercial attaché. Very well-educated fellow. Graduated from three universities. Or was it four? Swear to God! Two in Tokyo and two in Manchukuo. But there's one odd little quirk about him. Sheer trivia, a diplomat's whim. The main thing is not to pay any attention to it. You see, he likes to talk about starched collars, cuffs, shirts, things like that . . . It can't be helped, etiquette insists.

RITA: (*Impatiently.*) Where is he?

CHULANOV: Good grief, Rita, I did the best I could!

(*He opens the door. Behind it stands a man, smiling.*)

RITA: Chulanov!

CHULANOV: What?

RITA: This is no diplomat.

CHULANOV: He is a diplomat. On my word of honor!

RITA: This is no Jap.

CHULANOV: Swear to God, he is a Jap!

RITA: He's a Chinaman.

CHULANOV: A Jap from the embassy.

RITA: A Chinaman from the hand-laundry.

CHULANOV: (*In a lachrymose voice.*) I told you now isn't the season!

RITA: (*Shoving Chulanov out.*) Get out and don't come back without a foreigner! And make sure he's the genuine article. A European. From Paris. Understand? (*She hums.*) "Sous les toits de Paris," ta-ra-ram-tam-tam-tam.

CHULANOV: (*Picking up the tune.*) Ta-ra-ram-tam-tam-tam . . .

RITA: That's it, ta-ra-ram.

CHULANOV: (*Decisively.*) Laugh, clown, laugh, though your heart is breaking . . . So be it! I'm off to that party at the Popovs and I'll kidnap Peep.

RITA: You sure this Mister Peep isn't anything like the last one?

CHULANOV: Well, he knows what's what! Only got in yesterday from Philadelphia. Is there enough vodka? Better check. (*Exits through the back door.*)

MAMA: Never mind, Rita darling, since there's no foreigner, we might as well sit down at the table.

(*The guests take seats, raise their glasses. A solemn pause.*)

DOCTOR: (*About to make a toast.*) Well . . .

(*Deafening knocking at the door. Everyone crouches down in fear, as if cowering from a missile.*)

DOCTOR: (*Places his glass on the table.*) No, this is intolerable. I'll go and have a word with him. (*Exits.*)

(*Everyone waits tensely. The Doctor returns with a thoroughly disgruntled expression on his face.*)

NATA: What's the matter?

DOCTOR: (*Twirling his moustache.*) He's nothing but a scoundrel! (*Sits down in his chair.*)

(*Everyone lifts his glass. Banging again. The guests cower once more.*)

TOLSTOY: Have to punch him one in the kisser, I guess! Let's go, Chekhov.
CHEKHOV: (Removes his jacket.) Don't drink without us. We'll be right back. Come on, Tolstoy. Let's give him a going-over.

(*They leave. The guests wait in silence. A pause. The door slams shut. Utter silence. Behind the door the clamor of a violent skirmish erupts Silence again. Re-enter, weaving and reeling, Comrades Tolstoy and Chekhov.*)

TOLSTOY: Why didn't you hold on to him?
CHEKHOV: How could I hold on to him, when you let him go?
TOLSTOY: *I* let him go? You're the one that let him go.
CHEKHOV: Because of you, he practically strangled me. Outrageous! There's no way of getting him off the landing.

(*They sit down at the table while the knocking proceeds at regular intervals. Obviously, that awful Lifshits is kicking the door with both feet.*)

MAMA: Maybe we should play some records.

(*Bernardov winds up the Victrola, and the party gets under way to the sound of music and knocking.*)

TOLSTOY: I suggest you keep an eye on the vodka, Chekhov. There ain't enough. It happens every time.
CHEKHOV: (*Pours out some for himself and Tolstoy.*) In that case there's no point in wasting valuable time. (*Loudly.*) To the newlyweds' health! (*Drinks quickly and pours out another glassful.*) To the health of the company! (*They drink and refill their glasses.*) To our hostess's health! (*They drink and refill their glasses.*) To the newlyweds' future offspring! (*They drink; all this is carried out with incredible speed.*)
MAMA: What's the matter with you, gentlemen? We haven't yet had time to pour ourselves a glass, while you . . . You mustn't.
TOLSTOY: (*Paying no attention, raises a fresh glass.*) To the welfare of mankind! Am I right, Chekhov?
CHEKHOV: Right you are, Tolstoy. (*They drink.*) To mankind! The hell with it.
DOCTOR: (*Squinting at the guests.*) Yes, I see there's no time to lose! (*He drinks four glasses in a row. The fifth he clinks with Seguedilla Markovna.*)
SEGUEDILLA MARKOVNA: Doctor, I absolutely insist on having my husband

and myself injected with donkey-glands. I've heard the most wonderful things about them. A lady I know suffered such a loss of vigor last year she almost never left her house. And do you know, after just two injections of donkey-glands, she was completely transformed—she went off to market, sold her husband's overcoat and bought some marvelous imported beads.

DOCTOR: Yes, donkey-glands produce some remarkable effects. Just the other day an old woman dropped by my office—she was about sixty. And naturally, suffering from senescent debility, arthritis, marasmus . . . Well, I took her in hand forthwith . . . (*With sounds and gestures he acts out an injection.*) And a second time. (*Acts it out.*) Yesterday I ran into her on the street—she was rushing somewhere on business as fast as her legs could carry her. What was the matter? They had cancelled her pension. They didn't believe she was sixty. They claimed she was twenty. She had recovered her youth!

SEGUEDILLA MARKOVNA: Doctor, you're a wizard and a warlock! A wizard and a warlock!

A GIRL: I'll drink to that fact!

DOCTOR: (*Casts a sidelong glance at Tolstoy and drinks a few glasses, one after another.*) Ye—es . . . Another old woman came to see me; she was around eighty. No teeth, no hair, no, damned if she had anything at all . . . Well, I took 'er in hand . . . (*He acts out a triple injection.*)

A GIRL: I'll drink to that fact!

(*Enter Aleksandr Witoldovich Markhotsky.*)

DOCTOR: Who might this be?

RITA: I don't believe I know.

DOCTOR: Just let me take 'im in hand and . . . (*He acts out an injection, attempts to stand up. They hold him back.*)

STAN: (*Dumbfounded.*) Papa!

MARKHOTSKY: Good evening, Stanislav. I had a hard time finding this flat. Luckily, there's a nice young man waiting on the landing, and he showed me the way. Well, I'm delighted to see you at large. Good evening, comrades. (*General bowing.*) Where's your young lady? It's high time we got acquainted. Aha! (*Gallantly kisses Nata's hand.*) Very, very pleased to meet you. You know, I'm somewhat unaccustomed to the company of ladies. (*Introduces himself to the guests.*) Markhotsky, Markhotsky, Markhotsky . . .

NATA: (*To Stan.*) You never even told me you had a papa. Where does he live?

STAN: Wait a minute, wait a minute. (*Leads his father aside.*) How did you wind up here, Papa?

MARKHOTSKY: They gave me a furlough till tonight. The fact is, my condition has improved considerably and they're rehabilitating me with special privileges.

STAN: (*Stupefied.*) You mean you arrived with an escort?

MARKHOTSKY: You're way off the track. What kind of an escort! You haven't the slightest idea what the contemporary penitentiary system is like.

STAN: (*Tiresomely.*) Why haven't I the slightest idea? What am I, a moron or some sort of mental retard? Besides, this business has nothing to do with the system. Nobody knows that you're serving a term in prison. What will Nata and the guests think! And to top it off, they're expecting a foreigner. No, I must ask you to go somewhere else.

MARKHOTSKY: Where am I to git to? I've only got a twelve-hour pass.

STAN: Well, stroll around the streets. You ought to find that interesting.

MARKHOTSKY: (*Dolefully.*) You kicking me out, Stan?

STAN: Of all the bad luck . . . Go ahead and stay. But for pity's sake—not a word about that shabby business.

MARKHOTSKY: (*Livens up, cheerfully walks over to the table.*) What sumptuous rations!

STAN: Papa!

MARKHOTSKY: (*Sits next to Nata.*) What charming companionship! I'm out of the habit, quite out of the habit! At our place, you know, the women's . . . that is, the ladies' block is set up in isolation from the men's . . .

STAN: Papa!

NATA: I don't quite understand. Where is this? Why is it isolated?

STAN: (*Curtly.*) Papa's come out of a sanatorium . . .

NATA: I dream of taking a cure in a sanatorium.

BERNARDOV: Excuse me, but how did you get accepted into the sanatorium— by application or by pulling strings?

MARKHOTSKY: How can I explain it . . . You see, when they were on my trail

STAN: Papa!

MARKHOTSKY: (*Drinks.*) Yes, by application.

BERNARDOV: And is it a decent sanatorium?

MARKHOTSKY: Decent is an understatement. Foreigners visit it and they're enraptured when they finally leave. You begin with walking up and down the solitary confinement cell . . .

STAN: Papa!

MARKHOTSKY: And you know, people leave completely transformed. You wouldn't recognize them, simply wouldn't recognize them . . .

NATA: Do they put on weight?

MARKHOTSKY: What? Put it on? (*Drinks.*) Who's knocking like that? . . . Yes, weight too. But the main thing is the psychological change. The most stupendous rehabilitaion programs are carried on. And what a dental lab they've got! I had a whole set of false teeth made. (*Shows them.*) Lots of time on my hands, you know, why not have them put in? When you're at large you never have the time to think about your teeth, but in our place . . .

STAN: Papa, I asked you . . .

BERNARDOV: How much is the entrance fee?

MARKHOTSKY: Not a thing, it's all free. Not so long ago they even rehabilitated me with trousers, and they were free too. Who keeps banging away like that?

RITA: Don't pay attention!

BERNARDOV: That's fantastic! Without costing a penny! Are you staying for a month?

MARKHOTSKY: My dear boy! For three whole years . . .

NATA: You see, Stan, your papa's in complete control of his affairs, while you're simply a limp rag!

BERNARDOV: Please, let me ask you to get me in too!

GUESTS: (*In chorus.*) Me too! . . . Me too!

MARKHOTSKY: (*Flattered by the unanimous attention.*) Naturally, I'll do all I can, although I'm not in charge, so to speak, but, as an inmate under correction . . . that is, a patient undergoing treatment . . .

STAN: Papa, I beg you, once and for all . . .

MARKHOTSKY: We've got an exercise-yard . . .

STAN: Papa!

MARKHOTSKY: Lay off me, you b-bourgeois!

SEGUEDILLA MARKOVNA: (*To Stan.*) You don't understand how much the sanatorium system has improved these days . . .

STAN: (*Taking offense.*) Why don't I understand? Everybody else understands, but I'm the only one not to. Just what's going on!

(*The telephone rings.*)

RITA: (*Picks up the receiver.*) It's me . . . You're bringing him? In a taxi? Thank God! Hurry up! . . . No, Lifshits is still here. He keeps breaking into the apartment. I really don't know what'll happen. Disgraceful. Come up the back way. What a country! (*Hangs up the receiver.*) Mister Peep will be here any minute. Comrade Tolstoy, darling, Comrade Chekhov, Doctor, Seguedilla Markovna, girls, you should be ashamed of yourselves, leave some vodka for Mister Peep . . . Bernardov, please, you too . . . Wind up the Victrola instead. I suggest we dance now, and when Mister Peep gets here, we'll sit down to supper again . . . (*Dreamily.*) When Mister Peep gets here . . . (*Dances with Bernardov. All of the following conversation goes on as they dance.*)

BERNARDOV: I can't understand why girls are so fond of foreigners.

RITA: (*Singing.*) When Mister Peep gets here . . .

BERNARDOV: I'm interested in this Mister Peep, inasmuch as I'd like to buy his suit off him cheap. You know, my morale gets so low, not having a suit.

RITA: You're always crying poor, Bernardov. The one you're wearing isn't so bad. How much did you pay for it, in gold?

BERNARDOV: In gold—I don't know. I bought it at the Water Transport Workers' commissary for sixty-five rubles.

RITA: Are you really a Water Transport Worker?

BERNARDOV: No, I'm not. I belong to the Civic Committee of Writers.

RITA: You're a writer?

BERNARDOV: No, I'm not. I only eat in the Writers' cafeteria, but I'm more or less in the Railway Workers' Union.

RITA: Ah, you're a railroad man?

BERNARDOV: No, I'm not. I just pick up free train rides that way. But on the whole I'm closest of all to the Firemen.

RITA: You fight fires?

BERNARDOV: No, I only get milk there. You see, the firefighting profession is very detrimental to your health, so they hand out a lot of milk. So you arrange to go down to the main department every day with your buckets and collect the milk . . . Honestly, I'm going to demand to be sent to a more central location, to the Kropotkin depot.

RITA: Why don't you go down there every day on the trolley . . .

BERNARDOV: The trolley suits me fine—nothing wrong with it. I ride on the platform as a member of the Moscow Soviet of Workers' Deputies.

RITA: Ah, you're a Workers' Deputy?

BERNARDOV: No, I'm not. I only ride as a Workers' Deputy. But, actually, it's awfully exhausting. And if I don't get a vacation in a sanatorium for People's Commissars, I'm going to wear myself to a frazzle.

RITA: You're high up in the government?

BERNARDOV: By no means! I've been explaining it to you for half an hour, and you refuse to understand.

(Suddenly the din outside grows louder.)

STAN: This is all your fault. This nightmarish banging is destroying our wedding.

NATA: Is it my fault that he's so in love with me?

A GIRL: I'll drink to that fact!

RITA: We'll have to discuss it with him. Bernardov, go out and ask him what he wants once and for all. (*Bernardov exits. Everyone crowds round the door and waits. The knocking stops. Bernardov enters.*)

BERNARDOV: He says that Stan should clear the hell out of here on the double.

STAN: It looks like he's waiting for me to kick him down the stairs!

MAMA: Tell him that we'll call the police.

BERNARDOV: (*Goes out and comes back.*) He says that no policeman in the world can keep him from loving Nata . . . meaning you, Natalya Viktorovna.

NATA: (*Flattered.*) Tell him don't mention it!

STAN: Now do you see what you've gone and done with your idiotic beauty! Admit that you like it!

NATA: Beat it, the lot of you!

STAN: (*To Bernardov.*) Tell him that I'm going to kick him down the stairs this very minute!

BERNARDOV: (*Exits and instantly reappears in the doorway with a desperate shout.*) Lifshits has broken in!! . . .

(*The company lets out a wail. Stan and the ladies jump away from the door. The men rush to Bernardov's aid. They fall upon Lifshits in such a way that the audience hasn't even time to catch a glimpse of him. This human mass forms a sphere that rolls along the stage. Finally the sphere rolls out the door. Shouts: "Hold the door! . . . Don't let go! . . . My fingers! My fingers!" Chulanov enters the back way, dragging Mister Peep by the arm.*)

CHULANOV: Rita, here he is. What I've been through! You see, Madam Popov ran her manicure along my cheek. That was when I was dragging him down the stairs. Well, never mind, I gave her a good kick . . . Rita, come get acquainted, please, Mister Peep.

RITA: Haow-dew-doo, Meester . . . (*She stammers.*)

CHULANOV: Don't bother, don't bother. He speaks beautiful Russian. Say something, Mister Peep.

PEEP: Good evening, young gentlewoman. (*From the vestibule the men return, panting hard.*) Have these persons been moving a pianoforte?

RITA: May I present to you—Mister Peep, a European.

(*Introductions.*)

CHULANOV: (*Beaming.*) Well now? Is he the genuine article? Eh? "Sous les toits de Paris" ta-ra-ram-tam-ram-tam . . .

RITA: (*Gratefully.*) The genuine article. Ta-ra-ram-tam-tam . . .

CHULANOV: That's right, ta-ra-ram. And now what about me? I still love you.

RITA: Later, later.

(*Everyone is rudely scrutinizing the foreigner, who keeps turning and smiling bashfully.*)

BERNARDOV: (*Feeling the guest's suit.*) Genuine blended wool!

A GIRL: Say, what's the weather like in Europe just now?

SEGUEDILLA MARKOVNA: Come and meet the doctor.

(*The Doctor staggers over, bows and emits a sound, illustrative of an injection.*)

RITA: Citizens, comrades . . . (*Gently pushes the guests aside.*)

BERNARDOV: Say, Mister Peep, won't you sell me your suit?

(*Rita takes Peep by the hand and leads him aside. All the guests, headed by Chulanov, follow. Comrades Tolstoy and Chekhov are dozing at the table.*)

RITA: Yew spik Eengleesh?

CHULANOV: Why do you even bother asking? For heaven's sake, he's not a hick from the sticks. Of course he speaks English. And Russian too.

BERNARDOV: Won't you sell me your necktie? If you were to sell me your suit, that necktie would go along with it just dandy.

RITA: (*Trying to walk off with the foreigner.*) For ever so long I've been dying to have a conversation with a man of European culture.

NATA: (*Takes Peep by his other arm. Flirtatiously.*) Why are you so sad? . . .

BERNARDOV: (*On the move.*) If you were to sell me your shoes, they'd go just super with the suit and the tie. Do sell them!

CHULANOV: Stop pestering the poor man all at once. He hasn't even had time to answer you. What do you want, Seguedilla Markovna? A rumba? Nobody dances it any more. He told me so in the taxi. What else?

MARKHOTSKY: Tell me, what kind of a penitentiary system have you got in the West?

CHULANOV: That's boring. What else?

VOICES: Ask him . . . Let him tell . . . What about . . .

(*General racket.*)

CHULANOV: Wait a minute! Wait a minute! Why did he come here? I'll ask him right now. Your newfound friends, Mister Peep, would like to know what you intend to do in our country?

PEEP: I came hither to seek work, gentlemens.

RITA: What? What did he say, Chulanov?

PEEP: I do not possess a means of livelihood, gentlemens . . . (*He smiles.*) But I see that I do possess many good friends . . .

BERNARDOV: (*Goes back to the table.*) Obviously a shady character.

(*Chulanov goes to the table hurriedly. Rita is right on his heels.*)

RITA: I'll never forgive you for this!

CHULANOV: What can I do about it, Rita honey? He's been spawned by the Depression. Well, there's a depression on, get me? A worldwide depression. It's not my fault. Marx explained how it would happen. You'll take Marx's word for it, won't you?

RITA: (*Beaten down by his arguments.*) All the same you're a sonuvabitch.

(*The Guests abandon Peep and sit at the table. Peep stands alone.*)

MARKHOTSKY: (*Pouring out a drink.*) What a lot of tommyrot! We'd do far better to toast the penitentiary . . .

STAN: Papa!

MARKHOTSKY: Shut up, you young whippersnapper!

DOCTOR: (*Drinks.*) It's a dirty business, these donkey-glands. Dirty as they come. Nobody gets cured. Quite the contrary, they die off!

SEGUEDILLA MARKOVNA: Doctor, what's wrong with you?

DOCTOR: (*Imitating her.*) What's wrong with me! What's wrong with me! Cut out all this flibberty-gibberty . . . Wizard and warlock . . . I'm a quack. Q-U-ack! You don't like that fact? You think maybe *I* like it?

(*Peep walks over to the table, tries to sit down, but all the seats are taken.*)

PEEP: (*Tries to squeeze in between somebody's shoulders, but they don't let him in. He smiles.*) There's a wedding, it would seem? (*Silence. The guests are regaling themselves.*) There's somebody knocking. (*Silence.*) There's somebody knocking very loudly. You ought to open the door.

BERNARDOV: Listen, Peep, please don't get in our hair!

(*Peep smiles dazedly and walks over to one side.*)

MARKHOTSKY: (*Making a speech.*) In the last analysis, Stan, it's a good thing you got married. By the end of the month, I'll be out of jail . . .

STAN: Papa! What the hell are you . . .

MARKHOTSKY: Don't interrupt! We'll all live together . . . I'll play nursemaid to my grandchildren . . .

NATA: What is he saying? What's that about jail? Nursemaid to who? He's going to live with us? In one room?

STAN: Don't worry, Nata. There's . . . there's some misunderstanding! Papa, I must request you to leave at once.

MARKHOTSKY: What? Who do you think you're talking to, you dumbbell?

STAN: (*Beside himself.*) Papa, get out of here!

MARKHOTSKY: (*Stands up, rocking back and forth.*) Right away, right away! Straight out of this hellhole! Back to prison! (*He runs out, noiselessly followed by a hurried Mister Peep.*)

NATA: You were concealing all this from me! . . .

STAN: Insignificant trivia, Nata dear . . .

NATA: You can't possibly imagine what a bastard you are!

STAN: Why can't I imagine it? Haven't I got any imagination?

NATA: (*Decisively.*) Call in Lifshits!

(*Chulanov rushes out. The door opens, the Triumph of Lifshits ensues. He enters, a puny runt with a wan, ecstatic face. The guests form two lines.*)

TOLSTOY: (*Pushes his way through and shouts.*) Kiss the bride!

(*Lifshits and Nata kiss. Chulanov steals a kiss from Rita. Clamor.*)

CHEKHOV: (*Pushing his way through.*) Kiss the bride! To the power of Love! Hip-hip-hurray!

MAMA: They kept saying—there isn't enough vodka, but everybody managed to get blind drunk!

END

Sundown

A Play in Eight Scenes

(1928)

Isaak Babel

Characters:

Mendel Krik, owner of a commercial trucking firm, 62.
Nekhama, his wife, 60
Benya ⎞   a dandified young man, 26
Lyovka ⎟ their children   an hussar on leave, 22
Dvoira ⎠   an overripe spinster, 30
Arye-Leib, sexton in the transport-workers' synagogue, 65
Nikifor, head driver for Krik's firm, 50
Ivan Pyatirubel, blacksmith, a friend of Mendel's, 50
Ben Zkharya, a rabbi in Moldavanka, 70
Fomin, a contractor, 40.
Yevdokiya Potapovna Kholodenko, sells live and slaughtered poultry in the
    marketplace, a fat old woman with a wrenched hip. A drunkard, 50.
Marusya, her daughter, 20
Ryabtsov, a tavern-keeper.
Mitya, a waiter at the tavern.
Miron Popyatnik, flautist at Ryabtsov's tavern.
Madam Popyatnik, his wife.
Urusov, a confidential business consultant. He lisps.
Semyon, a bald peasant.
Bobrinets, a pushy Jew. He's pushy because he's rich.
Weiner, a rich man with a speech impediment.
Madam Weiner, the rich man's wife.
Klasha Zubareva, a pregnant peasant girl.
M'sieu Boyarsky, proprietor of a ladies' ready-to-wear factory bearing the
    trade-name "Shay Doover" [Chef d'Oeuvre].
Senka Topun, a friend of Benya's.
Cantor Zwieback.

The action takes place in Odessa in 1913.

SCENE 1

Dining-room in the Kriks' home. A shabby, lived-in, lower-middle-class room. Paper flowers, sideboards, a gramophone. Portraits of rabbis cheek by jowl with photographs of the Krik family: petrified, somber, with bulging eyes and shoulders as broad as cupboards. Preparations for entertaining guests have been made in the dining-room. The table, laid with a red cloth, has been set with wine, preserves, and pies. Old Lady Krik is brewing tea. Beside her, on a small end-table, a samovar is boiling away. In the room are Old Lady Nekhama, Arye-Leib, Lyovka in full-dress hussar's uniform. He wears a yellow visorless cap cocked over his brick-red face, a full-length coat slung over his shoulders. A curved sabre trails behind him. Benya Krik, bedecked like a Spaniard at a village fiesta, is straightening his cravat before the mirror.

ARYE-LEIB: Well, fine, Lyovka, that's wonderful . . . Arye-Leib, the Moldavanka matchmaker and shammes for the teamsters, now knows what the army means by hewing down rods . . . First they hew down rods, then they hew down human beings with them . . . Mothers play no part in our lives . . . But, Lyovka, explain to me why a hussar like you can't be a week late back from leave—just until your sister comes into her good fortune?

LYOVKA: (*Roars with laughter. Thunder rolls in his gruff voice.*) A week! . . . You're a born fool, Arye-Leib! . . . A week late! . . . The cavalry is none of your infantry. The cavalry spits on your infantry . . . If I were just a single hour late, the sergeant-major would summon me to his quarters, squeeze the sap out of my heart and punch the sap out of my nose, and then hand me over to be court-martialled. Three generals sit in judgment on every cavalry-man, three generals with medals from the Turkish campaign.

ARYE-LEIB: And do they do that to everybody or just to Jews?

LYOVKA: A Jew on horseback is no longer a Jew. He's turned into a Russian. You're such a numbskull, Arye-Leib! . . . What have the Jews got to do with it?

(*Dvoira's face peeps through the half-opened door.*)

DVOIRA: Mamma, a person could lose her mind looking for something in your house. Where did you stick my green dress?

NEKHAMA: (*Not looking at anyone in particular, mumbling under her breath.*) Look in the dresser.

DVOIRA: I looked in the dresser—it wasn't there.

NEKHAMA: Look in the chest of drawers.

DVOIRA: It wasn't in the chest of drawers.

LYOVKA: Which dress?

DVOIRA: The green one with the yoke.

LYOVKA: I think Poppa pinched it.

(*Dvoira, half-dressed, rouged, her hair frizzed, enters the room. She is tall and buxom.*)

DVOIRA: (*In a wooden voice.*) Och, I'll die!

LYOVKA: (*To his mother.*) Most likely you let him know that Boyarsky was coming by today to look Dvoira over, didn't you, you old hooligan? . . . She let him know! That did it! . . . I've been watching him since morning. He hitched Solomon the Wise and Muska to the dray, had a bite to eat, swilled some vodka like a pig, tossed something green under the seat and drove out of the yard.

DVOIRA: Och, I'll die! (*She bursts into loud sobs, tears the curtain off the window, tramples on it and throws it at the old lady.*) So there! . . .

NEKHAMA: You should all drop dead. You should drop dead this very day . . .

(*Snarling and sobbing, Dvoira rushes out. The old lady shoves the curtain into the sideboard.*)

BENYA: (*Adjusting his cravat.*) You can take my word for it, Poppa begrudges the dowry.

LYOVKA: An old man like that should be carved up and thrown to the hogs!

ARYE-LEIB: Is that any way to talk about your father, Lyovka?

LYOVKA: Then let him stop acting like a clod.

ARYE-LEIB: Your father is older than you by a Sabbath.

LYOVKA: Then let him stop acting like a filthy swine.

BENYA: (*Slipping a pearl stick-pin into his cravat.*) Last year Semka Munsh was interested in Dvoira, but, you can take my word for it, Poppa begrudged the dowry. He mangled Semka's face into hash and gravy and threw him downstairs a step a time.

LYOVKA: An old man like that should be carved up and thrown to the hogs!

ARYE-LEIB: It is decreed in Ibn-Ezra, concerning such a matchmaker as myself, "If thou dost decide, o mortal, to take up candle-making, the sun shall stand in the midst of the heavens like a curb-stone and never go down . . .''

LYOVKA: (*To his mother.*) The old man murders us a hundred times a day, but you never say a word to him, you're dumb as a block of wood. And any moment a fiancé might turn up . . .

ARYE-LEIB: It is decreed in Ibn-Ezra, concerning me: "Decide to sew shrouds for the dead, and from that day forth, no man will die for ever and ever, Amen!''

BENYA: (*Has arranged his cravat, brushed aside the raspberry-colored bandanna that keeps his hair in place, put on a very tight, very short jacket, and poured himself a slug of vodka.*) Good health to all here!

LYOVKA: (*In a gruff voice.*) Your health!

ARYE-LEIB: May all go well.

LYOVKA: (*In a gruff voice.*) May all go well.

(*M'sieu Boyarsky bounces into the room—a perky, roly-poly fellow. He chatters away nonstop.*)

BOYARSKY: Salutations! Salutations! (*Introducing himself.*) Boyarsky . . . Delighted, absolutely delighted! . . . Salutations!

ARYE-LEIB: You promised me for four, Lazar, and now it's six.

BOYARSKY: (*Sits down and takes a glass of tea from the old lady.*) For Heaven's sake, we live in Odessa and in our Odessa there are customers who extract the life out of your body the way a person extracts pits from a fig! There are close friends out to devour you, clothes and all, without salt! There's a carload of headaches, wholesale aggravation. Even if you manage to look after your health, why should a businessman be healthy? I barely made it to the hot salt-water baths—and then straight on to you.

ARYE-LEIB: You take salt-water baths, Lazar?

BOYARSKY: Every other day, like clockwork.

ARYE-LEIB: (*To the old lady.*) The very least you lay out for the baths is fifty kopeks.

BOYARSKY: For Heaven's sake, new wine is flowing through our Odessa. The Greek bazaar, Franconi's . . .

ARYE-LEIB: You frequent Franconi's, Lazar?

BOYARSKY: I frequent Franconi's.

ARYE-LEIB: (*Triumphantly.*) He frequents Franconi's! . . . (*To the old lady.*) At the very least it costs thirty kopeks to sit down at Franconi's, I might even say, forty . . .

BOYARSKY: Pardon me, Arye-Leib, if I, a younger man, interrupt you. Franconi's costs me a ruble a day, and sometimes even a ruble and a half.

ARYE-LEIB: So you're a regular spendthrift, Lazar, you're a playboy, the like of which the world has never seen! . . . A family can live on thirty rubles, and the children can even study the violin, and they can even manage to lay aside a kopek now and again . . .

(*Dvoira drifts into the room. She is wearing an orange dress, her mighty calves squeezed into shoes with tightly-laced uppers.*)

ARYE-LEIB: This is our Vera.
BOYARSKY: (*Leaping up.*) Salutations! Boyarsky.
DVOIRA: (*Hoarsely.*) Pleased to meet you.

(*Everyone sits down.*)

LYOVKA: Today our Vera was a trifle asphyxiated by fumes from a flat-iron.
BOYARSKY: Anyone can be asphyxiated from ironing, but not everyone can be a fine human being.
ARYE-LEIB: Thirty rubles a month, right down the drain . . . Lazar, you had no right to be born!
BOYARSKY: A thousand pardons, Arye-Leib, but you ought to know this about Boyarsky, he is not interested in money—money is irrelevant —Boyarsky is interested in happiness . . . I ask you, my dear friends, what do I care if my firm turns out a hundred, a hundred and fifty suits a month, plus pairs of pants, plus coats.
ARYE-LEIB: (*To the old lady.*) Figure five rubles net per suit, I might even say, ten . . .
BOYARSKY: What's the difference to me what a firm puts out, since I'm interested exclusively in happiness.
ARYE-LEIB: And let me tell you this, Lazar, that if we go about our business here like human beings and not like phonies, you will be stocked up with happiness till the day you die, may you live to a hundred and twenty . . . I tell you this as a shammes and not as a matchmaker.
BENYA: (*Pours out the wine.*) May each of us get his wish.
LYOVKA: (*In a gruff voice.*) Your health!
ARYE-LEIB: May all go well!
BOYARSKY: I was talking about Franconi's. M'sieu Krik, listen to a story about a Jew with chutzpah . . . I dropped by Franconi's today, the cafe was packed with people like a synagogue on the Day of Atonement. People were munching snacks, spitting on the floor, getting all upset . . . One is upset because business is bad for him, another is upset because business is good for his competitor. On top of that, not even a place to sit down . . . Then M'sieu Chapelon, the distinguishable Frenchman, stands up to greet me . . . Mind you, it's a great rarity, a Frenchman distinguishable by himself alone . . . stands up to greet me and invites me over to his table. M'sieu Boyarsky, he says to me in French, I respect you as a firm, and I happen to have a first-class topping for an overcoat . . .

LYOVKA: A topping?

BOYARSKY: Fabric for a hood on an overcoat . . . A first-class topping for an overcoat, he says to me in French, and I beg you as a firm to drink a couple of mugs of beer with me and polish off some lobsters . . .

LYOVKA: I love lobster.

ARYE-LEIB: Better you should tell me you love toads.

BOYARSKY: . . . And polish off some lobsters . . .

LYOVKA: (*Stubborn.*) I love lobster!

ARYE-LEIB: A lobster is nothing but a toad.

BOYARSKY: (*To Lyovka.*) You will forgive me, M'sieu Krik, if I tell you that a Jew should not be fond of lobster. I tell you this as an observation from life. A Jew who is fond of lobster might permit himself to go further with womankind than is permissible. He might talk smut at the dinner-table. And if he happens to have children, they'll grow up to be one-hundred-per-cent degenerates who hang around pool halls. I tell you this as an observation from life. Now listen to a story about a Jew with chutzpah . . .

BENYA: Boyarsky!

BOYARSKY: That's me.

BENYA: Boyarsky, make me an offhand estimate how much a first-class winter outfit would cost me?

BOYARSKY: Double-breasted or single-breasted?

BENYA: Single-breasted.

BOYARSKY: Would you prefer the tails rounded or cut-away?

BENYA: Rounded tails.

BOYARSKY: My cloth or yours?

BENYA: Your cloth.

BOYARSKY: What sort of goods do you have in mind—English, Lodz or Moscow?

BENYA: Which is best?

BOYARSKY: English cloth, M'sieu, is the finest cloth. Lodz is burlap with something painted on it, and Moscow is burlap with nothing painted on it.

BENYA: Let's have the English.

BOYARSKY: Your pattern or mine?

BENYA: Your pattern.

BOYARSKY: How much will it cost you?

BENYA: How much will it cost me?

BOYARSKY: (*Suddenly inspired with an idea.*) M'sieu Krik, we'll come to an agreement!

ARYE-LEIB: You'll come to an agreement!

BOYARSKY: We'll come to an agreement . . . I was talking about Franconi's . . .

(*The thunderous thump of hobnail boots is heard. Mendel Krik enters holding a whip, followed by his head driver, Nikifor.*)

ARYE-LEIB: (*Terrified.*) Mendel, come and be introduced to M'sieu Boyarsky
. . .

BOYARSKY: (*Leaping up.*) Salutations! Boyarsky.

(*Clumping noisily with his boots and not looking at anyone, the old man walks the length of the room. He throws down the whip, sits on the sofa and stretches out his long, stout legs. Nekhama gets down on her knees and pulls off her husband's boots.*)

ARYE-LEIB: (*Stammering.*) M'sieu Boyarsky was just now telling us about his firm. It turns out a hundred and fifty outfits a month . . .

MENDEL: What's that you were saying, Nikifor?

NIKIFOR: (*Has been leaning against the door-jamb and staring up at the ceiling.*) I was sayin', boss, folks is laughin' at us.

MENDEL: And why are folks laughing at us?

NIKIFOR: Folks is sayin', you got a thousand bosses down to the stable, you got seven Fridays in a week . . . Yesterday we carted wheat to the harbor, I ran over to the office to get the money, they says "Hold on!" They says, "The young boss was here, Benchik, he gave orders for the money to be paid to the bank, on a receipt."

MENDEL: He gave orders?

NIKIFOR: He gave orders.

NEKHAMA: (*Has pulled off one boot. Mendel proffers his other leg. The old lady raises her hate-filled eyes to her husband and mutters through clenched teeth.*) You shouldn't live to see daylight, you torturer!

MENDEL: What's that you were saying, Nikifor?

NIKIFOR: I say Lyovka talked rude to me today.

BENYA: (*Drinks wine, his little finger upraised.*) May each of us get his wish.

LYOVKA: Your health.

NIKIFOR: Today we took Maid-of-Honor to be shod, Lyovka barges into the smithy, opens his mouth wide as a washtub, orders Pyatirubel the blacksmith to line her horseshoes with rubber. So I pipes up. What are we, police-chiefs? says I, or tsars, Nicholas the Seconds, that we should line them with rubber? The boss didn't order it . . . And Lyovka turned red as a beet and shouts "Who's in charge here?"

MENDEL: And who *is* in charge, Nikifor?

NIKIFOR: (*Sullenly.*) You're in charge.

MENDEL: Then if I'm in charge (*he walks over to Nikifor and grabs him by the chest*), then if I'm in charge, smash anyone who sets foot in my stable, smash him in the heart, in the muscles, in the eyes . . . (*He shakes Nikifor and thrusts him away. Hunched over, scraping his bare feet on the floor, Mendel walks the length of the room to the door, followed by Nikifor.*)

NEKHAMA: You shouldn't live to see daylight, torturer . . .

(*Silence.*)

ARYE-LEIB: If I were to tell you, Lazar, that the old man never completed his courses at young ladies' finishing school . . .

BOYARSKY: . . . I would believe you without your word of honor.

BENYA: (*Proffering his hand to Boyarsky.*) Come back some other time, Boyarsky.

BOYARSKY: For Heaven's sake, anything can happen in a family. Sometimes hot, sometimes cold. Salutations! Salutations! I'll drop by some other time. (*He disappears.*)

(*Benya stands up, lights a cigarette, drapes a foppish cape over his arm.*)

ARYE-LEIB: Concerning such a matchmaker as myself, it is decreed in Ibn-Ezra: "If you decide to sew shrouds for the dead . . ."

LYOVKA: An old man like that should be carved up and thrown to the hogs.

(*Dvoira sinks against the back of her chair and starts shrieking.*)

LYOVKA: Hurray! Dvoira's having hysterics.

(*Nikifor re-enters the room. Benya transfers the cape to his left arm and with his right hand hits Nikifor in the face.*)

BENYA: Harness the bay to the droshky for me!

NIKIFOR: (*Blood hesitantly trickling from his nose.*) Gimme my severance pay . . .

BENYA: (*Walks over to Nikifor with measured stride and says in a caressing, quavering voice.*) I'll see you die today without your supper, Nikifor, old pal . . .

SCENE 2

Night. The Kriks' bedroom. Moonlight, shimmering and pale blue, streams through the window. The old man and Nekhama are in a double bed, covered by a single blanket. The dishevelled, dirty-gray old lady is sitting up in bed. She mutters volubly, mutters endlessly.

NEKHAMA: Other people behave like real people . . . Other people bring home ten pounds of meat for supper, they make soup, they make cutlets, they make stewed fruit. The father comes home from work, everyone sits down at the table, other people eat and laugh . . . But in our house? . . . God, dear God, how dark it is in my home!

MENDEL: Let a man live, Nekhama! Go to sleep!

NEKHAMA: . . . Benchik, that Benchik is like the sun in the heavens, he's into that kind of life for good. One policeman today, another policeman tomorrow . . . Today people have a crust of bread, tomorrow their legs will be shackled in irons . . .

MENDEL: Let me breathe, Nekhama. Go to sleep!

NEKHAMA: . . .That Lyovka too . . . The child will come back from the army and he'll end up a hoodlum too. Where else can he turn? His father's a degenerate, his father wouldn't let his children into the business . . .

MENDEL: Let it be night-time, Nekhama. Go to sleep!

(*Silence.*)

NEKHAMA: The Rabbi said, Rabbi Ben Zkharya . . . Comes a brand-new month, said Ben Zkharya, I won't let Mendel into the synagogue. The Jews won't stand for it . . .

MENDEL: (*Pulling off the blanket, sits up next to the old lady.*) What won't the Jews stand for?

NEKHAMA: Comes a new moon, said Ben Zkharya . . .

MENDEL: What won't the Jews stand for, and what did your Jews ever give me?

NEKHAMA: They won't let you in, they won't let you into the synagogue.

MENDEL: A silver ruble with a chewed-off corner your Jews gave me, you they gave me, you swayback mare, and this coffin full of bedbugs.

NEKHAMA: And what did your Russian cut-throats ever give you, what did your cut-throats give you?

MENDEL: (*Lying down again.*) Oh, get off my head, you swayback mare!

NEKHAMA: Vodka those cut-throats gave you, a mouth full of dirty words, a rabid mouth like a dog's . . . He's sixty-two years old, God, dear God, and he's as hot as a furnace, he's as hail as a furnace.

MENDEL: Pull out my teeth, Nekhama, pour some of your kike soup in my veins, bow my back . . .

NEKHAMA: Hot as a furnace . . . I'm so ashamed, God! . . . (*She takes her pillow and lies down on the floor in the moonlight. Silence. Then her grumbling is heard again.*) On Friday evenings people come out of their gates, people fool around with their grandchildren . . .

MENDEL: Let it be night-time, Nekhama.

NEKHAMA: (*Weeps.*) People fool around with their grandchildren . . .

(*Enter Benya. He is in his underwear.*)

BENYA: Maybe you'd like to call it a day, you newlyweds?

(*Mendel partially rises. He looks his son straight in the face.*)

BENYA: Or do I have to go to a hotel for a good night's sleep?

MENDEL: (*Has got out of bed. Like his son, he is in his underwear.*) You . . . you came in here?

BENYA: Do I have to fork over two rubles for a room to get some sleep?

MENDEL: At night, at night you came in here?

BENYA: She's my mother. You hear me, you bag of guts!

(*Father and son stand in their underwear facing one another. Mendel comes closer to Benya, gradually slowing down. Nekhama's dishevelled head trembles in the moonlight.*)

MENDEL: At night, at night you came in here . . .

SCENE 3

A tavern in Import Square. Night. The landlord Ryabtsov, a dour, sickly man, is reading the Gospel at the counter. His dusty hair is plastered down on both sides of his forehead. On a platform sits the puny flautist Miron (commonly known as Major) Popyatnik. His flute emits a feeble, quavering tune. At one of the tables some grizzled Greeks with black mustaches are tossing dice with Senka Topun, a friend of Benya Krik's. In front of Senka lie a sectioned watermelon, a Finnish knife and a bottle of Malaga. Two sailors are sleeping, their sculpted shoulders resting on the table. In the far corner, the contractor Fomin meekly sips soda water. Drunken Potapovna is trying to talk him into something. At the foremost table sit Mendel Krik, drunken, bloodshot, colossal, and Urusov, a confidential business consultant.

MENDEL: (*Slamming his fist on the table.*) It's dark! You're trying to keep me in a grave, Ryabtsov, in a pitch-dark grave! . . .

(*Mitya, the waiter, an old man with a silvery crew-cut, brings a lamp over, and places it in front of Mendel.*)

MENDEL: I ordered all the lamps! I asked for a choir! I ordered every lamp in this tavern!

MITYA: But, y'see, our brother can't get kerosene for free. That's the way things are, y'see . . .

MENDEL: It's too dark!

MITYA: (*To Ryabtsov.*) The gent insists on additional lighting.

RYABTSOV: One ruble.

MITYA: One ruble paid.

RYABTSOV: One ruble received.

MENDEL: Urusov!

URUSOV: Present.

MENDEL: How much blood did you say flows through my heart?

URUSOV: According to science, two thousand quarts of blood flow through the human heart every twenty-four hours. And in America they've invented a kind of . . .

MENDEL: Hold on! Hold on! . . . Suppose I wanted to go to America—anything holding me back?

URUSOV: Nothing at all. You get on board and off you go . . .

(*Wagging her crooked hip, Potapovna waddles over to their table.*)

POTAPOVNA: Mendel baby, not America, but Bessarabia, that's where we should be going, to buy orchards.

MENDEL: You say, you get on board and off you go?

URUSOV: According to science, you'll cross four bodies of water—the Black Sea, the Ionian, the Aegean, the Mediterranean and two world-wide oceans—the Atlantic and the Pacific.

MENDEL: And didn't you say a man could fly across the seas?

URUSOV: He could indeed.

MENDEL: And over mountains, could a man fly over high mountains?

URUSOV: (*Firmly.*) Indeed he could.

MENDEL: (*Pressing his palms to his shaggy head.*) No end, no brink . . . (*To Ryabtsov.*) I'll do it! I'll go to Bessarabia.

RYABTSOV: And what'll you do in Bessarabia?

MENDEL: Whatever I want to do, that I'll do.

RYABTSOV: And what do you want?

MENDEL: Listen to me, Ryabtsov, I'm still alive . . .

RYABTSOV: You're not alive if God has killed you.

MENDEL: And when was it God killed me?

RYABTSOV: How old are you?

VOICES: He's sixty-two if he's a day.

RYABTSOV: For sixty-two years God has been killing you.

MENDEL: Ryabtsov, I'm smarter than God.

RYABTSOV: You may be smarter than the Russian God, but not smarter than the kike God.

(*Mitya brings in another lamp. Behind him, in single file, appear four fat sleepy wenches. Each one carries a lighted lamp. Bright light streams through the tavern.*)

MITYA: Have yourself a bright Easter. In other words, Christ has arisen! Girls, set the lamps down around this mad dog.

(*The wenches place the lamps on the table in front of Mendel. The light shines on his wine-flushed face.*)

VOICE: We turning night into day, Mendel?

MENDEL: No end.

POTAPOVNA: (*Yanks Urusov by the arm.*) Begging your kind indulgence, have a drink with me, mister . . . Look at me, peddling my chickens in the market-place, all the peasants palm off last summer's fowl on me, and am I condemned to these chickens for life? My daddy dear was a gardener, an A-one gardener. If an apple-tree is growing wild, I can prune it . . .

VOICE: We making Sunday out of Monday, Mendel?

POTAPOVNA: (*Her jacket has pulled open on her fat bosom. Vodka, heat and ecstasy stifle her.*) Mendel will sell his business, we'll take the money, God willing, we'll go with our darling starlet to the orchards, linden blossoms, you listening, mister? linden blossom'll float on top of us . . . Mendel, my goldpiece, I'm my daddy's darling daughter! . . .

MENDEL: (*Walks over to the counter.*) Ryabtsov, the eyes I used to have . . . listen to me, Ryabtsov, my eyes used to be stronger than a telescope, and what did I do with my eyes? My legs used to be faster than locomotives, my legs could walk on water, and what did I do with my legs? I went from the hashhouse to the shithouse, from the shithouse to the hash-house . . . I swept floors with my snout, so now I'll plant orchards.

RYABTSOV: Go ahead. Who's stopping you?

VOICE: Watch out—someone won't allow it. Someone'll tread on your tail —it won't pull loose . . .

MENDEL: I ordered songs!! Give us a marching tune, musician . . . Don't tug at my heart-strings . . . Give me life! More! More!

MITYA: (*Whispering to Urusov.*) Should I send for Fomin or is it too soon?

URUSOV: Too soon. (*To the musician.*) Keep it up, Major!

VOICE: Don't have to keep it up, here comes the choir. Pyatirubel's bringing the choir.

(*The choir enters—blind men in red shirts. They stumble over chairs, wave rattan canes in front of them. They are lead by the blacksmith Pyatirubel, an excitable man and a friend of Mendel's.*)

PYATIRUBEL: I roused these devils out of their sleep. We won't play any more songs, says they. It's night, says they, over the whole blessed world, we're worn out with playing . . . Listen you, says I, you know the kind of man you're turning down, says I?

MENDEL: (*Flinging himself at the lead singer, a tall, pockmarked blind man.*) Fedya, I'm going to Bessarabia.

BLIND MAN: (*In a rich basso profundo.*) Good luck to you, boss!

MENDEL: A song, Fedya, play a song.

BLIND MAN: Shall we sing "Glorious Sea"?

MENDEL: Any song . . .

BLINDMEN: (*Tuning up their guitars. Their syrupy bassos start in:*)

> Glorious sea—blessed Lake Baikal,
> Glorious ship—a battered herring keg,
> Ho, stormy blasts, sweep the whitecaps all:
> For the youth swims his last brief leg.

MENDEL: (*Smashes a window with an empty bottle.*) Crash!

PYATIRUBEL: Och, a regular superman, the sonuvabitch!

MITYA: (*To Ryabtsov.*) How much do we charge for the glass?

RYABTSOV: One ruble.

MITYA: One ruble paid.

BLINDMEN: (*Sing.*)

> Long have I languished in fetters so strong,
> Long have I roamed the Akatui mountains,
> Faithful companions helped my escape along,
> I'm alive, freedom flows in my veins . . .

MENDEL: Crash!

PYATIRUBEL: He's a Satan, not an old man!

VOICES:

> —He's whooping it up in style! . . .
> —Style nothing . . . He's whooping it up as usual.
> —He don't usually do it like this. Anybody die up at his place?
> —Nobody died . . . He's whooping it up as normal.
> —But what's the occasion, what's he whooping it up *for?*

RYABTSOV: Go look for an occasion. One fellow has money—he whoops it up over his money. Another fellow has no money—he whoops it up over his poverty. A man can whoop it up for any reason . . .

(*The song keeps growing in volume. In the broken window, a star flickers. The sleepy wenches are standing in the doorway; they prop up their breasts on their toil-worn arms and sing along. A sailor sways on his huge, wide-spread legs and sings in a clear tenor.*)

> Shilka and Nerchinsk hold no terrors for me,
> The mountain patrols couldn't catch me.
> I ran into no hungry beasts in the brush,
> Sharpshooters' bullets flew right past me . . .

POTAPOVNA: (*Drunk and happy.*) Mendel, baby, have a drink with me! Let's drink to our little starlet!

PYATIRUBEL: He punched the guard at the post-office in the kisser. That's the kind of man for you! Stole telegraph poles and toted them home on his shoulders . . .

> I walked all the night and all the day bright,
> I kept a sharp lookout near cities,
> Peasant girls fed me with bread in my plight,
> And the lads kept me stocked with t'baccy . . .

MENDEL: Bow my back, Nekhama, pour kike soup in my veins! . . . (*He throws himself on the floor, rolls around, groans, laughs uproariously.*)

VOICES:

—A regular elephant!

—I once saw an elephant cry . . .

—That's a lie, elephants don't cry . . .

—I'm telling you it cried real tears . . .

—In the zoo once I teased an elephant . . .

MITYA: (*To Urusov.*) Should Fomin come over or is it too soon?

URUSOV: Too soon.

(*The singers sing their hearts out.*)

> Glorious sea—holy Lake Baikal,
> Glorious sail—a raggedy caftan,
> Ho, stormy blasts, sweep the whitecaps all.
> I hear the thunder rolling on . . .

(*The blind men sing the last verse with joyful, throbbing voices. The song over, they get up and leave, as if on command.*)

MITYA: That all?

LEAD SINGER: That'll do.

MENDEL: (*Leaps up from the floor and stamps his feet.*) Give me a marching song! Musician, give me life!

MITYA: (*To Urusov.*) Should Fomin come over or is it too soon?

URUSOV: Just the proper time.

(*Mitya winks at Fomin, who is sitting in the far corner. Fomin ambles over to Mendel's table at a trot.*)

FOMIN: Here's to a pleasant meeting!

URUSOV: (*To Mendel.*) Now, old chum, here's what we'll do—fun's over, now it's time for business. (*He draws out a sheet of paper covered with writing.*) Should I read it?

FOMIN: As the saying goes, if you don't care to dance, give reading a chance.

URUSOV: Shall I read the amount?

FOMIN: Most agreeable to your proposition.

MENDEL: (*Stares Fomin in the face and draws back.*) I ordered songs . . .

FOMIN: We'll sing too and we'll make merry and when it comes time to die, we'll die.

URUSOV: (*Reads, rolling his r's.*) ". . . In accord with which article, I concede full ownership of my commercial trucking firm, to Vasily Yeliseyevich

Fomin, said firm consisting, as hereinafter enumerated, of . . .''

PYATIRUBEL: Fomin, you clown, you realize what kind of horses you're getting? These horses have hauled a million loads of wheat, they've lugged half a world of coal. You take everything in Odessa from us, when you make off with these horses . . .

URUSOV: ''. . .for the sum total of twelve thousand rubles, one third due at the signing and the remainder . . .''

MENDEL: (*Points a finger at the Turk imperturbably smoking his hookah in the corner.*) That man's sitting there passing judgment on me.

PYATIRUBEL: True enough, he's passing judgment . . . Okay, let's get down to business! (*To Fomin.*) Good God, he'll kill somebody any minute now.

FOMIN: And maybe he won't.

RYABTSOV: Don't be a fool, you fool. That guest is a Turk, a holy man.

POTAPOVNA: (*Drinking her wine in small sips and laughing blissfully.*) Daddy's darling daughter!

FOMIN: Right there, my dear fellow, sign your name there.

POTAPOVNA: (*Slaps Fomin on the chest.*) That's where it lives, that's where Vaska's money lives!

MENDEL: Did you say, sign my name? (*He shuffles across the tavern to the Turk and sits down beside him.*) All the girls I've had in my lifetime, my dear man, and all the pleasure I've known. I built a house and I raised sons,—the price for this, my dear man, is twelve thousand rubles. And then they put the lid on you—drop dead!

(*The Turk bows, places his hand on his heart and his forehead. Mendel kisses him gently on the lips.*)

FOMIN: (*To Potapovna.*) Meaning he's making a monkey out of me?

POTAPOVNA: He'll sell, Vasily Yeliseyevich, I bet my life he'll sell.

MENDEL: (*Comes back, shaking his head.*) What a bore!

MITYA: So now he's bored—you better pay up.

MENDEL: Beat it!

MITYA: No kidding, you're gonna pay up!

MENDEL: I'll kill you!

MITYA: You'll have to pay for that too.

MENDEL: Beat it, I'm going to sleep . . .

MITYA: You won't pay up? Och, gents, I'll commit a murder!

PYATIRUBEL: Not so fast with your murdering. How much do you rook him per half-bottle?

MITYA: (*Losing his temper.*) I'm a naughty boy, I'll bite!

(*Mendel, without raising his head, jerks some money out of his pocket. The coins roll across the floor. Mitya crawls after, collecting them. A sleepy wench blows out the lamps. Darkness. Mendel sleeps, his head resting on the table.*)

FOMIN: (*To Potapovna.*) Poking your nose into it too soon . . . Yammering with your tongue like a dog on the run . . . You spoiled the whole deal!

POTAPOVNA: (*Squeezing tears from her filthy, crumpled wrinkles.*) Vasily Yeliseyevich, I'm sorry for my daughter's sake.

FOMIN: I'll give you something to be sorry about.

POTAPOVNA: The Yids have settled on us like lice.

FOMIN: A Yid's no stumbling-block to someone with brains.

POTAPOVNA: He'll sell, Vasily Yeliseyevich, he'll shoot off his mouth for a bit and then he'll sell.

FOMIN: (*Menacingly, slowly.*) And if he doesn't sell, then by the Lord God Jesus Christ our Savior Almighty, I swear to you, you old bag, we'll get you home and I'll strip the hide off your carcass!

SCENE 4

Potapovna's garret. The old woman, clad in a gaudy new dress, is leaning out the window, gossiping with a neighbor-lady. Through the window we can see the harbor and the glistening sea. On the table lie heaps of purchases—bolts of cloth, high-heeled shoes, a silken parasol.

NEIGHBOR'S VOICE: Why don't you drop over and chew the fat, show off your things over here?

POTAPOVNA: Fine, I'll stop by your place, see how you're doin' . . .

NEIGHBOR'S VOICE: For twenty years we peddled poultry side by side in the marketplace, then bang—she ain't there, no Potapovna.

POTAPOVNA: Yeah, seems as how I ain't sentenced to chickens no more. They sure won't be giving me grief for the rest of my life . . .

NEIGHBOR'S VOICE: Sure, not for the rest of your life.

POTAPOVNA: I reckon folks' eyes is popping at Potapovna?

NEIGHBOR'S VOICE: They're popping like nobody's business! Happiness don't come to everybody. You can't just take it out of the oven . . .

POTAPOVNA: (*Laughing, her fat body jiggling up and down.*) Y'see, not everybody's got a little girl.

NEIGHBOR'S VOICE: Some folks say the girl's scrawny.

POTAPOVNA: The meat's the sweetest next the bone, honey.

NEIGHBOR'S VOICE: I hear tell the sons are gettin' wise to you . . .

POTAPOVNA: One girl will outweigh the sons.

NEIGHBOR'S VOICE: Just what I say—she'll outweigh 'em.

POTAPOVNA: It ain't likely an old man'll throw over a young girl. What else do folks say?

NEIGHBOR'S VOICE: They don't say nothing much, just yackety-yak. Who can figger it out?

POTAPOVNA: We can. I can . . . What's the gossip about the linen?

NEIGHBOR'S VOICE: The gossip runs the old man set you up with twenty yards' worth.

POTAPOVNA: Fifty!

NEIGHBOR'S VOICE: A pair of shoes . . .

POTAPOVNA: Three pair!

NEIGHBOR'S VOICE: Old men fall in love mortal hard.

POTAPOVNA: Looks as how we ain't sentenced to the chickens . . .

NEIGHBOR'S VOICE: Looks like you ain't sentenced . . . Drop by and show off a bit, shoot the breeze with us.

POTAPOVNA: I'll be over. I'll see how you're doin' . . . Bye-bye, honey!

NEIGHBOR'S VOICE: Bye-bye, dearie.

(*Potapovna clambers down from the window. Waddling, humming, she rambles round the room, opens the cupboard. She climbs on to a chair in order to reach a bottle of applejack on the top shelf, drinks, munches an eclair. Mendel, dressed in his Sabbath-go-to-meetin' clothes, and Marusya enter the room.*)

MARUSYA: (*In clarion tones.*) Look where our birdie has flown to! Run over to Moiseika's, Mamma.

POTAPOVNA: (*Climbing off the chair.*) And what should I buy?

MARUSYA: Buy some melons, a bottle of wine, half-a-dozen smoked mackerel . . . (*To Mendel.*) Give her a ruble.

POTAPOVNA: A ruble won't cover it.

MARUSYA: Don't start in with your swindling! It'll cover it, there'll even be change left over.

POTAPOVNA: I don't think a ruble'll cover it.

MARUSYA: It will! Come back in an hour. (*She shoves her mother out, slams the door shut, and locks it with a key.*)

POTAPOVNA'S VOICE: I'll be sitting outside the gate. If you need me—give a yell.

MARUSYA: All right. (*She tosses her hat on to the table, lets her hair down, plaits her golden braid. In a voice vibrant with strength, health and merriment, she goes on with her interrupted anecdote.*) . . . We got to the cemetery, we look around—it's past noon. All the funerals have left, nobody in sight, just couples kissing in the bushes. Godfather's grave is so cute—it's fantastic! . . . I laid out the food, the madeira you gave me, both bottles, ran to fetch Father John. Father John is awful old, with tiny blue eyes, you must know him . . . (*Mendel gazes at Marusya adoringly. He rumbles and mutters something in reply, but his muttering is incomprehensible.*) The holy father recited the prayers for the dead, I poured him a shot of Madeira, wiped out the glass with a napkin, he drank it, I gave him another shot . . . (*Marusya has plaited her braid, smoothes down the end of it. She sits down on her bed, unlaces her hightopped yellow shoes, fashionable for the period.*) And there was Ksenka, all gussied up, as if it wasn't *her* father in the grave, all rouged and painted and powdered, her eyes devouring her fiancé, like a mouse does a grain of corn. But her Sergei Ivanych, he just keeping buttering sandwiches for me . . . I want to spite Ksenka, so I says . . . Sergei Ivanych, I says, why don't you pay some attention to your fiancée Ksenya Matveyevna? . . . I said it and it went right through her. We polished off every last drop of your Madeira . . . (*Marusya removes her shoes and stockings, walks barefoot to the window and pulls the curtains shut.*) Godmother was crying the whole time, and then she turned pink, as cute as a society girl—it was fantastic! I had a drink too—and I says to Sergei Ivanych: (*Marusya turns back the bedclothes.*) Come on, Sergei Ivanych, how about a dip in the Langeron! He says: Okay! (*Marusya chuckles, pulls off her dress, which is tight and difficult to remove.*) And I'll bet Ksenka's back is covered with pimples and she hasn't washed her feet in three years . . . So she starts bawling me out. (*Marusya is half-hidden from head down by the tightly-drawn dress.*) You, she says, you're setting your sights high, you schemer, you this, you that, aiming for the old man's money, well, some folks'll drag you away from that money. But I says to her: You know what, Ksenka,—here's what I says—don't you get my goat, Ksenka . . . Sergei Ivanych is listening in on us, he's collapsing with laughter! . . . (*Marusya's bare, beautiful, maidenly arm pulls Mendel to her. She removes his coat and tosses it on the floor.*) Now then, come here. Say—Marusichka . . .

MENDEL: Marusichka!
MARUSYA: Say—Marusichka is my sunshine . . .

(*The old man wheezes, trembles, half crying, half laughing.*)

MARUSYA: (*Affectionately.*) Ach, you chump!

SCENE 5

The teamsters' synagogue in Moldavanka. Friday evening services. Lighted candles. At the altar Cantor Zwieback stands in a prayer-shawl and boots. The congregation—deafeningly conversing with God—strolls round the synagogue, sways back and forth, spits. Suddenly stung by the bee of beatitude, they utter thunderous exclamations, frantically sing along with the cantor in experienced voices, subside, mutter under their breath for a long while and then bellow again, like goaded oxen. In the bowels of the synagogue, two ancient Jews, two rawboned, hunchbacked giants with yellow beards slung over their shoulders, are bowed over a volume of the Talmud. Arye-Leib, the shammes, struts grandly between the aisles. On the last bench sits a fat man with downy puffed-out cheeks, squeezing a ten-year-old boy between his knees. The father is poking the boy's nose into his prayer-book. On a side bench is Benya Krik. Behind him sits Senka Topun. They give no indication that they know one another.

CANTOR: Arboim shono okut bdoyr vo-oymar . . . (*In a muffled voice.*) Arye-Leib, rats!

ARYE-LEIB: Shiru ladonai shir khodosh. Oi, sing the Lord a different tune . . . (*Steps over to a praying Jew.*) How does hay stand?

JEW: (*Swaying back and forth.*) Gone up.

ARYE-LEIB: A lot?

JEW: Fifty-two kopeks.

ARYE-LEIB: We'll hold on a bit, it'll go up to sixty.

CANTOR: Lifney adonai ki vo mishpoyt ho-orets . . . Arye-Leib, rats!

ARYE-LEIB: Stop yelling, you roughneck.

CANTOR: (*In a muffled voice.*) If I spot just one more rat—I'll make trouble.

ARYE-LEIB: (*Imperturbably.*) Lifney adonai ki vo, ki vo . . . Oi, I stand, oi, I stand before the Lord . . . How about oats? . . .

SECOND JEW: (*Without interrupting his prayers.*) A ruble-four, a ruble-four . . .

ARYE-LEIB: You could lose your mind!

SECOND JEW: (*Frantically swaying back and forth.*) It'll be a ruble-ten, it'll be a ruble-ten . . .

ARYE-LEIB: You could lose your mind! Lifney adonai—ki vo, ki vo . . .

(*Everyone prays. In the ensuing silence can be heard the staccato but muffled remarks exchanged by Benya Krik and Senka Topun.*)

BENYA: (*Bent over his prayer-book.*) Well?

SENKA: (*Behind Benya's back.*) There's this store.

BENYA: No deal.

SENKA: A wholesale store.

BENYA: What's the heist?

SENKA: Cloth.

BENYA: A lot of cloth?

SENKA: A lot.

BENYA: How about the cop on the corner?

SENKA: There won't be any cop on the corner.

BENYA: The night watchman?

SENKA: The night watchman gets his cut.

BENYA: The neighbors?

SENKA: The neighbors agree to sleep.

BENYA: What do you want out of this set-up?

SENKA: Half.

BENYA: No deal.

SENKA: You counting on your Pop's estate?
BENYA: I'm counting on my Pop's estate.
SENKA: What *will* you give?
BENYA: No deal.

(*A gunshot rings out. Cantor Zwieback has shot a rat that was scampering past the altar. The praying men stare at the Cantor. The little boy, squeezed between his father's tiresome knees, struggles trying to break away. Arye-Leib stands aghast, his mouth agape. The Talmudic scholars lift their vast, apathetic faces.*)

FAT MAN WITH DOWNY CHEEKS: Zwieback, this is a bum trick!
CANTOR: I contracted to pray in a synagogue, not in a rat-infested outhouse.
  (*He opens the muzzle of the revolver and rejects the cartridge.*)
ARYE-LEIB: Ai, you bum, ai, you boor!
CANTOR: (*Aims his revolver at the dead rat.*) Take a look at this rat, Jews, summon
  the people. Let the people say whether or not it's a regular cow . . .
ARYE-LEIB: You bum, you bum, you bum!
CANTOR: (*Coolly*) So much for these rats. (*He swathes himself in his prayer-shawl
  and puts a tuning-fork to his ear.*)

(*At long last the little boy breaks out of the imprisonment of the paternal knees, rushes over
to the cartridge, picks it up and runs out.*)

FIRST JEW: You chase around all day after a kopek, then you come to the synagogue for a little relaxation—and this is what you get!
ARYE-LEIB: (*Screeches.*) Jews, this is a swindle! Jews, you don't know what's going on here! The milkmen are giving this bum ten rubles extra . . . Go to
  the milkmen, you bum, kiss the milkmen where you're supposed to kiss
  them!
SENKA: (*Thumps his fist on his prayer-book.*) Will you shut up! Go find yourselves
  a soapbox!
CANTOR: (*Solemnly.*) Mizmoyr l'Dovid!

(*Everyone prays.*)

BENYA: Well?
SENKA: There're these guys.
BENYA: What kind of guys?
SENKA: Georgians.
BENYA: They got guns?
SENKA: They got guns.
BENYA: Where'd they hail from?
SENKA: They live next door to your buyer.

BENYA: What buyer?

SENKA: The one who's buying your business.

BENYA: What business?

SENKA: Your business—the wagons, the house, the whole trucking firm.

BENYA: (*Turns around.*) You gone nuts?

SENKA: He said so himself.

BENYA: Who said so?

SENKA: Mendel said so, your father . . . He's going to Bessarabia with Marusya to buy orchards.

(*The droning of prayers.*)

BENYA: You're nuts.

SENKA: Everybody knows about it.

BENYA: Swear!

SENKA: May I never meet with good luck!

BENYA: Swear by your mother!

SENKA: May I find my mother dead!

BENYA: Swear again, you piece of shit!

SENKA: (*Scornfully.*) You jerk!

CANTOR: Borukh ato adonai . . .

SCENE 6

The Kriks' yard. Sundown. Seven o'clock in the evening. By the stable, seated on a cart with uplifted shafts, Benya is cleaning a revolver. Lyovka leans against the stable door. Arye-Leib is expounding the covert meaning of "The Song of Songs" to the same boy who ran out of the synagogue on Friday night. Nikifor aimlessly scurries about the yard. He is evidently worried about something.

BENYA: The time's coming. Make way for time!

LYOVKA: Carved up and thrown to the hogs!

BENYA: The time's coming. Step aside, Lyovka! Make way for time!

ARYE-LEIB: "The Song of Songs" teaches us—"By night on my bed I sought him whom my soul loveth . . ." And what does Rashi tell us about this?

NIKIFOR: (*Pointing out the brothers to Arye-Leib.*) Look at 'em standing beside the stable like a couple of oak-trees.

ARYE-LEIB: This is what Rashi tells us: "By night" means by day and by night. "On my bed I sought" . . . Who sought? asks Rashi. Israel sought, the people of Israel. "He whom my soul loveth . . ." And whom does Israel love? asks Rashi. Israel loves the Torah. The Torah is beloved of

Israel.

NIKIFOR: I ask you, why should they hang around the stable with nothing to do?

BENYA: Keep up the noise.

NIKIFOR: (*Scurries around the yard.*) I know why . . . My horse-collar's missing. Whoever I want to, him I'll suspect.

ARYE-LEIB: An old man is teaching a child the Law, while you keep butting in, Nikifor . . .

NIKIFOR: Why are they rooted to the stable like a couple of scruffy oaktrees?

BENYA: (*Takes his revolver apart and cleans it.*) I notice, Nikifor, that you seem awfully upset.

NIKIFOR: (*Shouts, but there's no force to his voice.*) I never took an oath on your horse-collar! If you want to know, I got a brother livin' in the country, still in his prime. If you want to know, my brother'll welcome me with open arms . . .

BENYA: Yell, yell before you die.

NIKIFOR: (*To Arye-Leib*) Old man, tell me, why are they doin' this?

ARYE-LEIB: (*Lifts his faded eyes to the driver.*) One man is teaching the Law, while another man is bellowing like a milch-cow. Is that how things should be in this world?

NIKIFOR: You've got eyes, old man, but what do you see? (*Exits.*)

BENYA: Our Nikifor seems upset.

ARYE-LEIB: "By night on my bed I sought." Sought whom? Rashi instructs me.

BOY: Rashi instructs me—sought the Torah.

(*Loud voices can be heard.*)

BENYA: The time's coming. Step aside, Lyovka, make way for time!

(*Enter Mendel, Bobrinets, Nikifor, Pyatirubel a bit tipsy.*)

BOBRINETS: (*In a deafening voice.*) If you don't haul my wheat to the harbor, Mendel, who is there to haul it? If I don't go to you, Mendel, who is there for me to go to?

MENDEL: There are people in this world besides Mendel. There are trucking firms in this world besides my trucking firm.

BOBRINETS: There's no trucking firm in Odessa outside of yours . . . Unless you send me to Butsis with his three-legged nags, or to Zhuravlenko with his broken-down washtubs?

MENDEL: (*Not looking at his sons.*) Somebody's hanging around my stable.

NIKIFOR: They're rooted there like a couple of scruffy oak trees.

BORBINETS: Tomorrow you'll harness up ten teams for me, Mendel, you'll

haul the wheat, you'll get the money, you'll drink a glass, you'll sing a song
. . . Ai, Mendel!

PYATIRUBEL: Ai, Mendel!

MENDEL: Why is somebody hanging around my stable?

NIKIFOR: Boss, for Christ's sake! . . .

MENDEL: Well?

NIKIFOR: Clear out of the yard, boss, git away from your sons . . .

MENDEL: What's that about my sons?

NIKIFOR: Your sons is plannin' to whup you.

BENYA: (*Leaps off the cart on to the ground. Bowing his head, he speaks, carefully enunciating each word.*) We happened to hear from strangers, me and my brother Lyovka, that you're selling the business, Poppa, in which there's a pennyworth of our sweat too . . .

(*Neighbors, working in the yard, move closer to the Kriks.*)

MENDEL: (*Looks at the ground.*) You people, neighbors . . .

BENYA: Did we hear right, me and my brother Lyovka?

MENDEL: You people, neighbors, take a look at my own flesh and blood (*he raises his head*) at my own flesh and blood, raising a hand against me . . .

BENYA: Did we hear right, me and my brother Lyovka?

MENDEL: Oi, you won't get me! . . . (*He jumps on Lyovka, knocks him off his feet, punches him in the face.*)

LYOVKA: Oi, we will too! . . .

(*The sunset fills the sky with blood. The old man and Lyovka roll behind a shed.*)

NIKIFOR: (*Leaning against a wall.*) Och, it's a sin . . .

BOBRINETS: Lyovka, your father?

BENYA: (*In a desperate voice.*) Nikishka, I swear to you by my happiness, our horses, our home, our life—he dumped them all at the feet of that whore!

NIKIFOR: Och, it's a sin . . .

PYATIRUBEL: I'll kill any man that tries to part 'em! Watch out, don't get between them!

(*Wheezing and groaning can be heard from behind the shed.*)

PYATIRUBEL: The man's not born yet who can beat Mendel.

ARYE-LEIB: Get out of the yard, Ivan.

PYATIRUBEL: I'll bet a hundred rubles . . .

ARYE-LEIB: Get out of the yard, Ivan.

(*The old man and Lyovka tumble out from behind the shed. They scramble to their feet, but Mendel knocks his son down again.*)

BOBRINETS: Lyovka, your father?
MENDEL: You won't get me! (*He tramples on his son.*)
PYATIRUBEL: I'll bet anybody a hundred rubles . . .
MENDEL: You won't get me!
BENYA: Oi, we will too! (*He drops the revolver butt heavily on to his father's head.*)

(*Silence. The blazing forests of the sunset sink lower and lower.*)

NIKIFOR: Now they done him in.
PYATIRUBEL: (*Bending over the inert Mendel.*) Mike? . . .
LYOVKA: (*Hoisting himself up a bit, clutching the ground with his fists. He's crying and stamping his foot.*) He hit me below the belt, the bastard!
PYATIRUBEL: Mike! . . .
BENYA: (*Turning round to the pack of bystanders.*) You lose anything here?
PYATIRUBEL: And I say—it's not nightfall yet. It's still a thousand miles from night.
ARYE-LEIB: (*On his knees before the downfallen old man.*) Ai, you Russian you, why are you shouting that it's not yet night, when you can see that this man is already gone from among us.
LYOVKA: (*Crooked rivulets of tears and blood course down his face.*) He hit me below the belt, the bastard!
PYATIRUBEL: (*Staggers away a few steps.*) Two against one . . .
ARYE-LEIB: Get out of the yard, Ivan . . .
PYATIRUBEL: Two against one . . . Shame, shame on all Moldava! (*He stumbles out.*)

(*Arye-Leib wipes Mendel's battered head with a damp handkerchief. At the back of the yard Nekhama moves about in tentative circles. She falls to her knees beside Arye-Leib.*)

NEKHAMA: Say something, Mendel.
BOBRINETS: (*In a choked voice.*) Stop kidding around, you old faker!
NEKHAMA: Yell something, Mendel!
BOBRINETS: Get up, you old teamster, gargle a drink, knock back a glassful . . .

(*On the ground, his bare feet spread apart, sits Lyovka. He casually dribbles long ribbons of blood from his mouth.*)

BENYA: (*Drives the onlookers into a cul-de-sac, shoves to the wall a lad of twenty who is crazed with panic and grabs him by the chest.*) Okay, stand back!

(*Silence. Evening. Blue-blackness, but beyond the blackness the sky is still crimson, scorching, pockmarked with flaming pits.*)

SCENE 7

The Krik coachhouse—horse-collars dumped in a heap, an unharnessed droshky, harnesses. Part of the yard is visible. Benya is writing at a small table in the doorway. The bald, clumsy peasant Semyon is arguing with him, while Madam Popyatnik darts to and fro. In the yard on the cart with the upturned shafts sits the Major, his legs dangling. Against the wall a new signboard is leaning. On it in gold letters: "Commercial Trucking Firm Mendek Krik and Sons." The sign is ornamented with garlands of horseshoes and intertwined buggy-whips.

SEMYON: I dunno 'bout that . . . Jest gimme my money . . .

BENYA: (*Continues to write.*) You're talking rudely, Semyon.

SEMYON: Gimme my money . . . I'll tear yer throat out!

BENYA: I'd enjoy spitting on you, my good fellow!

SEMYON: Where'd you stow the old man?

BENYA: The old man is sick.

SEMYON: Rightcher's the place on the wall where he writ it down, how much he owed for oats, how much for hay—all neat as a pin. And he paid up. Twenty years I drove for him and never saw no dirty work.

BENYA: (*Stands up.*) You drove for him, but you won't be driving for me. He wrote on the wall, but I won't write. He paid you, but maybe I won't pay you, because . . .

MADAM POPYATNIK: (*Surveying the peasant with the greatest disdain.*) When a man's a fool, it makes you want to puke.

BENYA: . . . because for all I care, you can die without your supper, my good man.

SEMYON: (*Frightened, but still swaggering.*) Jest gimme my money!

MADAM POPYATNIK: I'm no philosopheress, M'sieu Krik, but I can plainly see there are some people on this earth who shouldn't be living here at all.

BENYA: Nikifor!

(*Nikifor enters; he looks around sullenly, speaks unwillingly.*)

NIKIFOR: Nikifor's here.

BENYA: You'll settle up with Semyon and drive over to Groshev's.

NIKIFOR: The day laborers is here, they're askin' who'll be givin' them their orders from now on.

BENYA: I'll be giving them their orders.

NIKIFOR: Cook's raisin' Cain out there. She hocked her samovar with the boss. She wants to know who she pays for the samovar?

BENYA: She pays me . . . Now settle Semyon's account. Drive over to Groshev's and pick up nine tons of hay . . .

SEMYON: (*Flabbergasted.*) Nine tons? Twenty years I drove . . .

MADAM POPYATNIK: With his own money a man can buy hay and oats, and a lot nicer things than hay.

BENYA: Oats—two and a half tons.

SEMYON: I refuse to carry it.

BENYA: Lose my address, Semyon.

(*Semyon twists his hat in his hands, wrenches his neck, walks out, turns back again, once more walks out.*)

MADAM POPYATNIK: One stinking peasant and he gave you such a hard time . . . My goodness, if people started remembering who owed them money! This very day I was saying to my Major: hubby, hubby sweety-pie, Mendel Krik deserves that lousy two rubles he owes you . . .

MAJOR: (*In a rumbling, melodious voice.*) A ruble ninety-five.

BENYA: What two rubles?

MADAM POPYATNIK: Nothing worth mentioning, for Heaven's sake, nothing worth mentioning! . . . Last Thursday M'sieu Krik was in a wonderful mood; he ordered a march . . . How many times the march, Major?

MAJOR: The march—nine times.

MADAM POPYATNIK: And then dances . . .

MAJOR: Twenty-one dances.

MADAM POPYATNIK: It came to a ruble ninety-five. My goodness, paying off the musician—that was M'sieu Krik's primary intention . . .

(*Nikifor enters, dragging his boots. He looks askance.*)

NIKIFOR: Potapovna's here.

BENYA: What's it to me if somebody's here?

NIKIFOR: She's makin' threats.

BENYA: What's it to me . . .

(*Limping, Potapovna bursts into the room. The old woman is drunk. She turns on Benya her bleary, unblinking eyes.*)

POTAPOVNA: Powers that be . . .

BENYA: What's your problem, Madam Kholodenko?

POTAPOVNA: Powers that be . . .

NIKIFOR: She came to act foolish!

POTAPOVNA: Z-z-z, the Yid's little balls are buzzing . . . The little balls are hopping in my head, z-z-z . . .

BENYA: What's your problem, Madam Kholodenko?

POTAPOVNA: (*Bangs her fist on the ground.*) That's right, that's right! Let the man with brains lay down the law, while the pig wallows in booze . . .

MADAM POPYATNIK: A lady of discrimination!

POTAPOVNA: (*Scatters pennies over the floor.*) Here's the forty kopeks I just earned . . . I got up before daybreak, waited for the peasants on the Balt road . . . (*Turns her head skywards.*) What time would it be now? Would it be three?

BENYA: What's your problem, Madam Kholodenko?

POTAPOVNA: Z-z-z-z, he spun them balls . . .

BENYA: Nikifor!

NIKIFOR: Yeah?

POTAPOVNA: (*Wags her fat, wobbly, drunken finger at Nikifor.*) That little gal of ours is pregnant, Nikisha!

MADAM POPYATNIK: (*Drops into a chair and kindles with enthusiasm.*) A plot, ai, what a plot!

BENYA: What did you lose here, Madam Popyatnik, and what do you expect to find?

MADAM POPYATNIK: (*Drops a curtsey, her eyes dart to and fro, flashing sparks.*) I'm going . . . I'm going . . . God grant we meet again in happiness, in enjoyment, in a gracious hour, in a lucky minute! . . . (*She tugs at her husband's arm, backs out, turns around, her eyes have become crossed and gleam askance with a black flame.*)

(*The Major shuffles out after his wife and twiddles his fingers. At last they disappear.*)

POTAPOVNA: (*Smears the tears over her rumpled, flabby face.*) Last night I snuck over to her, felt her breasts, and they're already so swole up, wouldn't fit in my hand.

BENYA: (*His luster dimmed. He speaks quickly, glancing behind him.*) What month?

POTAPOVNA: (*Not batting an eyelash, looks up at Benya from the ground.*) The fourth.

BENYA: You're lying!

POTAPOVNA: Well, the third.

BENYA: What do you want from me?

POTAPOVNA: Z-z-z, he spun them little balls . . .

BENYA: What do you want?

POTAPOVNA: (*Ties her kerchief.*) Abortion costs a hundred rubles.

BENYA: Twenty-five!

POTAPOVNA: I'll call in the stevedores.

BENYA: You'll call the stevedores? . . . Nikifor!

NIKIFOR: Nikifor's here.

BENYA: Go upstairs to Poppa and ask him whether he authorizes me to give twenty-five . . .
POTAPOVNA: A hundred!
BENYA: Twenty-five rubles for an abortion or not?
NIKIFOR: I won't go.
BENYA: You won't go? (*He rushes over to the chintz curtains that divide the coachhouse in two.*)
NIKIFOR: (*Grabs Benya by the arm.*) Listen, kid, I ain't scared of God . . . I seen God and warn't frightened . . . I'll kill and not be frightened . . .

(*The curtain rustles and parts. Mendel enters. His boots are slung over his shoulder. His face is blue and puffy, like the face of a corpse.*)

MENDEL: Open the gate.
POTAPOVNA: (*Crawls on the floor.*) Ai, it's spooky!
NIKIFOR: Boss!

(*Arye-Leib and Lyovka approach the coachhouse.*)

MENDEL: Open the gate.
POTAPOVNA: (*Crawls on the floor.*) Ai, it's spooky!
BENYA: Go upstairs to your room and your wife, Poppa.
MENDEL: You'll open the gate for me, Nikifor, dear heart . . .
NIKIFOR: (*Falls to his knees.*) I'm beggin' you from the bottom of my heart, boss, don't disgrace yourself in front of me, a simple man!
MENDEL: Why don't you open the gate, Nikifor? Why won't you let me out of the yard where I spent my life? (*The old man's voice grows stronger; in the depths of his eyes a light flares up.*) This yard beheld me, it beheld me, the father of my children, the husband of my wife, the master of my horses. It beheld my strength, and my twenty stallions, and twelve wagons cinched with iron. It beheld my legs, hefty as house-timbers, and my hands, my wicked hands . . . So open the gate for me now, my dear sons, let today be as I want it. Let me leave this yard, which has beheld too much . . .
BENYA: Go upstairs to your room, to your wife, Poppa!

(*He draws near his father.*)

MENDEL: Don't hit me, Benchik.
LYOVKA: Don't hit him.
BENYA: You nasty people! . . . (*Pause.*) How could you . . . (*Pause.*) How could you say what you just said?
ARYE-LEIB: Why don't you see, you people, that you ought to get out of here?
BENYA: Animals, o you animals! . . . (*He exits rapidly. Lyovka follows him.*)

ARYE-LEIB: (*Leads Mendel to the stove-couch.*) We'll rest, Mendel, we'll sleep . . .

POTAPOVNA: (*Gets up off the ground and weeps.*) They've slain the falcon! . . .

ARYE-LEIB: (*Tucks Mendel into the stove-couch behind the curtain.*) We'll sleep, Mendel . . .

POTAPOVNA: (*Falls to the ground beside the couch, kisses the old man's lifelessly dangling hand.*) My sonny-boy, my little darling!

ARYE-LEIB: (*Covers Mendel's face with a kerchief, sits down and begins quietly from a long way away.*) Once upon a time there lived a man named David. He was a shepherd and then he was king, a king over Israel, over the hosts of Israel and over its sages . . .

POTAPOVNA: (*Sobs.*) My sonny-boy!

ARYE-LEIB: Wealth did David possess, and glory, but he never learned to be satisfied. Power thirsts, and only sorrow quenches the heart. When he grew old, David the King beheld on the roofs of Jerusalem, beneath the sky of Jerusalem, Bathsheba the wife of Uriah the leader of armies. Bathsheba's breast was fair, her feet were comely, her gaiety was great. And Uriah the leader of armies was sent off to battle, and the King lay with Bathsheba, with the wife of a husband who had not yet died. Her breast was fair, her gaiety was great . . .

SCENE 8

Dining-room in the Kriks' home. The room is brightly lit by means of a home-made hanging lamp, candles stuck in candelabra, and old-fashioned azure lamps fastened to the wall. Madam Popyatnik, arrayed in a silken gown, is fussing about the table which is decorated with flowers and laden with hors-d'oeuvres and wine. The Major sits silently at the back of the room. His paper dicky bulges out, his flute lies on his knees, he twiddles his fingers and wags his head. Many guests. Some wander through the suite of open rooms, others sit against the wall. The pregnant Klasha Zubareva enters the room. She wears a shawl, printed with gigantic flowers. Drunken Lyovka, wearing an hussar's full-dress uniform, stumbles in after her.

LYOVKA: (*Bellows cavalry commands.*) Cavalrymen, friends, forward! Forward at a trot! By the numbers. Water your horses.

KLASHA: (*Laughing out loud.*) Oi, my belly! Oi, I'll have a miscarriage!

LYOVKA: Left flank attention, and right turn!

KLASHA: Oi, you'll be the death of me! . . .

(*They cross the room, running into Boyarsky, in a frock-coat, and Dvoira.*)

BOYARSKY: Mam'zel Krik, I won't say of black that it's white, nor will I allow myself to say of white that it's black. With three thousand we set up an establishment on Deribasovskaya and we get legally hitched in a happy hour.

DVOIRA: But why the whole three thousand all at once?

BOYARSKY: Because when we go outside today, it's July, and July—that's no September. To me July means lightweight topcoats and September means ladies' overcoats . . . What have you got after September? Nothing. Septemb, Octob, Novemb, Decemb . . . I wouldn't say of night that it was day and I wouldn't allow myself to say of day that it was night . . .

(*They cross the room. Benya and Bobrinets appear.*)

BENYA: Are you all set, Madam Popyatnik?

MADAM POPYATNIK: Nicholas the Second wouldn't be ashamed to sit at such a table!

BOBRINETS: Tell me what's on your mind, Benya.

BENYA: Here's what's on my mind: a Jew who's not in his first youth, a Jew who went around all his life ragged and barefoot and dirty like a convict from Sakhalin Island . . . And now, thank God, when he's reached old age, we should put an end to this life-term hard labor; we should act so that the day of rest *is* the day of rest.

(*Boyarsky and Dvoira cross the room.*)

BOYARSKY: Septemb, Octob, Novemb, Decemb . . .

DVOIRA: And next, I want you to love me a little bit, Boyarsky.

BOYARSKY: And what would I do with you if not love you? Chop you up for mincemeat? For Heaven's sake, that's a funny one! . . .

(*They cross the room. Along the wall, beneath an azure lamp, sit a sedate dealer in livestock and a stout-legged youth in a three-piece suit. The youth is carefully cracking sunflower seeds and depositing the shells in his pocket.*)

STOUT-LEGGED YOUTH: One punch to the jaw, another punch to the jaw, and the old man's knocked off his high-horse.

LIVESTOCK DEALER: Even the Tatars respect their elders. Going through a lifetime ain't like crossing a meadow.

STOUT-LEGGED YOUTH: If only the guy had an angle on living, but that one . . . (*spits out a shell*), that one lives like life was goin' out of style. What's there to respect him for?

LIVESTOCK DEALER: What's the good of arguing with a fool?

STOUT-LEGGED YOUTH: Benchik bought fifteen tons of hay in a single order.

LIVESTOCK DEALER: The old man used to buy a couple tons at a time—and he was never short.

STOUT-LEGGED YOUTH: They'll slit the old man's throat, just the same.
LIVESTOCK DEALER: The *Yids* do that? To their father?
STOUT-LEGGED YOUTH: Slit his throat till he croaks.
LIVESTOCK DEALER: Talk to a fool . . .

(*Benya and Bobrinets cross the stage.*)

BOBRINETS: Just what are you after, Benya?
BENYA: I want the day of rest to be a day of rest. I want us to be no worse
   than other people. I want to walk with my feet on the ground and my head
   held high . . . You follow me, Bobrinets?
BOBRINETS: I follow you, Benchik.

(*Along the wall, next to Pyatirubel, sit the wealthy Weiners, husband and wife, puffed up
with their own importance.*)

PYATIRUBEL: (*Soliciting their sympathy, to no avail.*) He pulled off the constables'
   cartridge-belts, he beat up the guard at the central post office. He knocked
   down a quart's worth before supper, he held all Odessa in the palm of his
   hand . . . That's the kind of old man he was!

(*Weiner moves his heavy wet tongue for a long while, but it is impossible to make out what
he's saying.*)

PYATIRUBEL: (*Meekly.*) The gentleman can't talk straight?
MADAM WEINER: (*Fiercely.*) Isn't it obvious!

(*Dvoira and Boyarsky cross the room.*)

BOYARSKY: Septemb, Octob, Novemb, Decemb . . .
DVOIRA: And next, I want a baby, Boyarsky.
BOYARSKY: That's the ticket, a baby along with a firm—that's lovely, that
   looks good. But a baby without a firm—how would *that* look?

(*Madam Popyatnik, in a state of intense excitement, bursts in.*)

MADAM POPYATNIK: Ben Zkharya is here! The Rabbi . . . Ben Zkharya . . .

(*The room fills with guests. Among them Dvoira, Lyovka, Benya, Klasha Zubareva,
Senka Topun; drivers glistening with hair-oil, shopkeepers waddling, old women smirking
at one another.*)

STOUT-LEGGED YOUTH: Even the Rabbi comes a-runnin' where there's money. Right on cue.

(*Arye-Leib and Bobrinets wheel in a large armchair. It conceals in its tumbled-down innards the shrivelled body of Ben Zkharya.*)

BEN ZKHARYA: (*Shrilly.*) The dawn is just starting to sneeze, God is still washing Himself in red water . . .

BOBRINETS: (*Laughs loudly, anticipating an intricate answer.*) Why red, Rabbi?

BEN ZKHARYA: . . . I'm still lying on my back, like a cockroach . . .

BOBRINETS: Why on your back, Rabbi?

BEN ZKHARYA: In the morning, God turns me over on my back so that I'm not able to pray. God is fed up with my prayers . . .

(*Bobrinets roars with laughter.*)

BEN ZKHARYA: The chickens are still asleep, but Arye-Leib rouses me: hurry over to the Kriks', Rabbi, they're throwing a party, they're giving a banquet. The Kriks'll give you something to drink, they'll give you something to eat . . .

BENYA: They will give you something to drink, they will give you something to eat, whatever you want, Rabbi.

BEN ZKHARYA: Whatever I want? . . . And would you give me your horses?

BENYA: We'd give you my horses too.

BEN ZKHARYA: In that case, Jews, run over to the burial society, harness his horses to the hearse and drive me . . . where to?

BOBRINETS: Where to, Rabbi?

BEN ZKHARYA: To the second Jewish cemetery, you nitwit!

BOBRINETS: (*Roars with laughter, pulls off the Rabbi's skullcap, and kisses his bare pink bald-spot.*) Ai, you gangster . . . Ai, you smarty-pants! . . .

ARYE-LEIB: (*Introducing Benya.*) This is him, Rabbi, Mendel's son—Ben Zion.

BEN ZKHARYA: (*Gnaws his lips.*) Ben Zion . . . the son of Zion . . . (*He falls silent.*) A nightingale is not fed with fables, son of Zion, nor women with wisdom . . .

LYOVKA: (*In a deafening voice.*) Take a load off your feet, you crooks, park yourselves on the benches!

KLASHA: (*Shakes her head, smiles.*) Och, is he fresh!

BENYA: (*Casts an indignant glance at his brother.*) Dear friends, please be seated. M'sieu Bobrinets will sit next to the Rabbi.

BEN ZKHARYA: (*Fidgets in the armchair.*) Why should I have to sit next to this Jew who's as long as our exile? Let the State Bank (*points to Klasha*) sit next to me.

BOBRINETS: (*Anticipating a new wisecrack.*) Why the State Bank?

BEN ZKHARYA: She's better than a bank. You make the right deposit in her,— she'll yield you such a percentage that wheat will be green with envy. You make the wrong deposit,—she'll creak with all her innards to exchange your clipped kopek for a new-minted gold piece . . . She's better than a bank, she's better than a bank . . .

BOBRINETS: (*Lifts his finger.*) What he says has got to be taken in the proper interpretation.

BEN ZKHARYA: But where is our star over Israel, where is the master of this house, where is Reb Mendel Krik?

LYOVKA: He's sick today.

BENYA: Rabbi, he's in excellent health . . . Nikifor!

(*Nikifor appears in the doorway in his everyday peasant jacket.*)

BENYA: Let Poppa and his wife come down.

(*Silence.*)

NIKIFOR: (*In a voice of desperation.*) Most esteemed guests! . . .

BENYA: (*Slowly.*) Let Poppa in.

ARYE-LEIB: Benchik, we Jews don't shame our fathers in front of people.

LYOVKA: Rabbi, a man doesn't torture a pig the way he tortures Poppa.

(*Weiner splutters indignantly, spraying spittle.*)

BENYA: (*Leans toward Madam Weiner.*) What's he saying?

MADAM WEINER: He says—it's a shame and a disgrace!

ARYE-LEIB: Jews don't do such things, Benya!

KLASHA: You bring up sons . . .

BENYA: Arye-Leib, old man, old matchmaker, shammes at the teamsters' synagogue and cantor at the cemetery, are you trying to tell me how people manage their affairs? . . . (*He slams his fist on the table and says in measured tones.*) Let Poppa in here!

(*Nikifor vanishes. His head bowed, legs spread apart, Benya stands in the middle of the room. Slowly his face flushes with blood. Silence. And only the inane muttering of Ben Zkharya breaks the oppressive stillness.*)

BEN ZKHARYA: God in Heaven washes with red water. (*He falls silent, fidgets in his armchair.*) Why red, why not white? Because red is jollier than white . . .

(*The two halves of the side-door creak, groan and pull apart. All faces turn in that direction. Mendel appears, his powdered face covered with weals. He is in a brand-new suit.*

Beside him is Nekhama in a fancy turban and a heavy velvet gown.)

BENYA: Friends, assembled in my home! Allow me to raise this little glass to my father, the hard-working Mendel Krik, and his help-mate, Nekhama Borisovna, who for thirty-five years have walked down the road of life hand in hand. Dear friends! We know, we know all too well, that nobody has paved this road with asphalt, nobody has set up benches by the side of this long highway, and although hordes of people have traveled down this road, it hasn't made it any easier. In fact, it's made it that much harder. Friends, assembled in my home! I trust that you won't water down the wine in your glasses or the wine in your hearts . . .

(*Weiner mutters enthusiastically.*)

BENYA: What's he saying?

MADAM WEINER: He says—hooray!

BENYA: (*Not looking at anyone.*) You show me, Arye-Leib . . . (*Brings wine to his father and mother.*) Our guests are honoring us, Poppa. Say something to our guests.

MENDEL: (*Surveys the scene and says quietly.*) I wish you good health . . .

BENYA: What Poppa means is that he contributes a hundred rubles to some needy charity.

LIVESTOCK DEALER: And they try to tell me about the Yids . . .

BENYA: Poppa contributes five hundred rubles. Which charity, Rabbi?

BEN ZKHARYA: Which charity? The milk in a young girl's breasts shouldn't turn sour, Jews . . . You should contribute it to the fund for dowerless brides!

BOBRINETS: (*Bursts out laughing.*) Ai, you gangster! . . . Ai, you smarty-pants! . . .

MADAM POPYATNIK: I'll give the downbeat.

BENYA: Go ahead.

(*A plaintive fanfare fills the room. A row of guests holds out its glasses to Mendel and Nekhama.*)

KLASHA ZUBAREVA: Your health, Gramps!

SENKA TOPUN: A carload of pleasures, Pops, a hundred thousand for pocket money!

BENYA: (*Not looking at anyone.*) You show me, Arye-Leib!

BOBRINETS: Mendel, God grant that I have a son like that, like your son!

LYOVKA: (*Down the length of the table.*) Poppa, don't get mad! Poppa, you've had your fling . . .

LIVESTOCK DEALER: They try to tell me about the Yids! I know the Yids better than you ever will . . .

PYATIRUBEL: (*Thrusts himself at Benya and tries to kiss him.*) You'll buy us, you devil, and sell us, and tie us in knots!

(*Loud sobbing is heard behind Benya's back. Tears are streaming down Arye-Leib's face.*)

ARYE-LEIB: Fifty years, Benchik! Fifty years together with your father . . . He was a good father to you, Benya!

WEINER: (*Acquires the gift of speech.*) Take him out of here!

MADAM WEINER: God, what is this nonsense!

BOYARSKY: Arye-Leib, you're mistaken. Now's the time to laugh.

WEINER: Take him out of here!

ARYE-LEIB: (*Sobbing.*) He was a good father to you, Benya . . .

(*Mendel pales beneath his powder. He hands a brand-new handkerchief to Arye-Leib, who wipes away his tears. He weeps and laughs.*)

BOBRINETS: You dumbbell, you're not at your graveyard now!

PYATIRUBEL: You can travel the world over and you won't find one like Benchik, I'm willing to bet . . .

BENYA: Dear friends, please be seated!

LYOVKA: Park yourselves on the benches . . .

(*Thunder of chairs being pushed in. Mendel is seated next to the Rabbi and Klasha Zubareva.*)

BEN ZKHARYA: Jews!

BOBRINETS: Pipe down!

BEN ZKHARYA: The old nincompoop, Ben Zkharya, wants to say a few words . . .

(*Lyovka snorts scornfully, falls chest down on the table, but Benya shakes him upright and he falls silent.*)

BEN ZKHARYA: Day is day, Jews, and evening is evening. The day drenches us in the sweat of our toil, but the evening holds in readiness the fans of its divine coolth. Joshua the son of Nun, who stopped the sun in its course, was an evil madman. And behold, Mendel Krik, a member of our synagogue, has proved to be no saner than Joshua the son of Nun. He wanted to bask in the blazing sun all his life long, he wanted to stand in that spot where noonday had found him, all his life long. But God has policemen on every street-corner, and Mendel Krik had sons in his house. Policemen arrive on the scene and set things in order. Day is day and evening is evening.

Everything in its proper order, Jews. Let's have a glass of vodka!
LYOVKA: Let's have a glass of vodka! . . .

(*The tootling of the flute, the ringing of glasses, unrestrained shouting, thunderous laughter.*)

END

Ivan Vasilievich

A Comedy in Three Acts

(1935-36)

Mikhail A. Bulgakov

Characters

Timofeyev, an inventor
Georges Miloslavsky
Bunsha-Koretsky, the building superintendent
Anton Semyonovich Shpak
Ivan the Terrible
Yakin, a film director
A Scribe
The Swedish Ambassador
The Patriarch
Zinaida Mikhailovna, a film actress
Ulyana Andreyevna, Bunsha's wife
The Tsaritsa
Royal Guardsmen
Servitors
Dulcimer Players
Policemen

ACT I

An apartment in Moscow. Timofeyev's room next to Shpak's room, which is locked. In addition, an entrance hall with a radio loud-speaker in it. Chaos reigns in Timofeyev's room. Screens. A machine of enormous proportions and unusual construction, apparently a radio receiver on which Timofeyev is working. A myriad of lamps in the machine; different lights keep going off and on; Timofeyev's hair is dishevelled, his eyes bloodshot from lack of sleep. He is distraught.

TIMOFEYEV: (*Is pressing the buttons on the machine. We hear a pleasantly melodious tone.*) That tone's the same frequency again . . . (*The lighting alters.*) The light's gone out in the fifth lamp . . . Why is there no light? I can't figure it out. Let's get to the bottom of this. (*He computes.*) Two, three . . . the angle between two transverse axes . . . I can't understand it. The cosine, the cosine . . . Correct! (*Suddenly the radio transmitter in the hallway sends forth a cheery voice, saying: "You are listening to a performance of Rimsky-Korsakov's opera 'Ivan the Terrible'!" And next, the radio emits pealing bells and raucous music.*) Ivan gives me a pain, him and his bells! Besides, I should have unscrewed the head of the man who installed that radio. How many times have I told him to take it away. I'd fix it eventually, I haven't got the time now! (*He runs into the hallway and shuts off the radio; the speaker squawks and then is silent. He returns to his room.*) Where did I leave off? . . . The cosine . . . Ah, no, the building superintendent! (*He opens the window, leans out and shouts.*) Ulyana Andreyevna! Where's your gem of a husband? I can't hear! Ulyana Andreyevna, didn't I ask him to get rid of his radio! I can't hear. Get rid of his radio! Tell him to be patient, I'll repair the radio for him! He'll be able to get Australia! Tell him he's torturing me with his Ivan the Terrible! And besides, it's full of static! No, the *radio* is full of static! I haven't got the time! Bells are ringing in my head. I can't hear! Well, all right. (*He closes the window.*) Where did I leave off? . . . The cosine . . . My skull is throbbing . . . Where's Zina? I should have my tea now. (*He walks over to the window.*) What a funny-looking man, in black gloves . . . What's he after? (*He sits down.*) No, I'll try it out again. (*He pushes the buttons on the machine, which emits a faint melodious tone, while the lights in the lamps alter.*) Cosine plus bells . . . (*He writes on a piece of paper.*) Cosine plus bells . . . plus bells . . . I mean, cosine . . . (*He yawns.*) Chiming, pealing . . . there's a musical building super for you . . . (*He droops and falls asleep at the machine.*)

(*The lighting in the lamps alters. Then the lights go out. Timofeyev's room is plunged in darkness and all we can hear is the faint melodious tone. The entrance hall lights up. Zinaida Mikhailovna appears in the hallway.*)

ZINAIDA: (*In the hallway, listens to the melodious tone.*) He's home. I am seriously worried that machine has driven him crazy. Poor kid! . . . And he's got another blow in store for him . . . I've been divorced three times already . . . well, yes, three, Zuzin doesn't count . . . But I never felt so emotional about it before. I can imagine what'll happen this time! If only he doesn't make a scene! They're so exhausting, those scenes . . . (*She powders her face.*) Well, forward march! It's best to cut right through the Gordian knot . . . (*Knocks on the door.*) Koka, open up!

TIMOFEYEV: (*In darkness.*) Hey, what the hell! . . . Who's there?

ZINAIDA: It's me, Koka. (*Timofeyev's room lights up. Timofeyev opens the door. In place of the radio there stands a weird, outlandish machine.*) Koka, didn't you go to bed? Koka, that machine of yours is going to destroy you. This mustn't go on! And—you'll excuse me, Koka—all my friends insist that it's impossible to see the past and the future. It's simply a crazy notion, Kokochka. Never-neverland.

TIMOFEYEV: I am not of the opinion, Zinochka, that all your friends are adequate judges of such matters. You've got to be an expert.

ZINAIDA: I beg your pardon, Koka, some of them are fantastic experts.

TIMOFEYEV: Can't you understand there's a tiny error somewhere, an infinitesimal one! I feel it, I can sense it, it's in there somewhere . . . it's floating around inside! But I'll pin it down.

ZINAIDA: Honestly, he's one for the books!

(*Pause. Timofeyev is busy with his calculations.*)

ZINAIDA: Excuse me for disturbing you, but I've got some awful news to impart . . . No, I'm not up to it . . . Today in the commissary somebody swiped my gloves. Incredible! I put them down on the table and . . . I've fallen in love with somebody else, Koka . . . No, I can't . . . I suppose the guy was at the next table . . . Are you listening to me?

TIMOFEYEV: No . . . Which table?

ZINAIDA: Oh, for God's sake, that gadget has driven you nuts!

TIMOFEYEV: Well, your gloves . . . What about your gloves?

ZINAIDA: Forget the gloves, I fell in love with another man. It was bound to happen! . . . (*Timofeyev looks dully at Zinaida.*) Just don't give me a hard time . . . and let's not have any scenes. Why do people have to break up with dramatics, no matter what? You've got to agree, Koka, that they're not indispensable. This is the real thing, and everything else in my life was a delusion . . . Who is he, you'll ask? And you probably think it's Molchanovsky? No, get ready for this: he's a film director, really talented . . . Let's not play any more guessing games. It's Yakin.

TIMOFEYEV: So . . .

(*Pause.*)

ZINAIDA: This is odd, I must say! It's the first time in my life *this* has happened. They tell him his wife's been cheating on him—because I actually did cheat on you—but all he can say is—So! It's almost rude!

TIMOFEYEV: He . . . this guy . . . what's-his-name . . . tall and blond?

ZINAIDA: Well, this is really disgraceful! Taking such little interest in your wife! The blond is Molchanovsky, now don't forget it! But Yakin is the really talented one! (*Pause.*) I suppose you'll ask, where are we going to live? In five hours I'll be leaving with him for Gagri, to pick out a location for shooting, and when we get back, they're supposed to give him an apartment in a brand new building, if, of course, he's not making it up . . .

TIMOFEYEV: (*Dully.*) Sure he's making it up.

ZINAIDA: It's so stupid to insult the man out of jealousy! He can't be lying every single minute. (*Pause.*) I gave it a lot of thought the last few times I lay awake all night, and I came to the conclusion that we aren't suited to one another. My whole being is dedicated to the movies . . . to my art, while you're tied down to this machine . . . Honestly, I just can't get over your calm! I almost wish you'd make a scene. Well, so what . . . (*She goes behind a screen and brings out a suitcase.*) I'm already packed, so I won't get in your way. Please let me have some money for the trip. I'll send it back to you from the Caucasus.

TIMOFEYEV: Here's a hundred and forty . . . a hundred and fifty-three rubles . . . that's all I've got.

ZINAIDA: Look in the pocket of your jacket.

TIMOFEYEV: (*Having looked.*) None in my jacket.

ZINAIDA: Well, give me a kiss. Goodbye, Koka. Still and all, there's something sad about it . . . To think we've lived together a whole eleven months! . . . I can't get over it, positively can't get over it! (*Timofeyev kisses Zinaida.*) But don't you strike me off the list of tenants either. You never know what might happen. Besides, you'd never do such a low-down thing. (*She exits.*)

TIMOFEYEV: (*Starting after her dully.*) Alone . . . How could I have got married like that? To whom? What for? What kind of a wife is that? (*At the machine.*) Alone . . . And yet I don't blame her. Honestly, how could anybody live with me? Well, so what, if I'm alone, I'm alone! At least nobody will disturb me . . . Fifteen . . . sixteen . . . (*The melodious tone. The doorbell rings in the hallway. The ringing becomes insistent.*) How can a person work under such conditions! . . . (*He goes to the hallway and opens the front door. Ulyana Andreyevna enters.*)

ULYANA: Greetings, Comrade Timofeyev. Has Ivan Vasilievich dropped by your place?

TIMOFEYEV: No.

ULYANA: Tell Zinaida Mikhailovna that Marya Stepanovna said that Anna Ivanovna's been offered some imported fabric by her manicurist, so if Zinaida . . .

TIMOFEYEV: I can't tell Zinaida Mikhailovna anything, because she's gone.

ULYANA: Where did she go?

TIMOFEYEV: To the Caucasus with her lover, and afterwards they'll be living in a new building, that is, if he's not making it up . . .

ULYANA: What do you mean, with her lover? A fine state of affairs! And you can talk about it so calmly! You're a very peculiar man!

TIMOFEYEV: Ulyana Andreyevna, you're disturbing me.

ULYANA: Ah, pardon me! You're quite a character, Comrade Timofeyev! If I had been in Zinaida Mikhailovna's shoes, I would have left you too.

TIMOFEYEV: If you had been in Zinaida Mikhailovna's shoes, I would have hanged myself.

ULYANA: Don't you dare slam the door in a lady's face, you ruffian! (*She leaves.*)

TIMOFEYEV: (*Returning to his room.*) The devil's own doll-baby!

(*He presses the buttons on the machine and his room is plunged in total darkness. The front door opens quietly and in it Miloslavsky appears, badly dressed, with black gloves and the clean-shaven face of an actor. He listens at Timofeyev's door.*)

MILOSLAVSKY: Everybody's at work, but this guy sits at home. He'll be fixing the Victrola. (*He reads the nameplate on Shpak's door.*) Anton Semyonovich Shpak. Well, now, let's drop in on Shpak . . . What a ridiculous lock. I haven't run across one like this in a long time. Oh no, the widow on Meat Market Street had one like it. I'd better use number six. (*He takes out a skeleton-key.*) He's probably sitting in his office thinking: ''Ah, what a wonderful lock I installed on my door!'' But, as a matter of fact, a lock only serves one purpose: to show that the tenant isn't home . . . (*He opens the lock, goes into Shpak's room, and closes the door in such a way that the lock remains in place.*) Wow, very pretty furniture! . . . Lucky I stopped by . . . Wow, he's even got a private telephone. What luxury! And so precise, he's even written down his number at work. Well, since he wrote it down, I suppose my first duty is to phone him, just so there won't be any misunderstanding. (*On the telephone.*) Department of Interurban Transport. Merci. Extension 501. Merci. Comrade Shpak. Merci. Comrade Shpak? Bonjour, Comrade Shpak, will you be at work all day today? . . . This is an actress speaking . . . No, you don't know me, but I'm dying to make your acquaintance. So you'll be there till four? I'll phone you again, I'm very persistent . . . No, blonde. Contralto. Well, so long. (*Hangs up the receiver.*) He was awfully puzzled. Well now, let's get started . . . (*He breaks open a cupboard and removes a suit of clothes.*) Cheviot wool . . . Wow! . . . (*He takes off his own suit, wraps it up in newspaper and puts on Shpak's suit.*) Fits me like a glove . . . (*He breaks open the desk, picks up a watch and chain, puts them in the inner pocket of his coat.*) In the three years I've been out of Moscow, they've certainly managed to accumulate a lot of property! Makes it a pleasure to get back to work! Very nice Victrola . . . And a hat . . . My size. My lucky day! . . . Oof, I'm pooped! (*He breaks open the sideboard, takes out vodka and food, drinks.*) How did he make this liqueur? Superb vodka! . . . No, it's not absinthe . . . Fond of reading too . . . (*Takes a book, reads.*) ''Sans respite doth Ivan Vasilich the Terrible, the valiant, revel with his henchmen in the outskirts of Mother Moscow . . . The ranks of tables gleamed with golden flagons, behind them sate the guardsmen making merry . . .'' Marvelous poetry! Gorgeous poetry! . . . ''Hail to thee, lordings, guardsmen mine! Louder strum ye your strings, nightingale bards . . .'' I do like this poem. (*On the telephone.*) Department of Interurban Transport. Merci. Extension 501. Merci. Comrade Shpak. Merci. Comrade Shpak? It's me again. Tell me, what do you put in your vodka to make that liqueur . . . My name is a secret . . . From the Bolshoi Theatre . . . and what a surprise you'll be getting today! . . . ''Sans respite doth Ivan Vasilich, the Terrible, the valiant, revel with his henchmen in the outskirts of Mother Moscow . . .'' (*Hangs up the receiver.*) He was awfully puzzled. (*He drinks.*) ''The ranks of tables gleamed with golden flagons . . .''

(*Shpak's room is plunged in darkness, while Timofeyev's room lights up. Now the machine is emitting melodious tones more frequently and every so often the lighting in the machine alters.*)

TIMOFEYEV: It's lighting up! It's lighting up! Now that's a different story . . .

(*The front door opens and Bunsha enters. At first his attention is directed to the radio loud-*

speaker.)

BUNSHA: I exert an incredible amount of energy in order to bring culture to our building. I wire it for radio, but they stubbornly refuse to take advantage of the radio. (*He fiddles about with the plug and socket, but the machine remains silent.*) Must be intermission.(*He knocks on Timofeyev's door.*)

TIMOFEYEV: Now who's there? Come on in . . . it's enough to make you drop dead! (*Bunsha enters.*) That's all I needed! . . .

BUNSHA: It's me, Nikolai Ivanovich.

TIMOFEYEV: I can see that, Ivan Vasilievich. I'm surprised at you, Ivan Vasilievich! At your age you should be sitting at home, playing nursemaid to your grandchildren, but all day long you're prowling around the building with that greasy book . . . I'm very busy, Ivan Vasilievich, excuse me.

BUNSHA: This book happens to be the house register. I haven't got any grandchildren. And if I were to stop making my rounds, horrible things would happen.

TIMOFEYEV: The government would fall to pieces?

BUNSHA: The government will fall to pieces, if people don't pay their rent. Around this building they think they can get away without paying, but as a matter of fact they can't. By and large, ours is an amazing building. I walk around the yard and get goose-pimples. Every window is wide open, everyone's sprawled out on his window-sill, and talking such tommyrot, it's embarrassing to repeat it.

TIMOFEYEV: I can't follow any of this, for God's sake! Why don't you get treated for it, Prince!

BUNSHA: Nikolai Ivanovich, stop calling me Prince. I've already proved, with documentary evidence, that the year I was born, my papa was travelling abroad. Therefore I am obviously the son of our coachman Panteley. I even look like Panteley.

TIMOFEYEV: Well, if you're a coachman's son, all the better. But I haven't got any money, Ivan Panteleyevich.

BUNSHA: No. Call me Ivan Vasilievich, in accordance with the documents.

TIMOFEYEV: All right, all right.

BUNSHA: I implore you to pay your room rent.

TIMOFEYEV: I tell you I haven't any money at the moment . . . My wife walked out on me and now you come and apply the thumbscrew.

BUNSHA: Excuse me, but why didn't you inform me of this?

TIMOFEYEV: What business is it of yours?

BUNSHA: It's my business to strike her off the register immediately.

TIMOFEYEV: She asked not to be stricken off.

BUNSHA: I have to make a note of it all the same. (*He notes it in the book.*) I feel better now.

TIMOFEYEV: There's no reason for you to feel better. How can I make it clear to you that you mustn't disturb me while I'm at work?

BUNSHA: Well, try and make it clear. I'm a man of advanced ideas. Yesterday there was a lecture for us building superintendents and I derived enormous benefit from it. Understood practically all of it. About the stratosphere. By and large, our life is very interesting and useful, but they don't understand that in this building.

TIMOFEYEV: When you talk, Ivan Vasilievich, you give the impression that you're raving!

BUNSHA: By and large, our building is very strange. Shpak is constantly buying mahogany furniture, but is too tight to pay his rent. And you're always working on this outlandish machine.

TIMOFEYEV: This is torture, I swear!

BUNSHA: I implore you, Nikolai Ivanovich, make an official declaration about your gadget. It has to be registered with the police. What's more, the ladies in the annex have started saying that you're constructing a machine to demolish our whole building. And you know what—you'll get arrested, and I'll be in the same boat.

TIMOFEYEV: What filthy scum has been talking such drivel?

BUNSHA: I beg your pardon, my wife Ulyana Andreyevna was doing the talking.

TIMOFEYEV: Sorry! Why do women talk such crap? I know, it's your fault. You old stiff, you do nothing but loaf around the building, snooping, relaying tittle-tattle, and chiefly, telling lies!

BUNSHA: After those brutal insults, I intend to evacuate this apartment and wend my way to the police station. I am a person invested with the responsible position of building superintendent, and my duty is to keep an eye on things.

TIMOFEYEV: Hold on! . . . Forgive me, I was hasty. Well, fine, come over here. Quite simply, I'm conducting an experiment to explore time . . . Yes, and yet how can I explain to you what time is? You probably don't even know about four-dimensional space, motion . . . and in general . . . in short, you understand, not only won't it blow up, but it will bring the nation unheard-of advantages . . . Well, how can I put it simply? . . . To give you a for-instance, just now I want to penetrate space and go back into the past . . .

BUNSHA: Penetrate space? You can perform such an experiment only with police authorization. In my capacity as building superintendent, I am alarmed by such experiments going on in a building in my custody. Here stands a mysterious machine, locked with a key . . .

TIMOFEYEV: What!? A key? Ivan Vasilievich, thank you! Thank you! You're brilliant! A key! Ach, I'm an absent-minded nincompoop! I've been working on a locked circuit . . . Hold on! Look! Look at what'll happen now . . . Let's try it on a short distance . . . with a weak angle of incidence . . .

(*He turns the key and presses the button.*) Look, we're heading through space in-to time . . . backwards . . . (*He presses the button.*)

(*Ringing. Blackout. Then light. The party-wall between the two rooms has vanished, and in Shpak's room sits Miloslavsky, drinking, with a book in his hand.*)

TIMOFEYEV: (*Ecstatic.*) Did you see it?

MILOSLAVSKY: What the hell are you . . . What is this?

BUNSHA: Nikolai Ivanovich, what happened to the wall?!

TIMOFEYEV: Success! Success! I can't believe it! This is it! This is it! . . .

BUNSHA: A strange citizen in Shpak's room!

MILOSLAVSKY: I beg your pardon, but what's the matter? What's going on? (*He picks up the Victrola and his bundle and walks into Timofeyev's room.*) There was a wall there just now!

BUNSHA: Nikolai Ivanovich, you will answer for that wall to the law. You did it with your machine! Half the apartment's disappeared!

TIMOFEYEV: You can go to hell, you and your wall! Nothing will happen to it! . . .

(*He presses the button on the machine. Blackout. Light. The wall is standing in place, closing off Shpak's room.*)

MILOSLAVSKY: I've seen the wonders of technology, but never anything like this!

TIMOFEYEV: Oh God, my head's in a whirl! . . . Eureka, eureka! Oh, humanity, what's in store for you! . . .

BUNSHA: (*To Miloslavsky.*) I beg your pardon, but who might you be?

MILOSLAVSKY: Who might I be, you ask? I'm waiting for my friend Shpak.

BUNSHA: And how can you be waiting for him, when the lock on his door fastens from the outside?

MILOSLAVSKY: What's that you say? The lock? Oh, yes . . . he stepped down to the corner to buy a paper, and . . . locked me in . . .

TIMOFEYEV: Why don't you just go to hell! These questions are vulgar! (*To Miloslavsky.*) Do you realize I've conquered time! I've succeeded all on my own! . . .

MILOSLAVSKY: You mean to say that this can remove any wall whatever? Your ingenuity is priceless, citizen! My congratulations! (*To Bunsha.*) Why are you looking at me like that, my good man? There are no posies growing on me or patterns either.

BUNSHA: A vague suspicion is gnawing away at me. You're wearing the very same suit that Shpak has!

MILOSLAVSKY: What are you talking about? My suit? As if Shpak had the only striped suit in Moscow! We're close friends and we always buy our cloth in the same shop. Does that satisfy you?

BUNSHA: And the very same hat.

MILOSLAVSKY: The same hat.

BUNSHA: What's your name?

MILOSLAVSKY: I'm a performer at the State Bolshoi and Chamber theaters. What do you need my name for? It's too well-known for me to have to tell you.

BUNSHA: And the very same watch-chain as Shpak's.

MILOSLAVSKY: Hey, don't be such a pest! . . . The hat, the watch-chain . . . this is most annoying! "Sans respite doth Ivan Vasilich the Terrible, the valiant, revel with his henchmen . . ."

TIMOFEYEV: Why don't you leave the citizen alone. (*To Miloslavsky.*) Maybe you'd like to go back into Shpak's room? I'll open the wall for you.

MILOSLAVSKY: By no means. I'm put out with him. He probably went out for the paper and got lost. For all I know he may be wandering around for the next two hours. I'd rather watch this experiment, I'm delighted with it.

TIMOFEYEV: (*Shakes his hand.*) I'm so glad! You were the first to see it . . . You were the first witness, so to speak.

MILOSLAVSKY: I never had the chance to be a witness before! Delighted, absolutely delighted! . . . (*To Bunsha.*) Are you still staring? You'll drill a hole in me!

TIMOFEYEV: That's our building superintendent.

MILOSLAVSKY: Ah, now I catch on! . . . The hat, the watch-chain . . . what a repulsive job! If you only knew how many run-ins I've had with them, Citizen Scientist.

TIMOFEYEV: Don't pay any attention to him.

MILOSLAVSKY: You're right.

TIMOFEYEV: You understand, Citizen Actor . . .

MILOSLAVSKY: Why shouldn't I understand; say, is it possible to knock down a wall in a department store the same way? Ah, what a fascinating experiment!

BUNSHA: You came to Shpak's room with a Victrola?

MILOSLAVSKY: He's getting on my nerves! What is this anyway?

TIMOFEYEV: (*To Bunsha.*) Are you going to stop pestering the man or aren't you? (*To Miloslavsky.*) Bear in mind, the wall isn't the main thing, it's only the first step! The point is, once I have passed all these walls, I can penetrate time! Do you understand? I can move two hundred, three hundred years backwards or forwards! What am I talking about: three hundred! . . . No, the world has never known such an invention! . . . I'm getting over-excited! . . . My wife walked out on me today, but, you understand . . . Ah! . . .

MILOSLAVSKY: Citizen Professor, don't get upset. You can marry any woman you like! You can spit on her walking out!

BUNSHA: I've already stricken her from the register.

MILOSLAVSKY: (*To Bunsha.*) Spit on you too! "Sans respite doth Ivan Vasilich the Terrible, the valiant, revel . . ." Ah, what an invention! (*He knocks on the wall.*) You knock it down, walk in, walk out—and close it up! You're great, honest to God!

TIMOFEYEV: My hands are trembling . . . I can't stand it . . . How about it, shall we penetrate the past? . . . What do you say, shall we take a look at ancient Moscow? . . . Don't tell me you're scared? There's nothing to worry about!

BUNSHA: Nikolai Ivanovich! Think twice before you perform such experiments in a cooperative apartment-house.

MILOSLAVSKY: If you interfere with the Citizen Academician's experiment one more time, I'll let you have it! What kind of punishment is this? (*To Timofeyev.*) Roll 'em!

(*Timofeyev presses a button on the machine. Ringing. Blackout. Suddenly the throne-room of Ivan the Terrible springs up. Ivan, clad in royal robes and holding a staff, is sitting on the throne. Before him, hunched up on a chair, a Scribe is writing. Ivan is wearing a guardsman's cloak over his clothing. A church liturgy and the gentle pealing of bells can be heard in the distance.*)

IVAN: (*Dictating.*) . . . And to the superior . . .

SCRIBE: (*Writing.*) . . . And to the superior . . .

IVAN: Of the right blessed community, the most venerable Father Abbot Kozma . . .

SCRIBE: Kozma . . .

IVAN: . . . The Tsar and Grand Duke Ivan Vasilievich of All the Russias . . .

SCRIBE: . . . All the Russias . . .

IVAN: . . . Maketh obeisance . . .

TIMOFEYEV: Good Lord! Look! It's Ivan the Terrible himself! . . .

MILOSLAVSKY: Ye gods and little fishes! . . .

(*Ivan and the Scribe turn their heads toward the sound of voices. The Scribe leaps up and runs out of the throne-room. Ivan jumps and crosses himself.*)

IVAN: Begone! Avaunt! Woe unto me, a sinner! . . . Dolor unto me, the accursed! Grief betide the foul miscreant! . . . Begone!

(*In search of an exit, Ivan frenziedly rushes into Timofeyev's room, makes the sign of the cross all over the walls, gets flustered, runs out into the hallway, and disappears.*)

TIMOFEYEV: It's Ivan the Terrible! Where are you going? . . . Wait! . . . My

God, suppose anyone saw him! . . . Stop him! (*He runs after Ivan.*)

(*Bunsha hurries to the telephone.*)

MILOSLAVSKY: Who are you planning to phone?

BUNSHA: The police!

MILOSLAVSKY: Drop the receiver or I'll break your arm! He can't live a minute without the police!

(*A Guardsman breaks into the throne-room.*)

GUARDSMAN: Where be the cacodaemons? What ho! Slay them! (*To Bunsha.*) Where is the Tsar?

BUNSHA: I don't know! Help!

MILOSLAVSKY: Shut off the machine! Shut off the machine!

GUARDSMAN: (*Crossing himself.*) Ay, the cacodaemons! . . . (*He drops his halberd and disappears from the throne-room.*)

MILOSLAVSKY: Shut it off! Turn the key! The key! What a gadget! . . .

(*Bunsha presses the button, pulls out the key. At that moment, the ringing begins. The window curtain bellies out, sheets of paper blow around. Bunsha is pulled into the throne-room and drops his glasses.*)

BUNSHA: Save me! . . . Where is it dragging me?!

MILOSLAVSKY: How did you set the machine going, damn you?!

(*Miloslavsky is carried away. Blackout. Lights. No throne-room. The wall in place. In the room are neither Bunsha nor Miloslavsky. Only the Victrola, the bundle and the eye-glasses remain. Timofeyev appears.*)

TIMOFEYEV: He's locked himself in the attic! Help me get him out of there! . . . Good Lord, where are they? Huh? (*He runs to the machine.*) They reversed the current! Did it carry them away? . . . What's going to happen? . . . Bunsha? Bunsha! Ivan Vasilievich! (*A distant yell from Ivan.*) That one's howling in the attic! . . . But the key! Where's the key? . . . Good Lord, they've taken the key with them! What am I going to do, huh? . . . No key . . . That's what they did, they pulled out the key . . . Ivan Vasilievich! Why did you pull out the key? I don't suppose there's any point in shouting. They've taken the key with them. Suppose I bring the other one back to this room? (*He runs out.*)

(*Pause. The front door opens and Shpak enters.*)

SHPAK: I've been all hot and bothered since that blonde from the Bolshoi

Theatre phoned . . . I couldn't stay at work . . . (*He touches the lock on his door.*) Holy Moses! . . . (*Shpak's room lights up. Shpak enters and runs to the desk.*) Holy Moses! (*He runs to the cupboard.*) Holy Moses! (*On the telephone.*) Police! Police?! Number Ten Bathhouse Lane—grand larceny, comrade! . . . Who was robbed? Me, of course! Shpak! Shpak is my *name*! I was robbed by a blonde! (*Music starts playing on the radio.*) Comrade officer . . . That's the radio playing! An overcoat and a suit! . . . What are you getting angry for? Can you hear me? Well, I'll run right over to the station myself! Holy Moses, holy holy Moses! . . . (*Sobbing, he runs out of the room and disappears through the front door. Music is thundering out of the radio.*)

CURTAIN

ACT II

Timofeyev's room. In it, Ivan the Terrible. Both are very nervous.

IVAN: Oh Lord God Almighty!

TIMOFEYEV: Ssh . . . quiet, quiet! Just don't yell, I beg you! We'll get into awful trouble and there'll be a scandal, on top of it. I'm losing my mind too, but I make an effort to get a grip on myself.

IVAN: Alas, alack, ah, well-a-day! Utter it yet again, art thou no cacodaemon?

TIMOFEYEV: Oh, for heaven's sake, I explained to you up in the attic that I'm no demon.

IVAN: Nay, speak sooth! Thou liest to the Tsar! Not by man's desiring but by God's designing are we Tsar!

TIMOFEYEV: Nicely put. I realize that you're the Tsar, but I must ask you to forget that for the moment. I won't call you Tsar, but simply Ivan Vasilievich. Believe me, it's for your own good.

IVAN: Woe is me, Ivan Vasilievich, woe, woe! . . .

TIMOFEYEV: What can I do, I understand your desperation. It's a genuinely depressing turn of events. But who could have expected a catastrophe like this? They went and took the key with them! I can't send you back right now . . . Do you realize they're both there this minute, in your time! What'll happen to them?

IVAN: Harriers tear their flesh! Their heads shall be lopped off, and 'twill be an end on't!

TIMOFEYEV: What do you mean, lopped off? Good Lord, I've destroyed two human beings! This is appalling! This is monstrous! (*Pause.*) Do you drink vodka?

IVAN: Oh, alack the day! . . . With anise.

TIMOFEYEV: I haven't got any anise vodka. You'll have to drink zubrovka. It'll refresh you and you'll feel better. So will I. (*He takes out vodka and snacks.*) Have a drink.

IVAN: Taste thou of my goblet.

TIMOFEYEV: Why should I? Oh, I see . . . You suppose I want to poison you? Dear Ivan Vasilievich, that's not our way. Nowadays it's much easier to poison yourself with canned anchovies than with vodka. Drink it without fear.

IVAN: Well, to thy health.(*He drinks.*)

TIMOFEYEV: Thank you kindly. (*He drinks.*)

IVAN: How art thou yclept, warlock?

TIMOFEYEV: My name is Timofeyev.

IVAN: A prince?

TIMOFEYEV: That'll be the day! We've got only one prince in all of Moscow and he insists that he's the son of a coachman.

IVAN: Ah, the beggarly knave!

TIMOFEYEV: No, when I think that they're back then—I go out of my mind! . . . Have another drink. Take a piece of ham.

IVAN: 'Tis a fast day . . .

TIMOFEYEV: Well, an anchovy then.

IVAN: Thy châtelaine y-brewed the vodka?

TIMOFEYEV: Sure, let it be my châtelaine . . . it would take too long to explain . . .

IVAN: And so, methinks, thou hast wrought this contrivance thyself? . . . Oh ho ho! . . . I too didst possess a contrivancer like unto thee. He made himself wings . . .

TIMOFEYEV: And?

IVAN: I sate him in a keg of gunpowder, and let him fly! . . .

TIMOFEYEV: Really, why do you have to be so bloodthirsty?

IVAN: Thou dwellest here belike? Thy meadhall is cramped.

TIMOFEYEV: Yes, well, it's not much of a meadhall.

IVAN: And where is thy lady spouse? At church, mayhap?

TIMOFEYEV: I doubt it. My lady spouse ran off to the Caucasus with her lover Yakin today.

IVAN: Thou liest!

TIMOFEYEV: Cross my heart!

IVAN: Be they pursued? When that they are taken, Yakin shall be impaled upon a stake. 'Tis the first order of busyness . . .

TIMOFEYEV: No! What for? No . . . They love one another, so let them be happy.

IVAN: 'Tis just enow. Thou art a bounteous chiel . . . Ah, Lord God! Verily I be here . . . whilst the Swedes have bereft us of Kem! My lord, seek out the key! Dispatch me back!

TIMOFEYEV: Look, I'd run right over to the locksmith's myself, this very minute, but there's not a penny in the house. I gave it all to my wife.

IVAN: How now? Coin o' the realm? (*He takes gold coins out of his purse.*)

TIMOFEYEV: Gold? We're saved! First I'll go over to the jeweller's shop, then to the locksmith. He'll make me a key, and we can turn on the machine.

IVAN: I shall accompany thee withal.

TIMOFEYEV: On the street? Oh no, Ivan Vasilievich, it's out of the question! You stay here and don't show yourself. I'll even lock you in, and if anybody knocks, don't answer. Although nobody will come by. Thanks to Yakin, for carrying off my wife . . . In short, wait for me, and sit tight.

IVAN: Oh, Lord! . . .

TIMOFEYEV: I'll be back within the hour. Sit tight!

(*Timofeyev, having locked the door to his room, exits. Ivan, alone, rifles through the things in the room. The sound of an automobile is heard from the street. Ivan cautiously peeks out the window, then leaps back. He takes a swig of vodka.*)

IVAN: (*Humming softly.*) Grievous were the sins I committed . . . Succour me, Lord . . . succour me, ye miracle-workers, ye thaumaturges of Muscovy . . .

(*A knock at the door. Ivan gives a start, makes the sign of the cross on the door. The knocking stops.*)

ULYANA: (*Behind the door.*) Comrade Timofeyev, excuse me for making so bold as to disturb you again during your domestic tragedy . . . Listen, was Ivan Vasilievich with you? I've been looking for him all over the building. Comrade Timofeyev, you don't have the right to suffer in silence! Comrade Timofeyev, you're an uncouth person!

(*Ivan makes the sign of the cross on the door, and Ulyana's voice fades away.*)

IVAN: Praise the might of the salvatory cross! (*He drinks vodka.*)

(*Pause. Then a key turns in the lock. Ivan makes the sign of the cross on the door, but it doesn't work. Then Ivan retreats behind the screen. The door opens, and Zinaida enters. She throws down her suitcase. She looks frustrated.*)

ZINAIDA: What a bastard! It's all kaput! While I . . . why did I have to reveal everything to that sainted man? . . . (*She looks at the table.*) Why, of course, his grief drove him to drink! . . . Yes, he took to drink . . . A Victrola . . . where did the Victrola come from? Not a bad Victrola . . . Koka, aren't you here? I don't understand this! . . . Some kind of orgy's been going on here . . . He probably went out for more vodka . . . Who was he drinking with? (*She rifles through the bundle.*) A pair of pants! I don't understand a thing! (*She winds up the Victrola and sighs. Ivan squeezes up against the crack in the screen.*) And here I am back again . . . abused in the most offensive way . . .

(*After a brief pause, the front-door bell rings. Zinaida goes into the hallway and opens the door. Yakin enters, a young man in a beret and plus-fours, with a beard, sprouting from beneath his chin.*)

YAKIN: Zina, it's me.

ZINAIDA: What? You?! Get out! (*She goes into Timofeyev's room.*)

YAKIN: (*At the door.*) Zinaida Mikhailovna, are you alone? Open up, I implore you!

ZINAIDA: I categorically refuse to open the door to bastards.

YAKIN: Zina! I beseech you, Zina, I can explain everything to you in no time. Zina, listen to me. (*Zinaida opens the door. Entering Timofeyev's room.*) Zinochka, what happened? Why did you run away? I don't understand , . . .

ZINAIDA: Karp Savelevich, you're a louse!

YAKIN: Goodness, what language! Zinochka, there's some misunderstanding, I swear by the film studio!

ZINAIDA: Misunderstanding! . . . He'll explain! . . . I give my husband the brushoff. That sainted man is now getting drunk as all hell. I abandon these magnificent living-quarters. I walk out on a man who idolized me, shook off the dust of a . . . brilliant inventor! . . . I go to this sonuvabitch, and . . .

YAKIN: Zina, such language!

ZINAIDA: You haven't heard real language yet! And two hours before our departure, I find some strange woman in his room . . .

YAKIN: Zina! . . .

ZINAIDA: Whom he's holding tenderly by the hand! . . .

YAKIN: Zinochka, I was going over a scene with her! It's my professional responsibility!

ZINAIDA: To pinch her biceps? No, you try and explain pinching her biceps! (*She slaps Yakin.*)

YAKIN: Zinaida Mikhailovna! Comrade, what is all this?!

ZINAIDA: Out!

YAKIN: Zinaida, listen, she's an extra! She's got a snub nose!

ZINAIDA: What? She's going to be in the film?

YAKIN: A minor role . . . An itsy-bitsy, teeny-weeny walk-on! I can't shoot the picture without a snub-nosed woman! And anyhow, what are you doing hitting me! Your director?!

ZINAIDA: You can film snub-noses, no-noses, whatever you like! . . . I've had enough! I'm going to Kosoy, for his Boris Godunov production!

YAKIN: Kosoy's a hack! He won't be making any movies!

ZINAIDA: I beg your pardon, the production is confirmed! And I'm going to play the Tsaritsa! I am no longer interested in your "Golden Apples" in Gagri.

YAKIN: Don't you understand, they've got nobody to play the role of Ivan the Terrible! They'll keep the picture in the can till hell freezes over, and then you'll remember me, Zinaida!

ZINAIDA: No Ivan? I'm sorry, but I'm already in rehearsal with him.

YAKIN: Where were you rehearsing?

ZINAIDA: Right here, in my apartment . . . And when we got to the place where Boris is proclaimed Tsar, Kosoy, tough as he is, wept like a baby! . . .

YAKIN: Rehearsing behind my back? This is treason, Zinaida! Who's playing Boris, who's playing the Tsar? Who?

IVAN: (*Coming out from behind the screen.*) How now, Boris a Tsar? That suckling Boris?! (*Zinaida and Yakin are petrified.*) Come hither, sirrah!

ZINAIDA: Good grief, what is this?!

YAKIN: So, you really are rehearsing? God, what casting!

IVAN: Boris holding sway? . . . Thus doth he, the crafty villain, repay the Tsar's boons and bounties with base perfidy? . . . He doth covet the throne and yearns to 'stablish dominion o'er all! . . . He merits to die the death!

YAKIN: Bravo!

ZINAIDA: My God . . . Yakin, explain to me . . . Yakin, protect me! . . .

IVAN: Be it so! Boris shall chinchanter of this to the common headsman hereafter! (*To Yakin.*) Wherefore didst thou besmirch this noblewoman's honor, thou stinkard?

YAKIN: Remarkable! Incredible! Sensational! . . . I don't recognize you in your make-up. Who are you? Let me introduce myself—Karp Yakin. Twenty thousand rubles, and tomorrow morning at nine you'll sign your contract with the studio. I'll be your producer. What's your name?

IVAN: Ha, thou baseborn churl! Putrid excrescence!

YAKIN: Bravo! Zinaida, how did you manage to hide him from me? (*Ivan strikes Yakin with his staff.*) Stop it! You gone nuts? . . . Lay off! . . .

IVAN: To thy knees, grubworm! (*Grabs Yakin by the beard.*)

YAKIN: This is going too far! This is gangsterism!

ZINAIDA: I must be losing my mind . . . Who are you? Who are you?

IVAN: Prince Timofeyev, come to my avail! We have captured the miscreant, the whoreson Yakin!

YAKIN: Help! . . . Citizens! . . . Somebody . . .

ZINAIDA: Help! Who is he? Burglars! A burglar in the apartment! (*Shpak appears in the hallway and hearkens to the screams.*)

ZINAIDA: Oh, no! My God, I just realized! This is the Tsar for real! Koka's experiment worked! (*To Ivan.*) I beseech you, let him go!

IVAN: (*Draws a dagger from beneath his caftan and shouts at Yakin.*) Say thy prayers, thou son of a stockfish! (*Shpak peeps in at the door.*) Life be it or death, supplicate the noblewoman!

YAKIN: (*Screams.*) Life . . .

IVAN: Pick thyself up, thou misbegotten cockatrice!

YAKIN: What's going on, I ask you? (*To Shpak.*) Citizen, save me from this thug!

SHPAK: Are you rehearsing, Zinaida Mikhailovna?

ZINAIDA: We . . . we're rehearsing . . .

YAKIN: What do you mean rehear . . . Citizen!

IVAN: How now? . . . Kiss the royal hand! Thou hast been taught to, varlet!

YAKIN: Kiss your hand? I don't wan . . . Right away, right away . . . (*He kisses Ivan's hand.*)

ZINAIDA: (*To Ivan.*) Prithee, be seated!

(*Ivan sits down.*)

SHPAK: Your acting's so lifelike! What an ideal Tsar! Looks like our Bunsha. Only Bunsha's got a dumber look on his face. I've been robbed, Zinaida Mikhailovna! (*He bursts into tears.*)

(*Yakin makes an attempt to skulk away.*)

IVAN: Whither away?

YAKIN: Nowhere, nowhere . . .

ZINAIDA: (*To Shpak.*) Wait, I don't understand. What do you mean, you were robbed?

SHPAK: Plain and simple, Zinaida Mikhailovna! Pardon me, citizens, but did anyone run into a blonde from the Bolshoi Theatre carrying bundles, on the stairs? She's the one that robbed me . . . That's the sort of building we live in, Zinaida Mikhailovna! . . .

IVAN: Art thou afflicted, goodman?

SHPAK: Citizen Actor, why shouldn't I be afflicted? . . .

IVAN: What hath been bereaved from thee?

SHPAK: A Victrola, a cigarette-case, a lighter, a watch, a lightweight overcoat, a suit, a hat . . . all the things I had earned through backbreaking labor, everything's gone! . . . (*He weeps.*)

IVAN: Whose art thou?

SHPAK: Excuse me, what do you mean "whose"? I don't get it.

IVAN: Whose vassal, say I?

ZINAIDA: Oh Lord, what's going to happen now! . . .

SHPAK: That's a mighty odd question! . . .

IVAN: (*Taking out coins.*) Accept these, thrall, and render praise unto the Tsar and Grand Duke Ivan Vasilievich! . . .

ZINAIDA: What are you doing? You mustn't!

SHPAK: Excuse me, what is all this—thrall, shmall! Am I supposed to be your serf? What kind of talk is this?

ZINAIDA: He's kidding!

SHPAK: Jokes like that can land you in a mess in the people's court. And I don't need your small change either. It's stage-money.

IVAN: Dost thou, double-dealing stinkard, spurn the tsar's largess?

ZINAIDA: They're lines from his part, his role . . .

SHPAK: It's a foulmouthed role and I request him not to practice it on me. Goodbye, Zinaida Mikhailovna, and I'm sorry I dropped by. Where's Ivan Vasilievich? I want him to testify to the ghastly burglary in my apartment . . . (*He exits.*)

ZINAIDA: Listen to me, Karp, only, I beg of you, keep calm. This is the real Ivan the Terrible . . . Stop blinking your eyes.

YAKIN: Zinaida, you live in a loony bin! . . .

ZINAIDA: No, it's Koka's doing. I told you about his machine . . . how he wants to explore the past—or is it the future? . . . He's the one who summoned the Tsar from the past.

YAKIN: You're raving!

ZINAIDA: I *am* teetering on the brink of insanity . . .

YAKIN: (*Staring at Ivan.*) Comrades, what's going on? . . . (*To Zinaida.*) What? What? Are you telling the truth?!

ZINAIDA: I swear!

YAKIN: Come on now! In the twentieth century, right in the middle of Moscow! . . . No, it's . . . After all, he's dead!

IVAN: Who's dead?

YAKIN: I . . . I wasn't talking about you . . . somebody else it was . . . who died . . . who . . . call me a doctor! . . . I must be losing my mind . . . Why, he might slit my throat, you know!

IVAN: Draw nigh! Draw nigh and make answer! How long art thou to . . .

YAKIN: Odds bodkins, I doth . . . Prithee, don't pull out thine knife! . . . I must be asleep . . . Zinaida, phone somebody, save me! . . . Why is he picking on me? Where's your husband? He should get rid of him!

IVAN: Hast thou debauched this noblewoman?

YAKIN: I . . . I . . . my life . . .

IVAN: Ugglesome cur! What life?! Cast thine eyes upon thyself! O, heinous mortal! The Archfiend hath schooled thee to be a luxurious slugabed, agape in thy dreaming, thy head aching from potations pottle-deep and sundry other villainies immeasurable and inscrutable!

YAKIN: I'm done for! Zinaida, prompt me with something in medieval! . . .

Your husband doesn't have the right to perform such experiments! (*To Ivan.*) Forsooth, forsooth . . . Sumer is icumen in! . . . Your Majesty, have mercy!

IVAN: Repent thee, thou lust-ridden, whoremongering wen!

ZINAIDA: Just don't kill him!

YAKIN: I repent! . . .

IVAN: Bow thy scabrous head and fall at the unblemished feet of the noblewoman thou hast defiled . . .

YAKIN: With pleasure! You didn't understand me! You didn't understand! . . .

IVAN: How am I to understand thee, when thou hast not uttered a word!

YAKIN: I'm no good at languages, your Majesty! . . . Am I asleep or awake? . . .

IVAN: What was this snubnosed wench in thy chamber?

YAKIN: She's a walk-on, I swear by the film studio! Zinaida Mikhailovna didn't understand!

IVAN: Art thou enamoured of the noblewoman?

YAKIN: I'm madly enamoured over her! . . .

IVAN: How can one fail to be enamoured of her? The noblewoman is of a comely mien and most exceeding fair, with vermeil lips, her brows conjoined, her flesh abundant . . . What more canst thou require, cur?!

YAKIN: Not a thing! . . . not a thing!

IVAN: Then wed her, carcass! Her Prince repudiates her.

YAKIN: I ask your hand in marriage, Zina!

ZINAIDA: You aren't going to pull one over on me this time, Karp! I've been double-crossed far too often . . .

YAKIN: I swear by the film studio!

IVAN: Swear by the most blessed Sergius of Radonezh!

YAKIN: I swear by Sergius of the most blessed Radonezh!

IVAN: Now hark thee, beard of offenses unnumbered! Were I to hear of thy recusancy . . . then should I take thee . . . and . . .

YAKIN: I swear by Sergius . . .

IVAN: Interrompt not the Tsar! For as much as thou hast no ancestral demesnes, I bestow upon thee a fief in Kostroma.

YAKIN: (*To Zinaida.*) Another minute here, and they can lock me up in the funny-farm! . . . Let's get out of here right now! . . . Anywhere else! . . . Take me away! . . .

ZINAIDA: Tsar dear, it's time for us to catch our train.

IVAN: Fare thee well at once!

ZINAIDA: (*To Ivan.*) Forgive me for disturbing you . . . I don't understand how Koka never thought of it . . . You can't possibly stay here looking like that . . . Somebody might see you . . .

IVAN: Oh Lord Almighty! . . . Verily I did lose remembrance of my plight

. . . I did forget! . . .

ZINAIDA: (*Picks up Miloslavsky's suit.*) Don't get angry. I advise you to change clothes. I don't know where these rags came from. Karp, give him a hand.

YAKIN: May I please help you? Be so kind as to go behind the screen.

IVAN: 'Sblood, demoniacal garb! . . . 'Swounds, lead me not into temptacioun! . . .

(*Ivan and Yakin go behind the screen.*)

ZINAIDA: Meanwhile I'll write a note to Nikolai Ivanovich. (*She writes.*)

YAKIN: (*Behind the screen.*) Haven't you got any suspenders?

IVAN: (*Behind the screen.*) Avaunt!

YAKIN: Anything you say, sir . . .

ZINAIDA: (*Reading.*) Koka! I came back, but I'm leaving again. He practically cut Yakin's throat, and Yakin proposed. Don't take me off the house register . . . Zina . . . (*Ivan comes out from behind the screen in Miloslavsky's clothes. He is depressed.*) Now that's a horse of a different color! Goodness, you look just like our Bunsha! All you need are the glasses . . .

YAKIN: Here are some glasses on the floor . . .

ZINAIDA: I really think you ought to wear glasses. (*She puts the eyeglasses on Ivan.*) The spittin' image . . .

IVAN: (*Having looked in the mirror, spits.*) Tfoo, thou semblance! . . .

ZINAIDA: Well, let us thank you . . . You're a very temperamental guy!

IVAN: Am I to remain here henceforth? 'Tis weary, Lord! . . . Whence procedeth that entrancing musicke of the dulcimer?

YAKIN: If you'll deign to look, it's the Victrola . . .

IVAN: We did not ask of thee.

YAKIN: I won't say a word . . . I obey . . .

ZINAIDA: Very simple—place the needle here and wind it up. (*The Victrola plays.*) You see . . . You sit back and it plays . . . But Koka will be back, he'll help you out.

YAKIN: What's going on? . . . My thoughts are all in a tangle . . . Victrola . . . Koka . . . Ivan the Terrible . . .

ZINAIDA: Will you stop acting so nervous! Big deal, it's Ivan, big deal, it's the Terrible! . . . Well, what's so special? . . . Goodbye now!

YAKIN: My respects!

IVAN: Are ye sallying far afield?

ZINAIDA: Goodness yes!

IVAN: (*To Yakin.*) I bestow on thee the cloak from the Tsar's own shoulders.

YAKIN: Whatever for?

ZINAIDA: Ah, don't contradict him!

YAKIN: All right, all right . . . (*He dons the cloak.*)

(*Zinaida picks up her suitcase and exits with Yakin.*)

ZINAIDA: When all's said and done, I'm very happy. Kiss me!

YAKIN: We're stark, staring, raving mad! I swear by Sergius of Radonezh! . . . (*He throws off the cloak and leaves with Zinaida.*)

(*Ivan is alone. He walks over to the Victrola, sets it going. He takes a drink of vodka. Shortly thereafter the phone rings. Ivan goes over to it, examines the receiver at length, then picks it up. Horror is depicted on his face.*)

IVAN: (*Into the receiver.*) Where art thou secreted? (*He peeps under the table, crosses himself.*)

ULYANA: (*In the hallway.*) Anybody home? Have you seen Ivan Vasilievich? (*She knocks on Timofeyev's door, then enters.*) There you are, for heaven's sake! The whole building is searching for him, the plumbers have come and gone . . . His wife stands on line in a shop like a soul in torment waiting to buy him herrings, while he sits in other people's rooms and gets drunk! . . . Well, what's the matter with you, cat got your tongue? Shpak's been robbed, Shpak's racing around the yard looking for you, and here you sit! Why don't you say something? Saints alive, where did he get those clothes? (*Ivan, turning his back on her, winds up the Victrola.*) Just what's going on here? Have you ever seen the like of this? He's out of his wits! Saints alive, there's a hole in the seat of his pants! . . . Have you been in a fight with somebody or what? Why are you turning your face away from me? No, just you show me your black-and-blue marks! (*Ivan turns around.*) Heavens to Betsy! . . . You look like nothing on this earth! Your face is all swole up from drink! A person couldn't recognize you!

IVAN: Get thee hence. Dost hark to me?

ULYANA: What do you mean, hence? Just take a look at yourself in the mirror! . . . Take a good, hard look!

IVAN: Get thee gone, old crone. I am in doleful distress . . .

ULYANA: Old crone! Where do you get the nerve to talk to me that way, you lout? I'm five years younger than you!

IVAN: Nay, there thou liest . . . Bespeak my futurity, beldame, foretell the outcome with the Swedes.

ULYANA: What's this all about?

(*Shpak appears in the hallway, then enters the room.*)

SHPAK: Where can he be? Ivan Vasilievich, what kind of a building superintendent are you? Come and see how my room's been burgled!

ULYANA: No, just you feast your eyes on this lover-boy! . . . He's so drunk he can't even stand up straight!

SHPAK: What a superintendent! A person is robbed blind, while he drinks zubrovka! . . . I've been robbed by an actress! . . .

IVAN: Art thou here again? Thou art a pest!

SHPAK: What sort of language is that—a pest? This kind of building superintendent we don't need! . . .

ULYANA: Get a hold of yourself, you roughneck! You'll get fired from your job!

IVAN: By my halidom, thou witch! (*He snatches the herrings from Ulyana and flings them into the hallway.*)

ULYANA: Hooligan!

IVAN: (*Arming himself with his staff.*) 'Sblood, now shall I drum learning into thee!

ULYANA: Help! . . . A man is beating his wife, an educated woman! . . . (*She runs out through the front door.*)

(*Shpak is astounded.*)

SHPAK: Ivan Vasilievich, calm down . . . when a high-strung husband takes to drink . . . I fully understand . . . And yet I didn't realize you were that sort! . . . I thought you were henpecked . . . to tell the truth, that you were under her thumb . . . but you're a champion! . . .

IVAN: The witch! . . .

SHPAK: Quite frankly, yes, she is. You're right. In fact it's a good thing you set her straight . . . You should be stricter with her . . . I have to see you on business, Ivan Vasilievich.

IVAN: What dost thou require?

SHPAK: Here's a list of the stolen articles, respected Comrade Bunsha . . . I request that you attest it . . . I had stolen from me two suits, two overcoats, two watches, two cigarette-cases, herein recorded . . . (*He hands over the sheet of paper.*)

IVAN: Wherefore dost thou dare petition thy Tsar? (*He tears up the paper.*)

SHPAK: Ivan Vasilievich . . . you're under the influence, I understand . . . just stop acting like a hooligan . . .

IVAN: Thou gratest me! What was purloined from thee, speak!

SHPAK: Two Vict . . . I mean, one Victrola . . .

IVAN: 'Tis well, accept this Victrola. And be hanged to thee. Thou art a pest.

SHPAK: Excuse me, but how . . . of course this is somebody else's . . . exactly like mine . . . Well, anyway, thanks! . . . But what about the rest? I really ought to have your signature for it . . .

IVAN: Have I not bestowed gold-pieces upon thee? And thou didst not take them? Lackwit! . . .

SHPAK: That's the drink talking! What gold-pieces? You never gave me any money. Get a hold of yourself, Ivan Vasilievich . . . The collective is going to register a complaint about you!

IVAN: Eh, forsooth, thou art not steeped in wisdom, I perceive . . . Mayhap cacodaemons be rioting within thee? . . . (*He draws his knife.*)

SHPAK: Help! . . . The building superintendent is stabbing a tenant! . . .

(*Timofeyev runs into the hallway, then into the room.*)

TIMOFEYEV: What's happening? Where is he? Who dressed you up like that? Why did you let him in? . . . Didn't I tell you not to open the door! . . .

SHPAK: Take a good look at our building superintendent, Nikolai Ivanovich! . . . Help! . . . I'm going to the police! . . .

TIMOFEYEV: (*To Ivan.*) Stop it, or we'll both be goners!

(*Ivan puts the knife away.*)

SHPAK: (*Rushing into the hallway.*) I'm heading straight for the police! . . .

IVAN: Prince! . . . Thou shouldst scourge him along the way step by step!

TIMOFEYEV: (*Rushes after Shpak into the hallway.*) Please, wait up! . . . He isn't Bunsha! . . .

SHPAK: What do you mean, he's not Bunsha?

TIMOFEYEV: He's Ivan the Terrible . . . the bona fide Tsar . . . Wait a minute, hold on . . . I'm sane . . . I beg you, don't go off to the police! . . . It's my experiment, my time machine! . . . I summoned him . . . I'm letting you into a secret, because you're an honest man! . . . Don't destroy my experiment! A scandal would ruin everything! . . . I'll send him away right now . . . I'll just slip in the key . . . here's the key . . . Promise you won't say a word? Give me your word of honor!

SHPAK: Let me get this straight—so that is the Tsar?

TIMOFEYEV: The Tsar.

SHPAK: What's going on! . . .

TIMOFEYEV: Be quiet, I'll explain everything later, later . . . Give me your word that you won't tell a soul . . .

SHPAK: On my word, honor-bright.

TIMOFEYEV: Thanks, thanks. (*He runs into his own room. To Ivan.*) Why did you open the door? I asked you not to open it!

(*Shpak kneels down to peek through the keyhole.*)

IVAN: Wherefore didst thou not smite him in his ugsome mug?

TIMOFEYEV: What's the matter with you, Ivan Vasilievich? You mustn't go around hitting people in the mug, for God's sake! . . . Simmer down, simmer down! . . . Here's the key. Now let's try it out. (*He tries to insert the key.*) My hands are shaking . . . Damn, it's a bit too big . . . Well, never mind, it's all right. We can file it down in no time . . .

(*He pushes a button on the machine. Timofeyev's room dims out. Shpak's room lights up.*

Shpak closes the door behind him.)

SHPAK: Maybe the coins were real! . . . Oh dear, oh dear, oh dear! . . . (*He speaks into the telephone receiver.*) Police. Police? This is the man who was robbed today—I'm Shpak . . . No, don't get angry, I'm not on about the theft. There's something else going on here, something much juicier . . . Engineer Timofeyev has summoned Ivan the Terrible to his apartment, you know, the Tsar . . . I am not drinking . . . With his royal staff . . . The things that are going on! I give you my word of honor! Wait, I'll come right on over myself, I'll be right over! . . .

(*Blackout.*)

CURTAIN

ACT III

Ringing. Blackout. Ivan's throne-room lights up. Bunsha and Miloslavsky are propelled into the room.

MILOSLAVSKY: Damn you and your experiments! Talk about a mess!

BUNSHA: (*Hugging the wall.*) Comrade Timofeyev! Comrade Timofeyev! In my capacity as building superintendent, I demand an immediate halt to these experiments! Help! Where can we be?

MILOSLAVSKY: Stop yelling! We've been taken back to Ivan the Terrible's court.

BUNSHA: That's impossible! I protest!

(*Ominous noise and alarum.*)

MILOSLAVSKY: (*Locks the door with a key, looks out the window, for the noise grows louder outside. He jumps back.*) Looks like curtains for us!

BUNSHA: It only seems that way to us, but none of this actually exists. Nikolai Ivanovich, you'll pay for your anti-Soviet experiments!

MILOSLAVSKY: Don't be a jerk! Listen to the way they're shouting!

BUNSHA: They can't be shouting, because they're an optical and auditory figment, not unlike psychic manifestations. They died a long time ago. I appeal to you to keep calm! They're deceased.

(*An arrow flies through the window.*)

MILOSLAVSKY: You notice how the deceased are firing arrows?!

BUNSHA: I mean . . . excuse me . . . you don't think they might offer us a show of violence?

MILOSLAVSKY: No, I don't think so. I do think they'll bloody murder us. Listen, pals, why should you do this to us, huh? Pals! . . .

BUNSHA: This can't really be happening! Nikolai Ivanovich, call the police! The emergency number! To be cut down in the flower of one's prime! . . . Ulyana Andreyevna must be terrified! . . . I didn't tell her where I was going . . . the blood freezes in my veins! . . . (*Pounding on the door. A voice: "Open up, cur!"*) Who's he referring to?

MILOSLAVSKY: You.

BUNSHA: (*Through a chink in the door.*) I must request you not to use insults. I am not a cur! Bear in mind that you do not exist! This is an experiment of Engineer Timofeyev's! (*Clamor.*) In the name of the tenants of this building, I should like to ask—save me!

(*Miloslavsky opens the door to the next chamber.*)

MILOSLAVSKY: Clothing! The Tsar's wardrobe! Hurray, we've got it made! (*A voice: "Open yon portal, or we put the palace to the torch!" Putting on a caftan.*) Hurry up and put on the Tsar's bathrobe, or else we're dead ducks!

BUNSHA: This experiment has gone far enough!

MILOSLAVSKY: Get dressed or I'll beat your brains out!. . . (*Bunsha puts on the royal robes.*) Hurray! What a resemblance! Oops, there goes the resemblance! The profile spoils it . . . Put on the crown . . . You're going to be the Tsar . . .

BUNSHA: Not in a million years!

MILOSLAVSKY: I suppose you want me to get bumped off on your account? Sit on that throne, pick up that scepter . . . Hold on, I'll wrap this hanky round your jaw, otherwise you won't look like him . . . Ugh, what a dope! It'll never work! The other one had an intelligent face . . .

BUNSHA: I request you to leave my face out of this!

MILOSLAVSKY: Shut up! Sit down, start getting busy with affairs of State. Why have they stopped? The Tsar and Grand Duke . . . repeat after me . . . of all the Russias . . .

BUNSHA: The Tsar and Grand Duke of all the Russias . . .

(*The door is broken down, the Guardsmen rush in, accompanied by the Scribe. They stop, dumbfounded.*)

MILOSLAVSKY: (*To Bunsha.*) What were you saying . . . Tsar and Grand Duke? I've got that. Comma . . . Where did that secretary of ours get to? (*Pause.*) What's up, comrades? I'm asking you, sweethearts, what's up? What parasite dared break down the door to the royal suite? You think it was set up just so you could break it down? (*To Bunsha.*) Proceed, your Majesty . . . Maketh obeisance . . . semi-colon . . . (*To the Guardsmen.*) I'm waiting for an answer to my question.

GUARDSMEN: (*In confusion.*) The Tsar is here present . . . the Tsar is here present . . .

SCRIBE: Here present is the Tsar . . .

MILOSLAVSKY: And where else should he be? What are you carrying weapons for, my darlings? . . . I don't like it.

(*The Guardsmen drop their halberds.*)

SCRIBE: (*To Bunsha.*) Deign not to behead us, gracious my lord . . . Thou wert besieged by cacodaemons, and we sped to thy relief . . . We no sooner force entry, when the cacodaemons flee!

MILOSLAVSKY: There were a few demons, I won't deny it, but they were liquidated. So please call off this silly alarm. (*To the Scribe.*) Just who are you?

SCRIBE: Fedka . . . scribe of the ambassadorial chancellery . . . we engross at the Tsar's behest . . .

MILOSLAVSKY: Come over here. But I'd like the rest of you to clear out of the Tsar's quarters. To make a long story short, everybody out! Look at that, you scared the Tsar! Out! (*To Bunsha, in a whisper.*) Yell at them, or else they won't obey.

BUNSHA: Out!

(*The Guardsmen fall at his feet, then rush out. The Scribe prostrates himself at his feet several times.*)

MILOSLAVSKY: That'll do, that's enough somersaults. Flop once or twice, that's plenty.

SCRIBE: Gaze not upon me, like the wolf upon the lamb . . . Thou art choleric in thine ire against me, gracious my lord! . . .

MILOSLAVSKY: I should think so. But we'll forgive you.

SCRIBE: Wherefore, sire, hast thou thy jawbone enswathed? Hast an ailment befallen thee?

MILOSLAVSKY: (*In an undertone, to Bunsha.*) Don't shut up like a clam, will you! I can't manage this by myself.

BUNSHA: My teeth ache, I've got a painful inflammation of the gums.

MILOSLAVSKY: He's having root-canal work done, don't pester the Tsar.

SCRIBE: I hear and obey. (*Falls at his feet.*)

MILOSLAVSKY: Fedya, cut out the tumbling . . . At this rate you'll be at your acrobatics till tomorrow . . . Let's get acquainted. Why are you staring at my face?

SCRIBE: Wax not wroth, my lord, albeit I know thee not . . . Art thou a

Prince?

MILOSLAVSKY: It so happens I am a prince, yeah. What's amazing about that?

SCRIBE: Whence and in what wise didst thou enter the Tsar's abode? In sooth thou wast not here erewhile? (*To Bunsha.*) Our father the Tsar, what may he be? Torment me not!

BUNSHA: He is a close friend of Anton Semyonovich Shpak.

MILOSLAVSKY: (*In an undertone.*) Oh, you idiot! He takes the cake, even for a building superintendent! . . . (*Aloud.*) Well, yes, in other words, I am Prince Miloslavsky. You satisfied now?

SCRIBE: (*Dropping down in fear.*) Smite me not! Begone! . . .

MILOSLAVSKY: What is it now? Not again for God's sake? What's the matter?

SCRIBE: Verily, thou wert put to death two days afore . . .

MILOSLAVSKY: It's news to me! Cut the bull, how was I put to death?

BUNSHA: (*In an undertone.*) Oh dear, now it's starting! . . .

SCRIBE: Thou wert swinged and gibbeted on thine own portals, before the bedchamber, at the Tsar's bidding.

MILOSLAVSKY: Ah, thank you! (*To Bunsha.*) The name caused this mix-up . . . he says I was hanged . . . Get me out of this or else we've had it. (*In an undertone.*) Why don't you say anything, you louse? (*Aloud.*) Hey, I remember! You see, it wasn't me they hung! What was the hanged man's name?

SCRIBE: Vanka the Brigand.

MILOSLAVSKY: Aha! Whereas I, on the other hand, am called Georges. And this bandit was my first cousin. But I've disowned him. On the contrary, I'm the Tsar's favorite and right hand man. What have you got to say to that?

SCRIBE: Be it so! Belike I do perceive a semblance, but 'tis not proximate. And whence hast thou made thy way here?

MILOSLAVSKY: Hey, Fedya Scribe, you're awfully nosy! You should be working in the Criminal Investigation Department! I turned up on the spur of the moment, on a surprise visit, just when you started that goose-chase with the demons . . . Well, as you can imagine, I rushed into the throne-room to protect the Tsar, and safeguard his royal person from them.

SCRIBE: Hail to thee, Prince!

MILOSLAVSKY: And now everything's under control! (*Offstage noise.*) What are they clamoring about this time? Run over there, Fedyusha, and find out.

(*Scribe runs out.*)

BUNSHA: My God, where am I? What am I? Who am I? Nikolai Ivanovich!

MILOSLAVSKY: Can the hysterics!

(*The Scribe returns.*)

SCRIBE: The guardsmen wish to behold the rescued Tsar. They do rejoice.

MILOSLAVSKY: Oh no. Let's skip it. No time. No time. The rejoicings are postponed. (*To Bunsha.*) We've got to send them somewhere right away. He can't say a word, damn him! (*Aloud.*) Listen, Fedinka, have we got any war going on at the moment?

SCRIBE: Wherefore could it be otherwise, bounteous lord? Both the Cham of Crim Tartary and the Swedes do pillage and despoil us! The Cham of Crim Tartary maraudeth swingeingly on the Izyum Road!

MILOSLAVSKY: What's that you say? Why did you allow this to happen, eh? (*The Scribe falls at his feet.*) Get up, Fyodor, I'm not blaming you. Here, this is what we'll do . . . sit down and draw up a royal proclamation. Write. Let the guardsmen be sent to beat the Crim Tartary Cham off the Izyum Road. Put a period after it.

SCRIBE: Period. (*To Bunsha.*) Prithee affix thy hand and seal, great sovereign.

BUNSHA: (*In a whisper.*) In my capacity as building superintendent I haven't got the right to sign such papers.

MILOSLAVSKY: Write. Did you sign it, dumbbell? As building superintendent? And did you affix the seal of the cooperative apartment-house? What a winner! Write: Ivan the Terrible. (*To the Scribe.*) There.

SCRIBE: I cannot descry this word . . .

MILOSLAVSKY: Which word? Why, T . . . E . . . Terrible.

SCRIBE: Terrible?

MILOSLAVSKY: Why are you harping on every word, Fedka? Isn't he terrible, in your opinion? Not terrible? Go ahead and yell at him once and for all, great sovereign, stamp on him with your feet! Why doesn't he obey you?

BUNSHA: How dare you?! Listen, you! . . . I'll get you! . . .

SCRIBE: (*Dropping at his feet.*) Now I wot thee well! Thou art our father the Tsar, I ween . . .

MILOSLAVSKY: Well, that's better. Just you tell them that they shouldn't hurry back any too quickly. What more instructions do they need? Let them sing the joy of battle . . . deeds of olden times . . . the taking of Kazan . . . That reminds me: tell them that on the way back they should take Kazan, while they're at it . . . save making two trips . . .

SCRIBE: What dost thou purpose, sire . . . may it not enrage thee . . . verily Kazan is ours . . . forsooth we captured it eftsoons, long ago.

MILOSLAVSKY: Ah . . . That was very zealous of you . . . Well, since it's already captured, be sure it stays that way. Don't give it back. Well, go ahead and see that none of them are on the premises within five minutes. (*The Scribe runs out.*) Well, that's taken care of, more or less. What'll happen next though, I don't know. Why doesn't he use the machine to send us back?

BUNSHA: I've got to reveal a horrible secret to you. In my panic I made off with his key. Here it is.

MILOSLAVSKY: I hope you croak, damn you! This is all your fault, you moron! What are we going to do now? Well, all right, quiet, here comes the scribe.

SCRIBE: (*Enters.*) They have sallied forth, great sovereign.

MILOSLAVSKY: I'll bet they were surprised. Well, fine and dandy. What's next on the agenda?

SCRIBE: The Swedish ambassador craves audience.

MILOSLAVSKY: Show him in.

(*The Scribe shows in the Swedish Ambassador, who stares at Bunsha and gives a start. Then he begins a series of elaborate bows.*)

AMBASSADOR: Most potent, grave and reverend seignor . . . (*He bows. Bunsha shakes the Ambassador's hand. The Ambassador, in amazement, bows again.*) Der grosse Koenig des schwedischen Koenigsreich sandte mich, seinen treuen Diener, zu Ihnen, Tsar und Krandt Dook Ivan Vazilovich ov all der Roosias, damit die Frage von der shire ov Kem, die die rumvollwuerdige schwedische Armee erobert hat, freiwillig in Ordnung bringen . . .

MILOSLAVSKY: Yeah, yeah . . . this tourist is quite a talker . . . if only I could understand a word! We need an interpreter, Fedinka!

SCRIBE: We had an Allmand expositor, but we did boil him in a cauldron erewhiles.

MILOSLAVSKY: Fedya, this is an outrage! That's no way to treat interpreters! (*To Bunsha.*) Give him some kind of reply . . . can't you see the guy's all worn out.

BUNSHA: The only foreign words I know are revolutionary slogans, I've forgotten all the rest.

MILOSLAVSKY: Well then, why don't you say something revolutionary, instead of this dummy act . . . Looks like a fish on the throne! (*To the Ambassador.*) Go ahead, I agree with you one hundred percent.

AMBASSADOR: Die Frage von der shire ov Kem . . . Schwedische Armee hat sie erobert . . . Der grosser Koenig des schwedischen Koenigrsreich sandte mich . . . und . . . Das ist sehr ernste Fràge . . . Shire ov Kem . . .

SCRIBE: Sire, he speketh High Dutch. 'Tis no great matter to divine his purport. They do lay claim to the shire of Kem. They shall wage war, quoth he, lest that we do grant it them anon, quoth he! . . .

MILOSLAVSKY: Then why didn't he say so? The shire of Kem?

AMBASSADOR: Ach ja . . . ach ja . . .

MILOSLAVSKY: Is that all the conversation's about? Well, let 'em have it and keep it in good health! . . . I thought it was God knows what! . . .

SCRIBE: How then shall I make answer, bounteous lord?

MILOSLAVSKY: Who needs it? (*To the Ambassador.*) Take it, take it, the Tsar consents. Gut.

SCRIBE: O Lord Jesus!

AMBASSADOR: (*Delighted, bows.*) Kann ich mich frei zaehlen und in mein Vaterland zurueckkehren?

SCRIBE: He asketh, might he wend homewards?

MILOSLAVSKY: Why, of course! Let him leave this very day. (*To them, Ambassador.*) Au revoir.

AMBASSADOR: (*Bows.*) Was befehlt Tsar und Krandt Dook Ivan Vazilovich den grossen Koenig des Schwedens hinterbringen?

SCRIBE: He asketh, what is he to present to the King?

MILOSLAVSKY: My sincerest good wishes.

BUNSHA: I don't go along with sending a king sincere good wishes. The tenants' council would hound me to death.

MILOSLAVSKY: Shut up, you troublemaker. (*He embraces the Ambassador, and the bejewelled medallion disappears from the Ambassador's chest.*) Auf wiedersehen. My respects to the King and tell him not to send us anyone for a while. We don't need any. Nichts. (*The Ambassador, bowing, exits, followed by the Scribe.*) A nice guy. Plenty of foreign currency in his pockets, I'll bet! . . .

BUNSHA: I'm succumbing beneath the weight of all the major state offences we're committing. Oh, my God! What's poor Ulyana Andreyevna doing now? She's probably at the police station. She's weeping and moaning, while I have to reign as tsar against my will . . . How can I show my face at our next general assembly?

(*The Scribe enters and starts looking for something on the floor.*)

MILOSLAVSKY: Why are you crawling around, old boy?

SCRIBE: Deign not to behead me, sire . . . The Ambassador hath been bereaved of the royal effigy from off his bosom . . . 'twas inset with graven adamants.

MILOSLAVSKY: He shouldn't be so absent-minded.

SCRIBE: When that he came in, 'twas there. When that he went out, 'twas not . . .

MILOSLAVSKY: The same old story. In theatres it never happens anywhere but in the lobby. You ought to keep an eye on your belongings when you come into a room. Just why are you staring at me that way? I hope you don't think I took it?

SCRIBE: Say not so, say not so!

MILOSLAVSKY: (*To Bunsha.*) Did you steal it?

BUNSHA: Maybe it fell behind the throne. (*He looks.*)

MILOSLAVSKY: No, not there! Take a look under the table. Not there either.

SCRIBE: I shall run mad . . . Lackaday! (*He exits.*)

BUNSHA: These incidents keep getting more and more frightening. What I wouldn't give now to be myself again and make an official statement of what happened to me. There'd be dancing in the streets!

SCRIBE: (*Enters.*) The Patriarch craves audience, sire. He rejoiceth.

BUNSHA: Things are going from bad to worse.

MILOSLAVSKY: Tell him that we request his presence on the double.

BUNSHA: What are you doing? I can't be in the same room as an exponent of organized superstition and bigotry. I'm ruined.

(*A bell chimes. The Patriarch enters.*)

PATRIARCH: Peace be upon thee, Sire, within the year at hand and for the years to come! Brethren, let us sound the golden trumpets! Tsar and Grand Duke, may thy beauteous countenance forever shine upon us! Tsar, in the clutches of cacodaemons though thou wert, thou hast been restored to us. The Lord hath bestowed upon thee the might of Samson, the valor of Alexander, the wisdom of Solomon and the meekness of David! May all the nations and all men that draw breath praise thee now and forever and till the end of time!

MILOSLAVSKY: (*Applauding.*) Bravo! Amen! It's not in my power to add anything to your brilliant speech except the word—amen! (*A choir begins to sing "Long Life to the Tsar." Miloslavsky joins in, singing something rollicking and contemporary. To Bunsha.*) You see the way they're welcoming you! And you were snivelling! . . . (*To the Patriarch.*) Verily he has arisen, Father! Happy Easter! (*He embraces the Patriarch, in such a way that the bejewelled cross disappears from the Patriarch's chest.*) Thank you once again, Father, on behalf of the Tsar, and thank you for myself as well. You may return to the Cathedral and to your patron saints. You are absolutely, positively free, and we can do without the choir too. If anything urgent turns up, we'll let you know. Don't call us, we'll call you. (*He accompanies him as far as the door, saluting. The Patriarch and the Scribe leave. The Scribe immediately runs back in, in agitation.*) What's going on now?

SCRIBE: Utter sacrilege! The Cross from off the Patriarch's bosom . . .

MILOSLAVSKY: Don't tell me somebody pinched it?

SCRIBE: Pinched it is!

MILOSLAVSKY: Well, that's downright mystical! But what's eating you, hmmm?

SCRIBE: The Cross was of gold in its four ingles, with precious lapis lazuli, two emeralds . . .

MILOSLAVSKY: This is disgraceful!

SCRIBE: What art thy commands, Prince? We gibbet malefactors and hang them by their ribs, yet natheless cannot be rid of them all.

MILOSLAVSKY: Well, why hang 'em by the ribs? I tell you straight out I'm against it. This is typical deviationism. If you want to know, Fedya, you've got to treat thieves more gently. You go to the Patriarch and be a bit more delicate with him . . . buck him up . . . Tell me, was he very upset?

SCRIBE: He budgeth not, like Patience sitting on a monument.

MILOSLAVSKY: Well, that's understandable. This sort of thing can cause serious shock. I should know: in a theatre once I happened to see . . .

(*The Scribe runs out.*)

BUNSHA: Sinister suspicions are starting to gnaw at me. Shpak's suit, the Ambassador's medallion, the Patriarch's cross . . .

MILOSLAVSKY: What are you driving at? I don't know about other people, but I am personally incapable of stealing. It's the way my hands were constructed . . . they're abnormal. Prints of my fingers were taken in five different cities . . . by scientists, that is . . . and all the authorities unanimously conclude that a man with such fingers cannot misappropriate other people's goods. I even took to wearing gloves, I got so fed up with it.

SCRIBE: (*Enters.*) The Tartar prince Yedigey craves audience with the sovereign.

MILOSLAVSKY: Huh, no! I'm not up to it. I hereby proclaim a lunch break.

SCRIBE: The Tsar desireth to gormandize.

(*Immediately Servitors bring in food. They are followed by Dulcimer Players.*)

BUNSHA: This must be a dream! . . .

MILOSLAVSKY: (*To Scribe.*) What's that stuff?

SCRIBE: Hares' kidneys roasted on a spit and pikes' heads with garlic . . . Caviar, sire. Anise vodka, thy privy distillation, and cardamom vodka, as thou doth savor it.

MILOSLAVSKY: Beautiful! . . . Tsar, put on the feedbag, start in on the hot hors-d'oeuvres! . . . (*He drinks.*) "Stand by me, my lordings, guardsmen mine! . . ."

(*Bunsha drinks.*)

SCRIBE: The guardsmen have all been posted hence, beneficent Prince!

MILOSLAVSKY: And it was a good thing we sent them away, let 'em go to blazes! It turns my stomach just to think about 'em. That habit of theirs of hacking and chopping, at the drop of a hat! Those pole-axes . . . They're gangsters, Fedya. Excuse my outspokenness, your Majesty, but your guardsmen are nothing but gangsters! Votre santé!

BUNSHA: All the same my nerves have calmed down a bit under the influence of spiritous beverages.

MILOSLAVSKY: There, you see. But, Fedya, why are you planted there next to the kidneys? Have a drink, Fedyunya, don't stand on ceremony. We're informal. I'm really very fond of you. I confess, losing you would be like losing my right arm. Let's the two of us drink Bruderschaft. Let's be friends, I'll show you how to break into the theatre . . . Yes, your Majesty, we'll have to build a theatre.

BUNSHA: I've already mapped out a few projects. I've decided it would be better to start with cooperative apartment houses.

MILOSLAVSKY: Don't order me put to death, your Majesty, but in my opinion, a theatre is more important. I can just picture the way they're fighting on the Izyum Road right now! What do you think, Fedya? Listen, have they got any rubies for sale around here?

SCRIBE: Great Sovereign, the Tsaritsa craves audience.

BUNSHA: Now we're in for it! Somehow I didn't foresee this. I'm afraid there's going to be a falling-out with Ulyana Andreyevna. In our private conversations, she always takes a negative viewpoint on this topic. And yet, to hell with her! What am I afraid of her for anyway?

MILOSLAVSKY: Quite right. (*Bunsha takes the handkerchief off his jaw.*) There's no point in taking off your headband. To tell the truth, you don't have much of a royal expression.

BUNSHA: Is that so? I beg your pardon! Whom are you addressing?

MILOSLAVSKY: Attaboy! Why didn't you talk like that from the start!

(*The Tsaritsa appears and Bunsha puts on his pince-nez.*)

TSARITSA: (*Astonished.*) Sublime sovereign, my lord and master! Vouchsafe thy handmaiden leave, assuaged by thy graciousness . . .

BUNSHA: Glad to. (*He kisses the Tsaritsa's hand.*) Very happy to make your acquaintance. Allow me to introduce—the scribe and Citizen Miloslavsky. Please sit at our table.

MILOSLAVSKY: Stop clowning around! Take off your pince-nez, you creep.

BUNSHA: Tut-tut-tut! Waiter! How about a kidney for the Tsaritsa—just one! Excuse me, isn't your name Julia Vladimirovna?

TSARITSA: I am yclept Marfa Vasilievna . . .

BUNSHA: Wonderful, wonderful!

MILOSLAVSKY: Now he's on the loose! Eh-heh-heh! I'm keeping an eye on you, you playboy! That's what the mild-mannered types are like!

BUNSHA: A little glass of cardamom vodka, Marfa Vasilievna.

TSARITSA: (*Giggling.*) Go to, go to . . .

BUNSHA: We were just discussing an interesting topic. A question of cooperative apartment-houses . . .

TSARITSA: Thou art ever swinking and sweating, forever at thy travail, great sovereign, like unto the toilsome bee!

BUNSHA: Another glass, to wash down the pike's head.

TSARITSA: Marry, go to, I say . . .

BUNSHA: (*To the Scribe.*) What are you looking at me that way for? I know what's on your mind! You're wondering whether I'm the son of some coachman or somebody of that sort? Admit it! (*The Scribe falls at his feet.*) No, go on and admit it, you scoundrel . . . What's a coachman's son got to do with anything? That was sly of me. (*To the Tsaritsa.*) That's how I tricked them, esteemed Marfa Vasilievna. What? Keep still! (*To the Scribe.*) Tell me please, have you got a private dining-room here?

MILOSLAVSKY: I'll be doggone! Is he loaded! He hasn't been wasting his time! I'd better save the situation. (*To the Dulcimer Players.*) Why aren't you making any music, citizens? Strum us something.

(*The Dulcimer Players begin playing and singing.*)

DULCIMER PLAYERS: (*Sing.*) Yea, the mighty storm-wrack rears its head . . . Yea, the mighty thunderclap doth rumble . . . Whither wends that cur the Tsar of Crim Tartary . . .

BUNSHA: What cur is that? I won't allow such songs to be sung in the Tsar's presence! He may be a Crim Tartar, but he's no cur! (*To the Scribe.*) Are you responsible for these musicians? You've been taking over since I left?

(*The Scribe falls at his feet.*)

MILOSLAVSKY: Hey, Fedyusha, have you got any soda water?

BUNSHA: Have them play a rumba!

DULCIMER PLAYERS: Deign to tell us, sire, what it is . . . and we shall strive . . . we shall anon . . .

(*Bunsha hums a modern dance-tune. The Dulcimer Players vamp it.*)

BUNSHA: (*To the Tsaritsa.*) May I have this dance, Julia Vasilievna?

TSARITSA: Marry come up, thou shameless one! Wherefore dost thou so, our father the Tsar . . .

BUNSHA: Never you mind, never you mind. (*He dances with the Tsaritsa.*)

(*The Scribe tears out his hair.*)

MILOSLAVSKY: Never mind, Fedya, don't get all upset. The Tsar overindulged, so what . . . who doesn't! Join in! (*He dances with the Scribe. Tumult and clamor. The Dulcimer Players fall silent.*) I don't like this, now what's the matter? (*The Scribe runs out, then returns.*)

SCRIBE: Misery, misery! The guardsmen have risen in contumacious mutiny, they approach! They cry that the Tsar is not the veritable one. A pretender, quoth they!

TSARITSA: Woe is me, alack the day! I did tread a measure with the spurious one . . . Misery me, I must perforce get me to a nunnery and take the veil! . . . Alas, 'tis my ruination! . . . (*She runs out.*)

MILOSLAVSKY: What do you mean, the guardsmen? They're on their way to Izyum Road!

SCRIBE: They failed to reach it, good my lord. They were confounded and turned back from the gates.

MILOSLAVSKY: What skunk spread this slanderous rumor?

SCRIBE: The Patriarch, my lord, the Patriarch.

MILOSLAVSKY: Autocrat dear, we're done for!

BUNSHA: I demand that the dancing continue! What do you mean, done for? Citizens, what's going on? (*The Dulcimer Players disappear together with the Scribe.*) Nikolai Ivanovich, save me! (*The clamor draws nearer. Ringing. Blackout. Lights. The wall vanishes and Timofeyev's room appears next to the throne-room.*)

TIMOFEYEV: Hurry, Ivan Vasilievich!

IVAN: (*Fastening on the royal garments.*) Glory be unto thee, O Lord!

TIMOFEYEV: Here they are, alive!

MILOSLAVSKY: Alive, alive! (*To Bunsha.*) Move, move, move! (*He and Bunsha run into Timofeyev's room.*)

IVAN: (*At the sight of Bunsha.*) 'Sblood, begone, avaunt! Get thee behind me!

MILOSLAVSKY: Just a minute, just a minute, dad, don't get in a fret! (*Ivan runs into the throne-room.*) Ivan Vasilievich! Keep in mind we gave the shire of Kem to the Swedes! So that's all under control.

IVAN: Kem!—to the Swedes? How did ye dare, ye sons of stockfish? (*Guardsmen and the Scribe rush into the throne-room.*) Kem!—to the Swedes? And thou, thou caitiff scribe, where wast thy tongue?

(*The Scribe falls at his feet. Ivan in a rage flings the Scribe at the invention. The Scribe jumps up and immediately runs into the throne-room. Blackout. Lights. No throne-room.*)

TIMOFEYEV: My invention! My invention! It's smashed! Why did you do that? Why did you get him angry? . . . My invention is destroyed!

(*Shpak and a couple of Policemen appear in the hallway.*)

SHPAK: There they are, Comrade Officers, take a look!

TIMOFEYEV: Oh it's you, you bastard!

POLICE: Aha! . . . (*To Bunsha.*) Are you the one that's the Tsar? Your identification papers, citizen!

BUNSHA: I admit I was the Tsar, but under the influence of Engineer

Timofeyev's infamous experiment.

MILOSLAVSKY: Why do you listen to him, comrades? We're coming from a masquerade party, we've been to the Cultural Amusement Park. (*He takes off his boyar's garb.*)

(*Bunsha removes his royal garments. On Miloslavsky's chest are the medallion and the cross.*)

BUNSHA: My suspicions were correct! He robbed the Patriarch and the Swedish Ambassador!

SHPAK: Arrest him! That's my suit!

POLICE: Are you trying to confuse the police, citizens? Are they thieves?

SHPAK: Thieves, thieves! They go around stealing and passing themselves off as tsars!

(*Ulyana Andreyevna appears.*)

ULYANA: That's where he is! What's this, you've been arrested? Now you've really done it, you drunken bum!

BUNSHA: Ulyana Andreyevna! I'll make a clean breast of it. I confess that I was reigning as tsar, but I didn't cheat on you, dear Ulyana Andreyevna! They tempted me with a Tsaritsa, the scribe is my witness!

ULYANA: What scribe? What are you babbling about, you alcoholic? He's some tsar all right, comrade officers! He's the building superintendent!

TIMOFEYEV: Shut up everybody! Shut up, the lot of you! My invention, my machine is destroyed! While you go on about all these trifles . . . Yes, I did it! I performed the experiment, but disaster dogged me every step of the way . . . this nitwit superintendent had to show up and carry off the key! The old nincompoop, the clown prince . . . and then he has to go and make Ivan the Terrible lose his temper! And now there's nothing left of my machine! While you talk about twaddle!

POLICE: Have you finished, citizen?

TIMOFEYEV: I've finished.

POLICE: (*To Miloslavsky.*) How about your identification?

MILOSLAVSKY: Why, what identification? What's this about identification? I'm Miloslavsky—Georges Miloslavsky.

POLICE: (*Delighted.*) Ah! So you're back in Moscow, are you?

MILOSLAVSKY: I won't conceal the fact. I came back too soon.

POLICE: Well sir, everybody to the stationhouse, if you don't mind.

BUNSHA: With feelings of enthusiasm I hand myself over to our beloved police, in whom I place my hope and trust.

MILOSLAVSKY: Now, now, Kolya, my academician! Stop crying! Obviously, such is fate! But as for the cross, comrades, believe it or not, but the

Patriarch gave it to me.

(*The Police lead everyone out of the apartment. At that very moment, the lights go out in Timofeyev's room. A cheery voice on the radio in the hallway announces: "You are listening to Part Two of Rimsky-Korsakov's opera 'Ivan the Terrible!'" And instantly bells ring out and raucous music plays. Timofeyev's room lights up. Timofeyev is asleep in the same position he dozed off in in Act I. No strange, outlandish machine, just the same radio-receiver as before.*)

TIMOFEYEV: Quick, quick, Ivan Vasilievich . . . Oof, hell, I must have dozed off! God, what a ridiculous dream . . . Is the machine in one piece? Still in one piece. Good grief, my wife left me . . . Oh no, that was in the dream. Thank God, it was in the dream. All of a sudden . . . The cosine . . . damn, he's getting on my nerves with those bells . . .

(*The hallway lights up. Zinaida enters.*)

ZINAIDA: Kolya, I'm home.

TIMOFEYEV: You, Zinochka!

ZINAIDA: Haven't you gone to bed? Koka, you're losing your mind, I keep telling you. I'll get you some tea right away, then you'll lie down . . . You shouldn't work so hard.

TIMOFEYEV: Zina, I meant to ask you . . . don't you see, I admit I was wrong . . . I really was working so hard that I didn't pay much attention to you these last few days . . . the cosine . . . you understand me?

ZINAIDA: I don't understand a word.

TIMOFEYEV: Where were you just now?

ZINAIDA: At rehearsal.

TIMOFEYEV: Tell me, the truth now. Are you in love with Yakin?

ZINAIDA: Which Yakin?

TIMOFEYEV: Don't pretend. He's very talented . . . will they really give him an apartment? Well, you know who I mean, he's your film director.

ZINAIDA: We haven't got any director named Yakin.

TIMOFEYEV: Honestly?

ZINAIDA: Honestly.

TIMOFEYEV: And there's no Molchanovsky?

ZINAIDA: There's no Molchanovsky.

TIMOFEYEV: Hurray! I was just joking.

ZINAIDA: I tell you, you're going crazy! (*A knock at the door.*) Yes, come in!

(*Shpak rushes in.*)

TIMOFEYEV: Anton Semyonovich, I just dreamt that you were robbed.

SHPAK: (*Shedding tears.*) What do you mean, dreamt? I really was robbed.

TIMOFEYEV: What?

SHPAK: Plain and simple. While I was at work. Victrola, cigarette-case, clothing! Holy Moses! And they cut off the telephone! . . . Zinaida Mikhailovna, may I use your phone? Holy Moses! (*He runs to the phone.*) Police! Where's our building superintendent?

ZINAIDA: (*Throwing open the window; shouts.*) Ulyana Andreyevna! Where's Ivan Vasilievich? Shpak's been robbed!

(*The music on the radio swells even louder.*)

END

PAJ PLAYSCRIPT SERIES

General Editors: Bonnie Marranca and Gautam Dasgupta